• • • •

THINKING WITH ANIMALS

• • • •

THINKING

New Perspectives on Anthropomorphism

WITH ANIMALS

Edited by

Lorraine Daston and Gregg Mitman

COLUMBIA UNIVERSITY PRESS

NEW YORK

COLUMBIA UNIVERSITY PPRESS

PUBLISHERS SINCE 1893

NEW YORK, CHICHESTER, WEST SUSSEX

A version of chapter 6 was first published as "Anthropomorphism and Anthropomorphic Selection—Beyond the 'Cute Response,'" by James Serpell, in *Society and Animals* 11, no. 1. Permission to reprint from Brill Academic Publishers.

Library of Congress Cataloging-in-Publication Data
Thinking with animals : new perspectives on anthropomorphism /
edited by Lorraine Daston and Gregg Mitman.
p.   cm.
This book derived from a workshop held at the Max Planck Institute
for the History of Science in Berlin in May 2001.
Includes bibliographical references (p.   ).
ISBN 0–231–13038–4 (cloth : alk. paper)
1. Anthropomorphism.   I. Daston, Lorraine, 1951–   II. Mitman, Gregg.
BL215.T48 2004
590—dc22
2004055102

Columbia University Press books are printed on permanent and durable acid-free paper
Printed in the United States of America

c 10 9 8 7 6 5 4 3 2 1
p 10 9 8 7 6 5 4 3 2 1

CONTENTS

PREFACE

.

This book began as a workshop held at the Max Planck Institute for the History of Science in Berlin in May 2001. We would like to thank the institute for its hospitality and subsequent support of the project. We are grateful to all of the participants in the original workshop, speakers and commentators alike, for helping us to reshape our lively discussions of the original papers into a book and to Wendy Lochner of Columbia University Press for encouraging us to proceed with project. Carola Kuntze, Nathalie Huet, Erika Milam, and Benjamin Kristek have been very helpful in the coordination of far-flung authors and in the preparation of the final manuscript, and we thank them heartily.

• • • •

LORRAINE DASTON
GREGG MITMAN

· · · ·

THINKING WITH ANIMALS

· · · ·

The How and Why of Thinking with Animals

Lorraine Daston and Gregg Mitman

THE IRRESISTIBLE TABOO

We are animals; we think with animals. What could be more natural? The children's section of every bookstore overflows with stories about animal heroes and villains; cartoons and animated feature films show the adventures of Bambi, Mickey Mouse, and the Road Runner to rapt audiences; countless pet owners are convinced that their dogs and cats understand them better than their spouses and children; television wildlife documentaries cast the lives of elephants and chimpanzees, parrots and lions, in terms of emotions and personalities that appeal to human viewers around the world. The reflexive assumption that animals are like us, despite obvious differences of form, food, and habitat, is not confined to popular culture. From Aristotle to Darwin down to the present, naturalists have credited bees with monarchies, ants with honesty, and dogs with tender consciences, all on the basis of firsthand observation. In many cultures, the fundamental moral and prudential lessons of human life are taught via myths about animals, such as Aesop's fables, which have been told and retold for millennia. Literature from many epochs and societies explores the psyche of animals, and humans never seem so indelibly human as in fiction that turns them into animals, as in the case of George Orwell's allegorical novel *Animal Farm*. The weirdest aliens dreamed up by sci-fi filmmakers resemble humans more than most animals, and yet it is animals, not aliens, who evoke an immediate, almost irresistible pulse of empathy: humans past and present, hither and yon, think they know how animals think, and they habitually use animals to help them do their own thinking about themselves.

This is the double meaning of the title of this book, *Thinking with Animals*: humans assume a community of thought and feeling between themselves and a surprisingly wide array of animals; they also recruit animals to symbolize, dramatize, and illuminate aspects of their own experience and fantasies. This book is about the how and why of thinking with animals in both of these senses and how both humans and animals are transformed by these relationships.

Until recently, the how and why of thinking with animals were rarely posed as questions; far more attention has been paid to whether it is good or bad to do so. "Anthropomorphism" is the word used to describe the belief that animals are essentially like humans, and it is usually applied as a term of reproach, both intellectual and moral. Originally, the word referred to the attribution of human form to gods, forbidden by several religions as blasphemous.[1] Something of the religious taboo still clings to secular, modern instances of anthropomorphism, even if it is animals rather than divinities that are being humanized.[2] Although the focus of this book is mostly on what anthropomorphism is used for and how it works, it is important to understand why such a widespread practice is nonetheless so controversial.

If thinking with animals has become a focus for reflection and debate, it is in part because there has been so much thinking (and rethinking) *about* animals in the past decade. Among scholars and scientists, the biology, ethics, sociology, economics, anthropology, geography, and hermeneutics of animals furnish the stuff of a growing number of studies and surveys.[3] Among political activists, endangered species, laboratory animals, livestock, hunters' prey, and pets are the objects of vocal and occasionally violent protective campaigns. Among citizens at large, deliberations about what to wear and eat, the rights of pets and the responsibilities of their owners, and the legitimacy of zoos, aquariums, wildlife parks, and other sites of animal captivity open up a new area of practical morality with potentially vast economic, social, and political consequences.[4] Cultural critic Akira Mizuta Lippit suggests that animals are more present than ever in thought because they have never been less present in daily experience: "Modernity can be defined by the disappearance of wildlife from humanity's habitat and by the reappearance of the same in humanity's reflections on itself: in philosophy, psychoanalysis, and technological media such as the telephone, film, and radio."[5] Jennifer Ham and Matthew Senior take the more optimistic view that thinking with animals signals moments of historic cultural creativity: "To invent new languages and civilizations it was necessary to give animal voices to political, philosophical, and moral actors."[6] Yet anthropomorphism (and its converse, zoomorphism) remain matters of intellectual and ethical ambivalence: Why?

In the sciences, to impute human thoughts or emotions to electrons, genes, ants, or even other primates is to invite suspicions of sloppy thinking. Although a metaphor like the "selfish gene" might be tolerated in popularizations, to use the term literally is to be accused of making a category mistake. Genes (or radios or planets) are not the kind of things that can think or feel; to believe otherwise is considered a mark of childishness or feeblemindedness. Since the early nineteenth century, historians, philosophers, and anthropologists have repeatedly linked the rise of modern science with the waning of anthropomorphic attitudes toward the natural world. For example, the beliefs that the planets and stars were celestial intelligences or that heavy objects fell because they were seeking their natural place—beliefs held by many European natural philosophers before the Scientific Revolution of the seventeenth century—were regarded as signs of a "primitive" mentality. Despite the fact that the alleged analogy between the psychological development of children and the intellectual development of whole cultures has been largely discredited, the view that anthropomorphism of any kind is incompatible with modern science lingers.

The theory of evolution makes it more difficult to draw a hard-and-fast line between humans and animals, since common descent and the gradual process of natural selection on random variation make it plausible to assume some continuity of traits, including psychological traits, among closely related species. But ethologists who study animal behavior, including that of primates with close phylogenetic links to humans, have long made it a principle not to infer humanlike mental states from humanlike behavior. Indeed, until the recent emergence of the field of cognitive ethology, many scientists in this field frowned upon any discussion of animal mental states.[7] Their reasons were in part methodological (how can we know what animals are thinking, since they cannot talk to us?) and in part historical, a reaction against the sentimental animal stories cited so enthusiastically by earlier comparative psychologists. Few of these tales could be substantiated under laboratory conditions; moreover, the default assumption that other species thought and felt as humans did seemed lazy, a failure of scientific ingenuity to formulate and test alternative hypotheses. Hence not only in astronomy and physics but even in zoology, post-Darwin anthropomorphism became almost synonymous with anecdote and sloth and opposed to scientific rigor and care.

There is a moral as well an intellectual element to critiques of anthropomorphism. On this view, to imagine that animals think like humans or to cast animals in human roles is a form of self-centered narcissism: one looks outward to the world and sees only one's own reflection mirrored therein. Considered from a moral standpoint, anthropomorphism sometimes seems dangerously allied to anthropocentrism: humans project their own thoughts and feelings onto other animal species because they egotistically believe themselves to be the center of the universe. But anthropomorphism and anthropocentrism can just as easily tug in opposite directions: for example, the Judeo-Christian tradition that humans were the pinnacle of Creation also encouraged claims that humans, being endowed by God with reason and immortal souls, were superior to and qualtitatively different from animals. In this theological context, it made no sense to try to think with soulless animals. Even if anthropomorphism is decoupled from anthropocentrism, the former can still be criticized as arrogant and unimaginative. To assimilate the behavior of a herd of elephants to, say, that of a large, middle-class, American family or to dress up a pet terrier in a tutu strikes these critics as a kind of species provincialism, an almost pathological failure to register the wondrous variety of the natural world—a provincialism comparable to that of those blinkered tourists who assume that the natives of the foreign countries they visit will have the same customs and speak the same language as at home.

In recent years, another moral dimension of anthropomorphism has been opened up by the debate over animal rights. Should animals be treated as moral persons, with rights like those accorded to human beings? If so, would animal rights imply that humans ought to embrace vegetarianism, stop wearing fur and leather clothing, and abandon experiments on animals that do not serve the animals' own interests, for the same reasons that cannibalism and instrumental experiments on humans should be rejected as ethically repugnant? Since many (though not all) of the arguments pro and contra in this debate hinge upon the degree of analogy between humans and other animal species, and more particularly on the analogy between thoughts and feelings, the ancient and almost universal practice of thinking with animals has taken on new significance. If this practice is invalid—a childish illusion or a self-centered projection, as critics of anthropomorphism have claimed—then the position of those who support animal rights—at least for species that allegedly suffer pain, remember the past and plan for the future, and/or register kindred feelings—is weakened. And if the practice is valid—if further research were to confirm key commonalities among human and animal psychologies—then the acceptance of animal rights on this basis might well drive a wedge between the two senses of thinking with animals. That is, if humans were correct in their anthropomorphic assumption that, *grosso modo*, animals thought and felt as humans did, for that very reason humans would no longer be justified in using animals as stage props to act out certain ways of being human—no more than other humans may be used as a means to serve the ends of others.

The moral is not only central to debates over anthropomorphism, it is also at the core of epistemological and methodological debates in scholarship on animals and society. Can we ever really think *with* animals? The question raises important issues of representation and agency. Thinking with animals is not the same as thinking about them. Anthropological, historical, and literary analyses of animals in human culture have revealed much about changing human attitudes toward animals and the changing economic, political, and social relationships of human societies. But in what sense is the animal a participant, an actor in our analyses? Has the animal become, like that of the taxidermist's craft, little more than a human-sculpted object in which the animal's glass eye merely reflects our own projections? In thinking with animals, how might we capture the agency of another being that cannot speak to reveal the transformative effects its actions have, both literally and figuratively, upon humans?[8] Emphasis on the "textual, metaphor animal," Jonathan Burt observes, risks reducing "the animal to a mere icon," placing "the animal outside history." The difficulty becomes how to "achieve a more integrated view of the effects of the presence of the animal and the power of its imagery in human history."[9]

This is the highly electrified field in which current discussions about thinking with animals take place. The stakes are high and are being played for openly in science, art, politics, and global commerce. More subliminally but no less powerfully, ways of thinking with animals affect collective forms of feeling and seeing. The widening of the circle of human empathy and sympathy to include seals and elephants, whales and wolves, has altered both the subjective experience of identification with others and also its objective expression, as measured by contributions to organizations like the World Wildlife Fund.[10] The proliferation of animal images, accessible to viewers across boundaries of language and culture in global image banks and advertising campaigns, has recalibrated vision and attention: the anthropomorphized expressions of animals may now be viewed as more humanly intelligible than those of other humans. Throughout the world, pitched battles are being waged over wildlife management, livestock farming, scientific and medical experimentation on animals, the rights and responsibilities of pet owners, hunting, and forms of animal entertainment ranging from animated films to dolphin shows at aquariums. The outcome of all of them depends crucially not only on how we think *about* animals but whether, and above all how, we think *with* them.

The essays in this volume take for granted that humans think with animals and that they do so compulsively, whether or not they ought to by the lights of science and ethics. This is a book about the fact, not the value of anthropomorphism. From a variety of viewpoints—philosophical, historical, cross-cultural, political, economic, scientific, medical, and artistic—the authors explore what might be called the practice of anthropomorphism. What is it good for, and how is it done? The essays examine the mechanics of thinking with animals in different times and places—ancient India and contemporary cyberspace, the Victorian laboratory and the forests of Borneo—and in the here and now, in public and in private. When humans imagine animals, we necessarily reimagine ourselves, so these episodes reveal a great deal about notions of the human—the "anthropos" of anthropomorphism. But the "morphos" of anthropomorphism is equally important to the aims of this book: to track different modes of transformation, of shape-changing across species. These are the two axes around which the essays in this volume revolve: the performance of being human by animals and being animal by humans, and the transformative processes that make thinking with animals possible.

WHY THINK WITH ANIMALS?

Thinking with animals is useful. Cheryce Kramer explains how animal images sell products and create moods; James Serpell documents the fact that pets enhance the health and happiness of their owners; Gregg Mitman shows that animal personalities move the public and politicians more effectively than wildlife statistics; Sarita Siegel reports the editorial pressure on makers of wildlife films to "hook" audiences with a story of heroes and hope. Apparently people nowadays often find it easier to think with animals than to think with other people. Pet owners (especially dog owners) regularly profess themselves to be emotionally closer to their animal familiars than to friends and family and are further convinced that they and their pets understand one another's most intimate thoughts. Striking images of animals are in great demand by global advertisers because—in contrast to equally striking images of humans—age, race, class, and culture do not interfere with identification and the desire to acquire. In films, even films sold as documentaries, broadcasters like National Geographic International look for a "hero character" among the animals with whom viewers can identify. Environmental and conservation legislation sometimes pits the interests of humans against those of animals: the trappers whose livelihood is at risk when seals can no longer be hunted or the families who stand to starve when antipoaching laws deny them access to animals in newly created wildlife preserves. Yet the spectacle of suffering animals increasingly sways voters more strongly than that of suffering humans. No wonder that anthropomorphism has been assiduously cultivated: money, love, and power are all to be had by thinking with animals.

There are other, harder-to-name yearnings that are also expressed by thinking with animals. Wendy Doniger explores how ancient Indian myth uses a parallel cast of animals to try out alternative plots and personalities. The monkeys who echo but also alter the human configurations of lovers, rivals, allies, and enemies in the *Ramayana* epic act as a kind of narrative thought experiment: What would happen to the story if this detail of character or action were changed? Doniger likens this rearrangement of the pieces of the story into a similar but different pattern to dream work, according to Freud's account: the world of the monkeys turns into a projection of the human hero's unconscious, allowing him to act more freely there than in the conscious sphere of human society. The animal shadow plot opens up possibilities that no mere doubling by means of another human subplot could. The differences between the monkeys and the humans are as important as the similarities; otherwise, the animals could not serve as a kind of furry subjunctive case for the story, a "what would happen if" that ends up acting back on the indicative plot of the humans.

Thinking with animals can take the form of an intense yearning to transcend the confines of self and species, to understand from the inside or even to become an animal. Lorraine Daston notes that this is a desire with a long history and that it was once directed as ardently to angels as it now is to animals. In certain historical and cultural contexts, the longing to think with animals becomes the opposite of the arrogant egotism decried by critics of anthropomorphism. Instead of projection of one's own way of thinking and feeling onto other minds, submersion of self in the genuinely other is fervently attempted—but never achieved. It is a virtuoso but doomed act of complete empathy. Mitman relates how ethologists who have devoted their lives to the study (and often the preservation) of elephants, gorillas, and other at-risk animal species develop deep identifications with their chosen subjects. Among scientists who investigate animal behavior, such feelings are not uncommon, and even those who disapprove of anthropomorphism in ethology in principle admit that in practice the arduous life of the observer in the wild would hardly be tolerable without some such emotional bond. Siegel's film, *The Disenchanted Forest*, is in part a tribute to a group of scientists' dedication to and also identification with the orangutans to which they have devoted their lives. It is a commonly remarked phenomenon among ethologists that the tendency to anthropomorphize the animals under study increases rather than decreases with more experience in the field.[11] The yearning to understand what it would be like to be, say, an elephant or a cheetah scrambles the opposition between anthropomorphism and zoomorphism, that is, between humanizing animals and animalizing humans. This extreme form of thinking with animals is the impossible but irresistible desire to jump out of one's own skin, exchange one's brain, plunge into another way of being.

These longings for transcendence by taking thinking with animals to the limit often emerge in the context of field sciences like ethology, in which the researcher "goes native" in order to investigate animals in the wild. Laboratory studies of animals have usually stood opposed to anthropomorphizing tendencies: the proper scientific attitude is defined as cool, distanced, objective. But as Paul White shows, the situation in the nineteenth-century laboratory sciences of physiology and biology was considerably more nuanced. Much depended on which species was on the vivisecting table. Frogs were turned into scientific instruments and generally excited as little empathy or sympathy as other lab machines did. In contrast, experiments on dogs and other domestic animals not only triggered protests by anticruelty leagues, but also forced experimenters to steel themselves manfully against their own outbursts of sympathy in the service of science. Opponents of animal experimentation worried about the brutalization of the scientists caused by such emotional repression as well as the treatment of the beasts at their hands. Moreover, many if not most of the experiments were undertaken with the aim of understanding human biology and psychology better, so the analogy between humans and animals was a precondition for their validity. Hence, despite the official ban on anthropomorphism in science, thinking with animals permeated practice in the field and the lab. Both animal and human were transformed in the process. If nineteenth-century graphic methods morphed frogs into laboratory technologies, the participation of animals in experimental systems also altered the material, economic, and moral relationships of science. Similarly, while ethological studies have transformed elephants and orangutans into celebrities, the performative roles animals play in science has impacted the identity, careers, and practices of field biologists.

The advent of evolutionary theory, which posits phylogenetic continuities between humans and other animals, has made the ban on anthropomorphism difficult to sustain in principle as well as in practice in the life sciences. Elliott Sober reexamines the methodological rule that strongly discouraged anthropomorphism in comparative psychology until recently in the light of current thinking about evolutionary lineages and concludes that a more symmetric program of scientific inquiry into what animal and human cognitive capacities have in common would worry as much about committing the error of "anthropodenial" (underestimating commonalities) as "anthropomorphism" (overestimating them). Sandra Mitchell analyzes some of the most ingenious recent experiments to test whether humans and chimpanzees think alike and concludes that the jury is still out but that the matter can be decided empirically, albeit only on a case-by-case and species-by-species basis. Whether or not the scientific respectability of thinking with animals would survive the sort of comprehensive investigation Mitchell envisions is an open question, but the heuristic utility of anthropomorphism in generating hypotheses to test in the study of animal behavior is beyond question. The science of animal thinking makes constant, one is tempted to say necessary, use of thinking with animals.

HOW TO THINK WITH ANIMALS

Thinking with animals is eminently useful, and that is no doubt partly why it is so pervasive. But to say the habit is pervasive is not the same thing as saying that it is permanent. There is good evidence of multiple and changing ways to go about thinking with animals, with new ones being invented to exploit the possibilities of new forms of experience and new media. Animals are not "morphed" into humans in an Aesopian fable or a medieval bestiary in the same way they are in the latest nature film released for television. What it means to think with animals varies with time, place, and medium.

In fables animals are humanized, one might even say hyperhumanized, by caricature: the fox is cunning, the lion is brave, the dog is loyal. Whereas the same stories told about humans might lose the moral in a clutter of individuating detail of the sort we are usually keen to know about other people, substituting animals as actors strips the characterizations down to prototypes. Animals simplify the narrative to a point that would be found flat or at least allegorical if the same tales were recounted about humans. We are still avid for animal stories, but photography, film, and a distinctly modern preoccupation with the individual has transformed the way they are told. Pet owners, Serpell remarks, do not have a warm and trusting relationship with just any old dog or cat, no more than parents love a generic child: the mutual understanding is one between named individuals, and it presupposes idiosyncracies (endearing or not) on both human and animal sides. Mitman documents how naturalists trying to protect elephant herds from hunting and culling shifted from statistics and aerial photographs of animal aggregates to "pachyderm personalities": individual elephants, named rather than numbered, with biographies and photographs done in the style of high-fashion celebrity portraits. The latter way of presenting the elephants to legislators and citizens' groups was strategically more effective in winning converts to the conservation cause. But it was also the way in which the naturalists themselves had come to think about the animals they studied, despite the fact that their training had emphasized populations rather than personalities. Siegel makes a similar point about her film *The Disenchanted Forest*: National Geographic International may have had its own marketing reasons for wanting her to endow the orangutans with individual personalities, but Siegel acknowledges that this was also the way the naturalists who knew most about and cared most for the animals discussed them. In both scientific and popular contexts, thinking with animals is increasingly thinking with individual animals. That historical shift in the "morphos" of anthropomorphism, which can be readily traced to the late nineteenth century, has not only structured how we think with animals but how we act in relationship to them as well, fueling debates about the agency and moral standing of animals in human society.

It is also thinking about what it would be like to *be* that animal, as opposed to thinking about the structures and processes of animal cognition and emotion. The contrast roughly parallels that between an introspective approach to human thought, in which the psychologist turns inward and examines the contents of his or her own consciousness as data for understanding the workings of human consciousness, and the methods of the cognitive sciences, which attempt to model the mind with programs that could be executed by computers. The best-known example of the latter approach is artificial intelligence, which attempts to replicate what human intelligence can do (though not necessarily in the way that humans do it) with algorithms that can be executed by machines. In this case, it would make little sense to ask, What is it like to be a machine?—even if the robot or computer in question accurately mimicked human accomplishments. Only in certain fanciful science-fiction settings do we credit machines with a subjectivity that would warrant the question, What is it like to be one? There is no need, however, to have recourse to computer models in order to find examples of anthropomorphism practiced without appeal to subjectivities. Daston cites medieval angelologists as a case in point, who tried to understand angelic thought and emotion anthropomorphically but not subjectively. Only in the nineteenth century did the problem of understanding other minds, including those of animals, come to be formulated as seeing the world from the perspective of another, experiencing its experiences. Although this is, historically and logically, only one way of thinking with animals (or with aliens), it has become the dominant mode.

Before either animal individuality or subjectivity can be imagined, an animal must be singled out as a promising prospect for anthropomorphism. We do not choose to think with any and all animals. There seems to be no simple explanation as to why some species are singled out as good to think with and others not. Phylogeny may be part of the answer, and domestication, another: chimps and dogs are prime candidates, amoebas and eels are not. Evolutionary biologists, such as Stephen Jay Gould, have also suggested that we identify with certain species or animal characters like Mickey Mouse that display neotenic features similar to those of humans. Disney animators knew well that the large eyes of Bambi would elicit an emotional response from audiences more akin to the affection displayed toward a human child than if they had drawn the deer's eyes to scale.[12] Baby fur seals display similar neotenic features, but what about elephants? Why should they, or dolphins for that matter, become favored species? Doniger observes that although the attribution of language to animals in Indian myth humanizes them (and, conversely, the denial of language to humans animalizes them), there are very few anthropomorphic stories featuring parrots. There are strong evolutionary grounds for using chimpanzees for studies in comparative human-animal psychology, as in the experiments analyzed by Mitchell, but a great deal of the research in this field has been conducted on dogs, starting with Darwin himself.

Once again, medium can make the message. Just as the studio-like portraits of individual elephants created a different relationship between them and humans than aerial photos had, the right photographic angle can spotlight a species in human imaginaries. White describes how frogs became the "Job of physiology" because they inspired so little creaturely spirit among Victorians, yet Kramer recounts how photographer Tim Flach's brilliant staging of a frog peering out from a leaf—or bats wrapped in their wings like opera cloaks—can unleash a floodtide of identification in viewers. The animals to be found in the Getty Images archives inhabit a technological environment of temperature-controlled rooms, enormous light fixtures, and digital image banks as complex as any scientific laboratory or slaughterhouse. The articles by White, Kramer, Mitman, and Siegel all point to how thinking with animals also entails thinking about technology. If the technologies of factories and farms and laboratories and zoos were the predominant modes through which animal-human relationships were mediated in the nineteenth century, the explosion of new scientific, communication, and manufacturing technologies in the twentieth and twenty-first centuries has created new avenues of relationships. Technology, Akira Lippit writes, "and more precisely the technological instruments and media of the [late nineteenth and early twentieth centuries] began to serve as virtual shelters for displaced animals."[13] How these technological environments have transformed the habitats and ecologies of animals and animal-human relationships remains relatively unexplored.[14]

PERFORMING ANIMALS

Thinking with animals casts animals in performances. By this we do not just mean bears riding bicycles at the circus or thoroughbred horses showing off dressage or even cartoon dalmatians. But we do mean outward spectacle, a way of making something abstract, hidden, or conjectural visible and concrete. The frog "demonstrated" in the laboratory, the talking monkeys in myth, the orphaned orangutans on film, the poster elephant for a conservation campaign, even the chimpanzee following the gaze of a human around a barrier—each of these animals serves to reveal something that would have remained unconscious, unknown, or unarticulated. In each case, it is possible to imagine a nonperformative version of the revelation: a textbook explanation of reflex action, a literary gloss on the unconscious motives of the human actors, an impassioned plea for the preservation of orangutans and their habitats, a magazine article reporting observations on elephant behavior, an analysis of the cognitive and perceptual competences required to possess a theory of mind. These versions would be at least as informative and almost always more detailed and explicit than the performances. But something would be missing, the something that makes animals good to think with, in the sense that fingers are good to count with.

Animals are not just one symbol system out of many, one of the innumerable possibilities to externalize and dramatize what humans think. They are privileged, and they are performative. They do not just stand for something, as a word stands for a thing or a rhetorical trope figures something else; they do something. Even in cases of complete ventriloquism, in which thinking with animals is reduced to a blatant projection of human thoughts, feelings, and fantasies, there is some added value in the fact that the blank screen for these projections is an animal. To take an egregious example cited by Serpell, dog breeders who pander to human tastes in cuteness by selecting pugs with faces so flattened that breathing is impeded are guilty of anthropomorphism and anthropocentrism bordering on cruelty; ditto the doting pug owners who encourage these breeding practices. Why do they do it? Why can the craving for flat-faced cuteness not be satisfied by dolls or cartoons? Why make live animals perform these fantasies? The answer seems to lie in the active reality of animals. Plants are beautiful, endlessly varied, and marvels of organic adaptation. Yet they radiate none of the magnetism animals do for humans. Even the most enthusiastic fancier of orchids or ferns rarely tries to think with them, in either sense of the phrase. As Aristotle observed, the distinctive mark of the animal is self-locomotion; they move themselves, with all of the roaming autonomy movement implies. Unlike dolls or robots or any other product of human skill, however ingenious, animals are not our marionettes, our automata (which originally meant "puppet" in Greek). They are symbols with a life of their own. We use them to perform our thoughts, feelings, and fantasies because, alone of all our myriad symbols, they can perform; they can do what is to be done. We may orchestrate their performance, but complete mastery is illusion. Eyes peer through the human mask to reveal another life, mysterious—like us or unlike us? Their animated gaze moves us to think.

This is why the final essay in this volume is a reflection on how animals are performed: in this case, filmmaker Sarita Siegel's candid reflections about the making of her documentary on the rehabilitation of orangutans captured as pets and then abandoned in Indonesian Borneo. All of the promises and pitfalls of anthropomorphism are abundantly clear to Siegel; for her, they are daily dilemmas that have to be solved in specific scenes on film. Although the issues she grapples with in making the film are momentous, they are anything but abstract. Do the orangutans have culture? Should they be allowed to adopt the culture of their human caretakers? Is it scientifically true, is it ethically right to highlight cute shots of humanized orangutans washing the dishes and brushing their teeth? How can the film satisfy the template dictated by National Geographic International and be faithful to the plight of the animals? Above all, how can the film mobilize political support to stop the capture and killing of orangutans and the destruction of their habitat? These are questions of action as well as reflection, and ultimately their answers must be performed by orangutan and human alike: thinking with animals in action.

NOTES

1. A. Marmorstein, *The Old Rabbinic Doctrine of God: Essays in Anthropomorphism* (London: Oxford University Press, 1937).

2. John S. Kennedy, *The New Anthropomorphism* (New York: Cambridge University Press, 1992); Robert W. Mitchell, Nicholas S. Thompson, and H. Lyn Miles, eds., *Anthropomorphism, Anecdotes, and Animals* (Albany: State University of New York Press, 1997).

3. For a sampling of this literature, see Arnold Arluke and Clinton R. Sanders, *Regarding Animals* (Philadelphia: Temple University Press, 1996); Stephen Baker, *Picturing the Beast: Animals, Identity, and Representation* (Urbana: University of Illinois Press, 2001); Jonathan Burt, *Animals in Film* (London: Reaktion Books, 2003);

Jenifer Ham and Matthew Senior, *Animal Acts: Configuring the Human in Western History* (New York: Routledge, 1997); Donna Haraway, *The Companion Species Manifesto: Dogs, People, and Significant Otherness* (Chicago: Prickly Paradigm, 2003); Akira Mizuta Lippit, *Electric Animal: Toward a Rhetoric of Wildlife* (Minneapolis: University of Minnesota Press, 2000); Aubrey Manning and James Serpell, eds., *Animals and Human Society: Changing Perspectives* (London: Routledge, 1994); Harriet Ritvo, *The Animal Estate: The English and Other Creatures in the Victorian Age* (Cambridge: Harvard University Press, 1987); Nigel Rothfels, ed., *Representing Animals* (Bloomington: Indiana University Press, 2002); Mary J. Henninger-Voss, ed., *Animals in Human Histories: The Mirror of Nature and Culture* (Rochester: University of Rochester Press, 2002); Gregg Mitman, *Reel Nature: America's Romance with Wildlife on Film* (Cambridge, Mass.: Harvard University Press, 1999); Jennifer Wolch and Jody Emel, eds., *Animal Geographies: Place, Politics, and Identity in the Nature-Culture Borderlands* (New York: Verso, 1998).

4. Wolch and Emel, *Animal Geographies.*

5. Lippit, *Electric Animal*, 2–3.

6. Ham and Senior, *Animal Acts*, 5.

7. See, for example, Eileen Crist, *Images of Animals: Anthropomorphism and Animal Mind* (Philadelphia: Temple University Press, 1999).

8. See., for example, Erica Fudge, "A Left-Handed Blow: Writing the History of Animals," in *Representing Animals*, ed. Nigel Rothfels (Bloomington: Indiana University Press, 2002), 3–18, for an entry point into these debates.

9. Jonathan Burt, "The Illumination of the Animal Kingdom: The Role of Light and Electricity in Animal Representation," *Society and Animals* 9 (2001): 205.

10. Jody Emel and Jennifer Wolch, "Witnessing the Animal Moment," in *Animal Geographies: Place, Politics, and Identity in the Nature-Culture Borderlands*, ed. Wolch and Emel (New York: Verso, 1998), 1–24.

11. See, for example, Marc Bekoff, *Minding Animals: Awareness, Emotions, and Heart* (New York: Oxford University Press, 2002); Jane Goodall and Mark Bekoff, *The Ten Trusts: What We Must Do to Care for the Animals We Love* (San Francisco: HarperSanFrancisco, 2002); Caroline A. Ristau, ed., *Cognitive Ethology: The Minds of Other Animals. Essays in Honor of Donald R. Griffin* (Hillsdale, N.J.: Lawrence Erlbaum, 1991).

12. Stephen Jay Gould, "Mickey Mouse Meets Konrad Lorenz," *Natural History* 88 (1979): 30–36; Elizabeth A. Lawrence, "Neoteny in American Perceptions of Animals," in *Perceptions of Animals in American Culture*, ed. R. J. Hoage (Washington, DC: Smithsonian Institution Press, 1989).

13. Akira Mizuta Lippit, ". . . From Wild Technology to Electric Animal," in *Representing Animals*, ed. Nigel Rothfels (Bloomington: Indiana University Press, 2002), 125.

14. The laboratory is one environment where such human-animal interactions have been explored within scientific studies. See, for example, Haraway, *The Companion Species Manifesto*; Robert Kohler, *Lords of the Fly: Drosophila and the Experimental Life* (Chicago: University of Chicago Press, 1994); Karen Rader, "The Multiple Meanings of Laboratory Animals: Standardizing Mice for American Cancer Research, 1910–1950," in *Animals in Human Histories: The Mirror of Nature and Culture*, ed. Mary J. Henninger-Voss (Rochester: University of Rochester Press, 2002), 389–438.

PART I

THINKING WITH ANIMALS
IN OTHER TIMES AND PLACES

CHAPTER 1

Zoomorphism in Ancient India
Humans More Bestial Than the Beasts

•

Wendy Doniger

Ancient Indian Sanskrit texts are rich in anthropomorphism, projecting human qualities upon animals, but they more particularly abound in zoomorphism, imagining humans as animals. Anthropomorphism, though more common than zoomorphism in India (as elsewhere), tells us comparatively little about animals; an anthropomorphic text assumes a basic identification, such as lion as king, and then, although the object of discourse is, theoretically, an animal, the text imagines the animal as behaving the way the human does, betraying the fact that it is interested only in kings and not at all in lions. Zoomorphism is more complex: although this time a human being is the explicit object, the bestial qualities imputed to the human usually reveal an observation of animals more detailed (if no more accurate) than that of anthropomorphism, and the text teaches us simultaneously what sort of person it thinks that animal is like and what sort of animal it thinks that sort of person is like. And where anthropomorphism simply leaps over our knowledge that most animals cannot speak (there are, significantly, relatively few anthropomorphic stories about parrots), zoomorphism seizes upon language as a point of potential difference between humans and animals and worries that point in various ways, imputing human speech to certain individual animals and either muteness or, on the other hand, the ability to understand animals to certain individual humans.

Let us begin with a quick survey of the relatively straightforward texts of anthropomorphism and progress to the more challenging texts of zoomorphism.

India is a particularly good place to look for such texts, as ancient Sanskrit literature, composed in India from about 1000 B.C.E. to 1000 C.E. (when, arbitrarily, medieval literature might be said to begin), abounds in animal imagery. India is famous for its beast fables, in which animals stand for human types and point to human morals: the lion as king, the cunning jackal as his chief minister, clever monkeys and foolish donkeys, the ongoing battle of the crows against the owls. The most famous collection of these stories is the *Panchatantra*, probably composed about 500 C.E. but drawing upon much older Buddhist sources. These tales, known to Europeans from Aesop's fables, were tracked to their lair by nineteenth-century German folklorists: a Pahlavi (literary Persian) translation perhaps as early as 550 C.E. was translated first into Syriac and then into Arabic c. 750, whence it entered European literature through Moorish contacts in Spain and elsewhere. The *Panchatantra* is a textbook of political science, probably intended for the education of princes, but its cast of characters was widely diffused into all levels of Indian literature, from folktales in the vernaculars to court poetry in Sanskrit. The heron or the cat, for instance, is a widespread image of the religious hypocrite: a cat pretended to be a vegetarian ascetic and ate the mice until one day mouse bones were discovered in the cat's feces; the heron seems to be meditating, until he gobbles up a fish.[1] Animals also serve as metaphors more broadly in Indian culture: the dominant metaphor, indeed cliché, for anarchy is the law of the fishes (*matsyanyaya*): the big fish eat the little fish.

Indian mythology also used fish as a metaphor for an alternative consciousness. One such myth is an Indian parallel to a famous Daoist story of sages on a bridge, arguing about their ability to know if fish are happy. This is the Daoist story:

> Chuang Tzu and Hui Tzu had strolled on to the bridge over the Hao, when the former observed, "See how the minnows are darting about! That is the pleasure of fishes." "You not being a fish yourself," said Hui Tzu, "how can you possibly know in what consists the pleasure of fishes?" "And you not being I," retorted Chuang Tzu, "how can you know that I do not know?" "If I, not being you, cannot know what you know," urged Hui Tzu, "it follows that you, not being a fish, cannot know in what consists the pleasure of fishes." "Let us go back," said Chuang Tzu, "to your original question. You asked me how I knew in what consists the pleasure of fishes. Your very question shows that you knew I knew. I knew it from my own feelings on the bridge."[2]

In addition to the obvious twists and turns of the epistemological argument, the Chinese text conceals yet another level. For the word "How" in "How do you know?" also means "From what? From what position? Whence?" The answer, "*From* my feelings on the bridge," suggests a metaphor: we know because of the inexplicable bridge of emotion ("my feelings") that connects us with the fish. But the bridge is also a metaphor for all that *separates* us from the fishes. We never can be certain that we know their happiness.

The corresponding Indian tale, in a Sanskrit text, assumes that we can know about the happiness of fish, but that this very understanding may lead to a problem—not the problem of intellectual isolation, as in the Chinese parable but, on the contrary, the problem of human involvement:

> There was once a sage named Saubhari, who spent twelve years immersed in a pond. In that pond there lived a great fish who had many children and grandchildren. The young fish played around the great fish all day, and he lived happily among them. Their games began to disturb the sage's meditations; he noticed them and thought, "How enviable is that fish, always playing so happily with his children. He makes me want to taste that pleasure, too, and to play happily with my own children." And so the sage got out of the water and went to the king to demand a bride. He married the king's fifty daughters and had a hundred and fifty sons, but eventually he realized that his desires were self-perpetuating and hence insatiable, and that he must return to the meditations that the fish had disturbed. So he abandoned his children and his wives and returned to the forest.[3]

The Hindu sage is not depicted, like one of the Daoist sages, as mistaken in his empathy: the fish *are* happy, taking pleasure in the same thing that humans take pleasure in, playing with their children. We might ask if the sage could have been made aware of the pleasures of child rearing by a vision not of fish but of humans and their children, but the text implies that the sage has left human company and hence would not see human children. Moreover, the sage understands the fish (where he might not have understood his fellow men and women) because he has become, in effect, a kind of animal himself: fishlike, he lives underwater, in a transhuman condition made possible by his extraordinary ascetic powers. But the sage is mistaken in believing that he personally can be happy like a fish, or rather that such happiness is desirable for him: he comes to learn that though other people may be like fish (in enjoying their children), he himself is not like them (in his special powers of meditation), and hence, though fishlike (in being nonhuman), not like a fish (in procreation).

A more extensively developed anthropomorphism pervades the *Rama-yana*, composed by Valmiki in Sanskrit between the second century B.C.E. and the second century C.E.[4] Like the *Panchatantra*, this text is ostensibly about a king, though it is a continuous epic narrative rather than a collection of moral lessons. And, like the beast fables, the *Ramayana* was widely diffused throughout Indian culture, far beyond the world of kings. The central characters of this text—Rama the perfect prince, Sita his perfect wife, and Lakshmana his perfect brother (later to form the template for the perfect worshipper of the now deified Rama)—were born to be paradigms, squeaky clean goody-goodies (or, in the case of the perfectly demonic demon king Ravana—who steals Sita from Rama and keeps her captive on the island of Lanka for many years—a baddy-baddy). If that were all there was to the *Ramayana*, it would have proved ideologically useful to people interested in enforcing moral standards or rallying religious fanatics—as, alas, it has proved all too capable of doing, to this day, in India—but it would probably not have survived as a beloved work of great literature, as it has also done. Rama may or may not be God in the original Sanskrit text—often he seems to forget that he is and has to be reminded of it, and more often it does not seem to be an issue at all—but even in Sanskrit, god is in the details, and the details of the *Ramayana* are what give its characters their character. More precisely, each of the major human characters has a double among the monkeys who help Rama kill Ravana and retrieve Sita. These doubles are, ironically, more flesh and blood, as we would say, more complex and nuanced than the human characters that they mirror. Or, rather, added to those original characters, they provide the nuances of ambiguity and ambivalence that constitute the depth and substance of the total character, composed of the original plus the shadow. All the fun is in the monkeys.

There are a number of parallels between monkeys and people in general in the *Ramayana*, both explicit and implicit.[5] The appropriateness of these parallels is supported by such factors as the human characters' failure to remark that—though they cannot understand the language of the deer (Rama explicitly laments this fact when he runs off after a golden deer that he suspects—rightly—to be a demon in disguise)—they can understand the language of monkeys, who are called "the deer of the trees." Hanuman, the commander in chief of the monkeys, not only speaks human languages but speaks Sanskrit. When he approaches Sita on the island of Lanka (5.30), he anxiously debates with himself precisely what language he will use to address her: "If I assume a human form and speak Sanskrit like a sage, Sita will think I am Ravana [as she mistook the real Ravana, a notorious shape-changer, for an ascetic sage] and will be terrified. But I must speak with a human tongue, or else I cannot encourage her. Yet she will think I am Ravana, who can take any form he wants. And she'll scream, and we will all be killed." He finally does address her in Sanskrit, and she is suitably impressed. She does not scream.

Monkeys are like people, and special monkeys are the sons of gods, as special people are. Sugriva is the son of Surya (the sun god), Valin is the son of Indra (king of the gods), and Hanuman, the great general of Sugriva's army, is the son of Vayu, the wind. In this, the monkeys particularly resemble the human heroes of the other great Sanskrit epic, the *Mahabharata*, in which Surya is the father of Karna, Indra the father of Arjuna (the enemy of Karna), and Vayu the father of Bhima. Monkeys function as the shadows of Lakshmana, Rama, and a third brother, Bharata. In the human world, Rama's father Dasharatha has put Bharata, the younger brother, on the throne in place of Rama, the eldest, and exiled Rama to the forest; Lakshmana and Sita go with him. In the forest, where humans understand the speech of monkeys, after the demon Ravana has stolen Sita, Rama and Lakshmana meet Sugriva, who used to be king of monkeys and claims that his brother Valin stole his wife and throne. Rama sides with Sugriva and murders Valin by shooting him in the back, an episode that has troubled the South Asian tradition for centuries, to this very day. Why does he do it? Apparently because Rama senses a parallel between his situation and that of Sugriva and therefore sides with Sugriva against his brother. But if Sugriva is Rama, who is Valin?

The answer to this question lies in the more specific parallels between the things that happen to the monkey brothers and the things that happen to the human brothers. After Lakshmana has told Hanuman of Rama's troubles, Hanuman says to Rama, speaking of Sugriva, "He is exiled from his kingdom and is hated by his brother Valin, who has stolen his wife and left him abandoned in the forest." Now, this is not exactly true of Sugriva; the first point is pretty true (he is exiled); but the second is not (Valin does not hate Sugriva; Sugriva hates Valin); and the third is not exactly true either: Sugriva carried off Valin's consort first, and when Valin retaliated, Sugriva fled out of guilt and terror. Nor is any of this true of any single enemy of Rama (if we take Rama as a parallel to Sugriva); it was Dasharatha who exiled Rama and caused him to flee to the forest; there is no enmity between Rama and Bharata, though Bharata occupies Rama's throne; and it was Ravana who carried off Rama's consort. If the monkey king is to be taken as the simian counterpart of Rama, then, the usurping monkey brother is a combination of Rama's father, the demon Ravana, and Rama's brother Bharata. This is hardly a neat parallelism. No, Rama sides with the wrong monkey: the usurping monkey, like Rama, is the *older* brother, the true heir; the "deposed" king had originally taken the throne from the "usurping" brother. Valin, not Sugriva, is the legal parallel to Rama. Yet the main implication of Hanuman's speech is true: Rama sympathizes with Sugriva because each of them has lost his wife and has a brother occupying the throne that was to be his. The situations are the same, but the villains are entirely different—and this is what Rama fails to notice.

The monkeys' access to human language also grants them access to human ethics, or *dharma*. On another occasion when Rama behaves badly, the monkeys remind him that he is a man (that is, higher than a monkey), just as he is elsewhere reminded, when he behaves badly, that he is a god (that is, higher than a man). When Rama kills Valin, hitting him in the back when he is fighting with Sugriva, the dying Valin reproaches Rama, saying, "I'm just a monkey, living in the forest, a vegetarian. But you are a *man*. I'm a monkey, and it is against the law to eat monkey flesh or wear monkey skin." That is, as a human, Rama should have higher ethics than a monkey and should obey human laws against the mistreatment of monkeys; it may also be implied that monkeys, in particular, are protected by human *dharma*, perhaps because of their perceived proximity to humans. But Rama defends himself against the charge of foul play by saying, "What does it matter whether you were fighting me or not, since you are nothing but a monkey? And here is the crowning argument: snares and hidden traps are always used to catch wild animals; and I don't think there is anything wrong about this. Even sages go hunting. That is why I struck you while you were fighting with your brother." But Rama is whistling in the dark here; the text judges him to have violated human *dharma* in his treatment of the monkey.

Rama is driven to this unethical act because the rage and resentment that he *should* feel toward his brother and father, but does not, is expressed for him by his monkey double—the deposed monkey king, Sugriva—and vented by Rama on that double's enemy, Valin, who doubles for Rama's brother and father. This is the sense in which the monkeys are the shadows of the human brothers, or rather, *side-shadows*, to use the term coined by Gary Saul Morson (after Bakhtin): they suggest what might have been.[6] The monkeys are not merely Valmiki's projections, nor projections from Rama's mind; they are, rather, literary fractions, symbolic layers, parallel lives. The monkey story is not merely accidentally appended; it is a telling variant of the life of Rama. But it does not mirror (dare one say monkey?) that life exactly; it is a mythological transformation, taking the pieces and rearranging them to make a slightly different pattern, as the dream work does, according to Freud. Freud (in *The Interpretation of Dreams*) and Ernest Jones after him (in *On the Nightmare*) wrote about the ways in which animals often replace, in dreams, people toward whom the dreamer has strong, dangerous, inadmissible and hence repressed emotions.[7] Or, to put it differently, the dreamer displaces emotions felt toward people whom he cannot bear to visualize directly in his dreams and projects those emotions onto animals. Thus Rama's cultural role as the perfect son and brother prevents him from expressing his personal resentment of his father and brother, and so the monkeys do it for him. In the magical world of the monkey forest, Rama's unconscious mind is set free to take the revenge that his conscious mind does not allow him in the world of humans.

TALKING ANIMALS, LISTENING HUMANS

A liminal space between anthropomorphism and zoomorphism is marked out by a mythological cluster about talking animals and humans who commit the fatal error of mistaking sexual humans for animals.[8] This corpus is found in both of the great Sanskrit epics, the *Ramayana*, which we have just considered, and the *Mahabharata* (composed between the third century B.C.E. and the third century C.E.).[9] These myths argue that we often mistake animals for people, and the reverse, in sexual (or quasi-sexual) situations. They also imply that people become animals, and therefore in a sense unrecognizable, in the sexual act that Shakespeare's Iago imagined as a "beast with two backs" (*Othello* 1.1.121). And finally, they imply that hunting, like sex, is a vice of lust; the *Arthasastra*, the ancient Indian textbook of political science, lists hunting (along with sex, gambling, and drinking) under the vices of desire,[10] and we have seen Rama, defending himself against charges of foul play against an animal, argue, "Even sages go hunting." The ultimate result of this conflation is that human hunters often mistake other humans for animals, particularly when they are mating—a mistake that has fatal consequences not only for the animals but for the unlucky hunter.

At the beginning of the *Mahabharata* (1.109), Pandu, the father of the Pandavas, is cursed to die in the embrace of his own wife because he killed a sage whom he mistook for a stag when the sage was mating with his wife (they had taken the form of a stag and a doe to do this because they were too embarrassed to do it as humans). Elsewhere in the *Mahabharata* (1.173), another king, who has been cursed to become a man-eating demon, devours a sage who is making love to his wife (still in human form), and the wife, furious because she had not "finished," curses the king to die if he embraces his own wife. These mistakes are not limited to the sexual arena. Later in this text (8.20), the warrior Karna kills a young calf by mistake (presumably mistaking it for a wild animal) and is cursed to fail in a crucial battle. And at the end of the story (17.5), the incarnate god Krishna dies when a hunter named Old Age mistakes him for an animal and shoots him in the foot, the only part of him that is mortal, like Achilles' heel.

In the *Ramayana,* Rama's father, king Dasharatha, mistakes a boy for an elephant and is cursed to lose his own son (2.57–8). Later, when Ravana plots to capture Sita, he gets another demon to take the form of a marvelous golden deer that captivates Sita and inspires her to ask Rama to pursue it for her. Rama suspects that it is a demon in disguise (this is where he expresses his wish that he could talk to it), but Sita insists. The deer leads Rama far away from Sita, and, when Rama kills the deer and it assumes its true demonic form, Rama realizes that he has been tricked and has thereby lost Sita, whom Ravana has captured in Rama's absence (3.41–44). Thus, once again, the killing of a human (or, here, a demon) in animal form causes the hunter to suffer the curse of separation from his sexual partner.

The theme of language first enters this corpus in the outside frame of the *Ramayana*, where we learn that the author, the poet Valmiki, was searching for a poetic language in which to tell the story when he went to bathe in a river. There he saw a hunter kill the male of a pair of mating cranes (Indian saras cranes), and when the hen grieved, Valmiki cried out, "Hunter, since you killed one of these birds at the height of its passion, you will not live very long." Then Valmiki realized that he had instinctively uttered this curse in verse, in a meter (the meter in which both epics are composed) that he called the *shloka,* because it was uttered in sorrow (*shoka*) (1.1–2). With this link added to the narrative chain, the corpus of stories combines five major themes: succumbing to the lust for hunting; mistaking a human for an animal and killing the "animal"; interrupting the sexual act (by killing one or both of the partners); understanding the language of animals; and creating a poetic language. Killing an animal interrupts the sexual act, the animal act, killing sex, as it were, and producing in its place the characteristic human act, the making of language.[11]

Another tale in the *Ramayana* also ties together the themes of the interruption of sexuality, the curse of separation from a beloved, the deadly nature of erotic love, and the language of birds:

A king, the father of Rama's evil stepmother, had been given the boon of understanding the cries of all creatures, but he was warned that he must not tell anyone about it. Once when he was in bed with his wife he heard a bird[12] say something funny and he laughed. She thought he was laughing at her, and she wanted to know why, but he said he would die if he told her. When she insisted that he tell her nevertheless, he sent her away and lived happily without her for the rest of his life.

$(2.32)^{13}$

As an indirect result of his ability to comprehend the language of birds, this king hears a bird talking when he is in a sexual situation and laughs, which exposes him to the danger of death and separates him from his mate. This story is in many ways the inversion of the story of Valmiki, who sees a bird who is killed in a sexual situation, hence separated from his mate, which makes him cry and inspires him to invent an unusual language of humans. Or, to forge another link, this king (Rama's step-grandfather, as it were) is forced to become separated from his wife, just as Rama's father is cursed to become separated from his son. The two episodes are related: the stepmother, daughter of the woman who wanted to know why the bird laughed, is the paradigmatic evil co-wife, who uses sexual blackmail to force Rama's father to disinherit Rama, an act that is regarded as directly responsible for the father's death; so she does kill her husband, as her mother failed to do.

Significantly, the man in this story is allowed to understand the speech of animals, and the woman is not. This is in keeping with the underlying Hindu misogyny of the Sanskrit mythological texts that depict men as more gifted with special powers than women are; it may also reflect the actual sociological fact that men in India were allowed to read and speak Sanskrit, while in general women were not.[14] In a broader sense, as we will see, all hypersexualized women are represented as talking animals—but not as talking *with* animals. In this corpus as a whole, there are logical links between, on the one hand, killing a human (who has human speech) whom you mistake for an animal (which lacks human speech) or who has become an animal (to express the bestial sexual impulse) and, on the other hand, becoming a human who has a uniquely poetic language. That is to say, these stories express the idea that the possession of human speech is a prerogative that may deprive humans of their sexuality but may deprive animals of their lives—and may deprive of their lives humans who resort to animal sexuality. Or, to put it differently, there are logical links between, on the one hand, sexual transformation (humans becoming animals in the sexual act, regarded as an animal act) and, on the other hand, linguistic transformation (the creation of speech, which distinguishes humans from animals and, sometimes, women from men). That is to say, sexuality makes humans into animals; language makes animals into humans.

We have now seen one reason why, in Hindu myths, humans become animals: to partake of animal sexuality. But there are other reasons why humans—and even gods—become animals, and this takes us deeper into the realm of zoomorphism. Let us begin with the gods. At the end of the *Mahabharata* (17.2–3), the great *dharma* king, Yudhishthira, the son of Dharma (incarnate as a god), is walking on the path to heaven, followed by a dog who has joined up with him:

> Yudhishthira went on, never looking down. Only the dog followed him—the dog that I have already told you about quite a lot. Then Indra, king of the gods, came to Yudhishthira in his chariot and said to him, "Get in." Yudhishthira said, "This dog, O lord of the past and the future, is constantly devoted to me. Let him go with me; for my way of thinking is not cruel." Indra said, "Today you have become immortal, like me, and you have won complete prosperity, and great fame, your majesty, as well as the joys of heaven. Abandon the dog. There is no cruelty in that. There is no abode for dog-owners in the world of heaven; for the evil spirits called Overpowered-by-anger carry off what has been offered, sacrificed or given as an oblation into the fire, if it is left uncovered and a dog has looked at it. Therefore you must abandon this dog, and by abandoning the dog you will win the world of the gods." Yudhishthira said, "Handing over someone who has come to you for refuge; killing a woman; confiscating the property of a Brahmin; and betraying a friend: these four acts, Indra, are equaled by the act of abandoning someone who is devoted to you; this is what I think." When he heard these words spoken by the king of dharma, the god (who had been there in the form of the dog) took his own form, Dharma, and spoke to king Yudhishthira with affection and with gentle words of praise: "Great king, you are well born, with the good conduct and intelligence of your father, and with compassion for all creatures. And now you abandoned the celestial chariot, for you insisted, 'This dog is devoted to me.' Because of this, there is no one your equal in heaven. And because of this, you have won the supreme destination of going to heaven, and with your own body."

The moral law, *dharma*, absolutely forbids Hindus to have any contact with dogs, who are regarded as unclean scavengers, the parasites of Untouchables. What is most striking about this passage is that the god of Dharma himself becomes incarnate in this animal; it is as if the God of the Hebrew Bible became incarnate in a pig. Clearly animals, real animals, not animal symbols or anthropomorphic animals, are being used here to make a powerful ethical point. All good Hindus go to heaven, but they do so after dying and being given a different, heavenly body; Yudhishthira is unique in being given the gift of going to heaven in his own body, without dying at all. There may well be an implication here that in acknowledging his bond with animals—treating his dog like "someone who has come to you for refuge" or "a friend"—Yudhishthira has somehow preserved the animality of his own body (that very animality denied by the sages who regard both dogs and sexuality as dirty) and enters heaven not merely as a disembodied spirit but as his entire self.[15]

Humans are animals in a very different sense in the *Kamasutra* of Vatsyayana, composed in north India probably at the very end of the epic period, in the third century C.E.[16] Here, humans are distinguished from animals precisely by their sexuality, in the argument that the author puts forward to justify his text:

> Scholars say: "It is appropriate to have a text about religion, because it concerns matters not of this world, and to have one about power, because that is achieved only when the groundwork is laid by special methods, which one learns from a text. But since even animals manage sex by themselves, and since it goes on all the time, it should not have to be handled with the help of a text." Vatsyayana says: Because a man and a woman depend upon one another in sex, it requires a method, and this method is learnt from the *Kamasutra*. The mating of animals, by contrast, is not based upon any method, because they are not fenced in, they mate only when the females are in their fertile season and until they achieve their goal, and they act without thinking about it first.
>
> (1.2.16–20)

The commentary by Yashodhara, composed a thousand years later, in the thirteenth century, expands upon these ideas:

> Even animals like cows, whose intellects are shrouded in torpor, visibly manage sex without instruction from a textbook; how much more must this happen among humans, whose intellects consist primarily of passion? As it is said:
>
> For desire is satisfied without instruction,
> and does not have to be taught.
> Who is the guru for deer and birds, for the methodology
> to give and take pleasure with those they desire?

And desire goes on all the time, because the qualities of wanting and hating are always there in the soul. There is no guarding or any other form of concealment, because the females of the species are loose. Animals mate only during their fertile season. Humans who want children, however, do it during a woman's fertile season but also outside her fertile season, in order to enjoy and please the woman. So animals and humans are not the same. And so the law book says:

You may have sex with a woman in her fertile season
—or any time when it is not expressly forbidden.

And animals engage in sex just until they achieve a climax; they do not wonder, "Has he reached his climax or not?" and therefore wish to mate a second time. And so, since the goal of animals and humans is not the same, animals need no method for sex. Animals, moreover do not first think, before engaging in sex, "What will happen to religion, power, sons, relatives, and the prosperity of our faction?" Sex just happens to animals in their own way.

The commentator here alludes to the Hindu belief that matter consists in three "strands" (torpor, passion, and lucidity) and that different creatures are made up of different proportions of these strands: cows have an abundance of torpor, where human beings abound in passion. (Only higher creatures like gods have a preponderance of lucidity.) Here again human language is explicitly contrasted with animal sexuality: humans, whose sexuality is more complex, more repressed ("fenced in," as the text puts it), require language (a textbook), where animals do not.

Humans, therefore, have a different sexuality from animals and need a text for it, where animals do not. But when we move from the world of science to the world of metaphor, within this same text, the *Kamasutra*, it appears that some humans are very much like animals precisely in their sexuality. The text offers a sexual typology according to size:

The man is called a "hare," "bull," or "stallion," according to the size of his sexual organ; a woman, however, is called a "doe," "mare," or "elephant cow." And so there are three equal couplings, between sexual partners of similar size, and six unequal ones, between sexual partners of dissimilar size. Among the unequal ones, when the man is larger there are two couplings with the two sexual partners immediately smaller than him and one, when he is largest, with the smallest woman. But in the opposite case, in a coupling when the man is smaller, there are two sorts of couplings with the two women immediately larger than him and one, when he is smallest, with the largest woman. Among these, the equal couplings are the best, the largest and the smallest are the worst, and the rest are intermediate. Even in the medium ones, it is better for the man to be larger than the woman. Thus there are nine sorts of couplings according to size.

(2.1.1–4)

As usual, the commentary is enlightening:

The sexual organ is called the "sign" [*linga*], because it is the sign of femaleness and so forth. From texts and from experience it is known that the male organ is convex and the female organ concave. If the man's penis is small, like a hare's, he is called a "hare"; if medium, a "bull"; if large, a "stallion." The word "however" indicates that women are distinct; they have a different nomenclature because they have a different sexual organ. Knowing this, scholars called them "doe" and so forth instead of "hare" and so forth.

The horse, hyper-sexualized, is the only animal that appears in both the male and female terminologies, though these two are not regarded as equal; the stallion is the largest male, while the mare is merely a middle-sized woman. Yet, in Hindu mythology, the mare is regarded as sexually enormous, bigger than the bull (with whom the *Kamasutra* pairs her) and an image of repressed violence: the doomsday fire is lodged in the mouth of a mare who wanders on the floor of the ocean, waiting for the moment when she will be released, to burn everything to ashes.[17] Moreover, the largest woman—the "elephant cow"—is encouraged to employ the one sexual position associated with a mare, one involving dangerous tightness, not daunting enormity: "In the 'mare's trap,' which can only be done with practice, she grasps him, like a mare, so tightly that he cannot move"(2.6. 21). And the cow does not appear here as one of the three sexual types at all, though she epitomizes the "animal" position in sexual intercourse, the equivalent of the English term "doggy style": "When she gets on the ground on all fours and he mounts her like a bull, that is 'sex like a cow.'" (2.6. 39.) Clearly the six paradigmatic animals are chosen for their size rather than their established cultural symbolism, but the disparity in their sizes reveals their deeper symbolic implications for the relationship between men and women. The nomenclature as a whole also constantly implies that despite the text's insistence that the sexuality of animals is different from that of humans, there is a very basic sense in which sex, even when done according to the book, as it were, is bestial.

Thus there are two conflicting agendas embedded in these passages: ideally, "equal is best," but in fact the man has to be bigger. This is because women are by nature bigger, in the sense that their sexuality is bigger; they are harder to satisfy. Just as elephants are bigger than stallions, so, as the commentator points out in the context of an argument about female orgasm, women have far more desire than men: "Women want a climax that takes a long time to produce, because their desire is eight times that of a man. Given these conditions, it is perfectly right to say that 'a fair-eyed woman cannot be sated by men,' because men's desire is just one eighth of women's" (2.1.19). Here he is quoting a well-known Sanskrit saying:

A fire is never sated by any amount of logs,
nor the ocean by the rivers that flow into it;
death cannot be sated by all the creatures in the world,
nor a fair-eyed woman by any amount of men.

In another text, a serial female-to-male bisexual says, when she is a woman, that a woman has eight times as much pleasure (*kama*) as a man, which could also be translated as eight times as much desire.[18]

Later in the *Kamasutra*, the greater animality of women is assumed in a passage that makes them, in contrast with men, creatures both explicitly likened to animals and said to speak a meaningless animal language:

There are eight kinds of screaming: whimpering, groaning, babbling, crying, panting, shrieking, or sobbing. And there are various sounds that have meaning, such as "Mother!" "Stop!" "Let go!" "Enough!" As a major part of moaning she may use, according to her imagination, the cries of the dove, cuckoo, green pigeon, parrot, bee, nightingale, goose, duck, and partridge. He strikes her on her back with his fist when she is seated on his lap. Then she pretends to be unable to bear it and beats him in return, while groaning, crying, or babbling. If she protests, he strikes her on the head until she sobs, using a hand whose fingers are slightly bent, which is called the "out-stretched hand." At this she babbles with sounds inside her mouth, and she sobs. When the sex ends, there is panting and crying. Shrieking is a sound like a bamboo splitting, and sobbing sounds like a berry falling into water. Always, if a man tries to force his kisses and so forth on her, she moans and does the very same thing back to him. When a man in the throes of passion slaps a woman repeatedly, she uses words like "Stop!" or

"Let me go!" or "Enough!" or "Mother!" and utters screams mixed with labored breathing, panting, crying, and groaning. As passion nears its end, he beats her extremely quickly, until the climax. At this, she begins to babble, fast, like a partridge or a goose. Those are the ways of groaning and slapping.   (2.7.1–21.)

It is worth noting that these women make the noises of birds, never of mammals, let alone the mammals that characterize the three paradigmatic sizes of women. Birds, as we have seen, are implicated in the Hindu mythology of fatal sexuality linked with language. Moreover, one of the birds whose babbling the sexual woman imitates—the parrot—appears elsewhere in the *Kamasutra* as one of the two birds who can be taught to speak like humans: teaching parrots and mynah birds to talk is a skill that both a man and a woman should learn (courtesans, in particular, often have parrots in Indian poetry and paintings) and that a man can use to lure a woman to his home (the ancient Indian equivalent of coming up to see his etchings) (1.3.15, 1.4.8, 6.1.15).

The passage about slapping and groaning inculcates what we now recognize as the rape mentality—"her mouth says no, but her eyes say yes"—a dangerous line of thought that leads ultimately to places where we now no longer want to be: disregarding a woman's protests against rape. And this treatment of women is justified by a combination of the official naming of women after oversized animals with oversized desire and the expectation that in the throes of passion women will become animals and lose their human speech. Thus, the commentator assures us, speaking of the woman who has the most sexual energy (of three types) and lasts longest (also of three types): "The passion even of a long-lasting woman whose sexual energy is fierce is quelled when she is slapped" (2.7.11).

The behavior of the woman—making her animal noises—is a ritualized, performed action regarded as appropriate for her gender. At this point, the text tells us that men, too, may do this—but, again, only in performance, and only for a moment:

A man's natural talent is
his roughness and ferocity,
a woman's is her lack of power
and her suffering, self-denial, and weakness.
Their passion and a particular technique
may sometimes lead them even to exchange roles;
but not for very long. In the end,
the natural roles are reestablished.

(2.7.22–3)

> Sometimes, but not always, there is an exchange when they make love, out of the pull of passion or according to the practice of the place. Then the woman abandons her own ways and changes to what the man has a natural talent for, doing the slapping, while the man abandons his own way, of slapping the woman, and takes up her ways, moaning and screaming. But after a short time, they change back. And in the absence of passion or this particular technique, they do it just as before, and there is no occasion to switch.

In the *Ramayana*, as we have seen, the fact that Hanuman can speak Sanskrit and that monkeys in general can speak human languages forces humans to apply human ethical considerations to monkeys alone among animals. The natural zoomorphism of women is the other side of the coin of this liminal anthropomorphism of the epics, in which some animals speak human languages and some humans—males, contrasting with females—are privileged to understand the language of animals. In the full spate of sexuality, women lose their human language and become like animals. To compare this scenario with the paradigm of the death of copulating animals, we might say that in an inversion of the myth of the creation of poetic language by the violent interruption of sex, violent sex implies the suspension of language.[19] Men may, sometimes, become like women who have become like animals, moaning and screaming instead of using male human speech. But a modern feminist would say that it is not at such moments of role reversal but when men expect women to behave like animals, while they themselves behave like men, that the men are truly behaving like animals.

BEYOND SEXUALITY:
LANGUAGE AND COMPASSION FOR ANIMALS

Language is the place from which compassion springs. Now we know that dolphins and whales can talk not only to one another but to us. This knowledge brings to life the myth of the fish and the bridge and makes us wonder if perhaps someday dolphins will tell us their myths. But since dolphins are not fish but look like fish and since they are animals but they talk to us as other animals cannot, they doubly straddle the boundary between our own categories of mammals and fish and thereby threaten our definition of what it is to be human. This accounts, in part, for some peoples' reluctance to call what dolphins do "speech." And in fact the language that people use to talk to dolphins is neither the language in which dolphins talk to one another nor the language in which we talk to one another—it is a Rosetta stone language. Yet it is a language, and it joins us with the fish.

The belief that all animals may be in some sense less other than they seem to be is the source of the ever-enchanting myth of a magic time or place or person that erases the boundary between humans and animals.[20] The time of this animal paradise finds a close parallel in the myth that tells of the time when gods walked among people or people walked among gods. The place, like the magic place in the Looking-Glass forest where things have no names, where Alice could walk with her arms around the neck of a fawn, is like the high mountains where people mingle with the gods. And the particular individual with these special powers finds a parallel in the myth of a particular person (often a shaman or a priest) who has the special ability to traffic with the gods.

Famous examples of such people who live at peace among animals would include Enkidu in the *Gilgamesh* epic, Francis of Assisi, and the many mythical children who are raised as cubs by packs of animals, like Romulus and Remus, Mowgli, and Tarzan, like Pecos Bill (suckled by a puma) and Davy Crockett (raised among mountain lions). Our list might also include the women of Euripides' *Bacchae*, who suckle at their breasts fawns or wolf cubs, while snakes lick their cheeks. It is significant that the Bacchae abandon their own nursing children and dismember tame cattle; it is only in the wild that they are at home.[21] T. H. White (who once translated a medieval bestiary) imagined the young King Arthur's education by Merlin the magician as taking place among ants and geese and owls and badgers, whose language Arthur understood.[22] Siegfried in German mythology and Fionn in Irish mythology gain the ability to understand the language of animals by licking their fingers after touching a part of a magic animal—for Siegfired, the blood of a dragon, for Fionn, the drippings of a magic salmon. Significantly, they do not eat the animals, though the animals are killed. The myths in which we speak the language of animals are generally myths about friendships with wild animals that we normally hunt, not the tame animals that we sacrifice, but it might be extended to include children born and raised among domestic animals: Oedipus raised among sheep and Jesus born in a manger.

In the parallels to these stories in which we commune with gods rather than animals, the gods do not become human; a human becomes one of the gods. So, too, the ideal state of humans among animals is not one in which wild animals become tame (as they often do in reality, as in the story of Elsa the lioness in *Born Free*); it is a state in which a human becomes an animal. Nietzsche's Zarathustra encountered a sage in the forest who urged him, "Do not go to man. Stay in the forest! Go rather even to the animals! Why do you not want to be as I am—a bear among bears, a bird among birds?" But the human who becomes part of the society of animals usually remains a human; the adopted child remains human and must eventually return to the human world. Zarathustra mocked and rejected the "saint."[23]

To be a bird among birds means, among other things, not eating birds. It is difficult, though not impossible, to torment—or eat—the people we speak with. Elaine Scarry made the first point, in reverse, when she argued that torture takes away speech,[24] and Lewis Carroll made the second when the Red Queen, having introduced Alice to the roast ("Alice—mutton: Mutton—Alice"), commanded: "It isn't etiquette to cut any one you've been introduced to. Remove the joint!"[25] This compassion-inducing language need not be even the signing of chimps, let alone the whistles of dolphins or the body language of primates; it may be no more than the silent language of the eyes. Emmanuel Levinas once said that the face of the other says, "Don't kill me."[26] This is the language that inspires empathy, the language that is denied by people who defend the right to treat animals as things through a self-serving tautology.[27]

Anthropomorphism and zoomorphism are two different attempts to reduce the otherness between humans and animals, to see the sameness beneath the difference. But sameness, just like difference, may lead to the inhuman treatment of both humans and nonhumans.[28] The ethical decision to treat animals according to the basic standards of human decency is one that must be taken regardless of whether we prefer to emphasize the qualities that they share with us—such as their sexuality—or those that they do not—their language.

NOTES

1. For the cat, see *Tantrakhyana*, tale 1, cited in Wendy Doniger and Brian K. Smith, trans., *The Laws of Manu* (Harmondsworth: Penguin Books, 1991), 92, verse 4.195. For the heron, see *Manu* 4.196 and *Panchatantra of Vishnu Sharma*, trans. Chandra Rajan (Harmondsworth: Penguin, 1995), 1.6.

2. Chuang Chou, *Chuang-tzu*, book 17, paragraph 13, "Chuang-tzu and Hui-tzu dispute on their understanding of the enjoyment of fishes." See Herbert A. Giles, trans., *Chuang Tzu: Mystic, Moralist, and Social Reformer* (London: B. Quaritch, 1926), 218–19.

3. *Vishnu Purana* (Calcutta: Sanatana Shastra, 1972), 5.3.

4. *Ramayana of Valmiki*, 7 vols. (Baroda: Oriental Institute, 1960–75).

5. J. L. Masson, "Fratricide and the Monkeys: Psychoanalytic Observations on an Episode in the Valmikiramayanam," *Journal of the American Oriental Society* 95 (1975): 454–59.

6. Gary Saul Morson, *Narrative and Freedom: The Shadows of Time* (New Haven: Yale University Press, 1994).

7. Ernest Jones, *On the Nightmare* (London: Hogarth Press, 1949).

8. See Wendy Doniger, *The Bedtrick: Tales of Sex and Masquerade* (Chicago: University of Chicago Press, 2000), 118–22.

9. *Mahabharata of Vyasa*, 18 vols. (Poona: Bhandarkar Oriental Research Institute, 1933–69).

10. *Arthasastra of Kautilya*, vol. 2, ed. and trans. R. P. Kangle (Bombay: University of Bombay, 1960), 8.3.38–55.

11. These themes are also combined in the story of Cephalus and Procris that Ovid tells in the *Metamorphoses* 7.700–865.

12. The creature is a *jrimbha*, a rare word (related to the verb for "to yawn, expand, or have an erection") that probably refers to a bird.

13. *Ramayana* passage rejected by critical edition at 2.32, appendix 1, no. 14, 36–54. Cf. *Jataka* 386 (the *Kharaputta Jataka*) about a cobra woman and talking animals.

14. There are exceptions to this rule, such as an explicit statement in the *Kamasutra* that some women were capable of reading such texts, but in general it prevailed.

15. I owe this realization to Lorraine Daston's response to an earlier stage of this paper.

16. *Kamasutra of Vatsyayana*, with the "Jayamangala" commentary of Shri Yashodhara. (Bombay: Lakshmivenkateshvara Steam Press, 1856). *Kamasutra of Vatsyayana*, trans. Wendy Doniger and Sudhir Kakar (New York: Oxford University Press, 2002).

17. Wendy Doniger O'Flaherty, *Siva: The Erotic Ascetic* (London: Oxford University Press, 1973), 289–92.

18. Wendy Doniger, *Splitting the Difference: Gender and Myth in Ancient Greece and India* (Chicago: University of Chicago Press, 1999), 287–92 (the tale of Chudala, in the *Yogavasistha*). Some Greek texts maintain that Teiresias, too, said that women have not just more pleasure, but *nine times* as much pleasure as men—thereby one-upping the ante. See Doniger, *Splitting the Difference*, 293.

19. This was the excellent insight of Fernando Vidal, in his response to the presentation of this paper in Berlin.

20. The ideas in this and the following two paragraphs are further developed in Wendy Doniger O'Flaherty, *Other Peoples' Myths: The Cave of Echoes* (New York; Macmillan, 1988; reprint, Chicago: University of Chicago Press, 1995), chapter 4.

21. Euripides, *Bacchae*, ed. and trans. E. R. Dodds (Oxford: Oxford University Press, 1989) 699–702.

22. T. H. White, *The Once and Future King*, part 1, "The Sword in the Stone" (New York: Putnam, 1958). The culmination of the animal education comes in chapter 23.

23. Friedrich Nietzsche, *Also Sprach Zarathustra* (Stuttgart: A. Kröner, 1975), part 1, prologue, para. 2. Friedrich Nietzsche, *Thus Spoke Zarathustra*, in *The Portable Nietzsche*, trans. Walter Kaufman (Harmondsworth: Penguin, 1976), 123.

24. Elaine Scarry, *The Body in Pain: The Making and Unmaking of the World* (New York: Oxford University Press, 1985).

25. Lewis Carroll, *Through the Looking-Glass*, chapter 9, "Queen Alice."

26. Emmanuel Levinas, *Totality and Infinity: An Essay on Exteriority*, trans. Alphonso Lingis (The Hague: Martinus Nijhoff, 1979), 198–99.

27. This paragraph is reworked from my essay, Wendy Doniger, "Compassion Toward Animals," in *The Lives of Animals*, by J.M. Coetzee, ed. Amy Gutmann (Princeton, N.J.: Princeton University Press, 1999), 93–106.

28. For this argument, see Wendy Doniger, *The Implied Spider: Politics and Theology in Myth* (New York: Columbia University Press, 1998), 31–33.

· ·

CHAPTER 2

Intelligences

Angelic, Animal, Human

· ·

Lorraine Daston

INTRODUCTION:
ANTHROPOMORPHISM AND ITS DISCONTENTS

It is notoriously difficult to imagine one's way into another person's way of thinking, feeling, being. It is allegedly impossible to imagine one's way into the lived experience of other life forms—not only that of bats and Martians, but even of dogs and monkeys. Tolstoy's imagining of the inner life of Anna Karenina pales beside the prospect of reconstructing from within what it is like to be an ape—or an angel. Yet the specter of impossibility has not discouraged some doughty writers from the attempt: consider two examples by authors of genius, John Milton and Franz Kafka. Here is Milton's explanation, put into the mouth of the archangel Raphael in conversation with Adam, of how angels think:

> "So from the root
> Springs lighter the green stalk, from thence the leaves
> More aery, last the bright consummate flower
> Spirits odorous breathes: flowers and their fruit,
> Man's nourishment, by gradual scale sublimed,
> To vital spirits aspire, to animal,
> To intellectual, give both life and sense,
> Fancy and understanding, whence the Soul
> Reason receives, and Reason is her being,
> Discursive or intuitive: discourse

Is oftest yours, the latter most is ours
Differing but in degree, of kind the 'same."[1]

And now Kafka's account, written in the form of a report by an ape to an
unnamed academy, recalling his caged transport from Africa to Europe:

> I did survive this period. Hopelessly sobbing, painfully hunting for
> fleas, apathetically licking a coconut, beating my skull against the
> locker, sticking out my tongue at anyone who came near me—that
> was how I filled in time at first in my new life. But over and above
> it all only the one feeling: no way out. Of course what I felt then as
> an ape I can represent now only in human terms, and therefore I
> misrepresent it, but although I cannot reach back to the truth of the
> old ape life, there is no doubt that it lies somewhere in the direction
> I have indicated.[2]

Neither of these trapeze acts of the imagination shakes free of anthropomorphism: Milton depends on a continuum of being, stretching from body
to spirit and from discursive to intuitive reason, in order to make the life
of angels comprehensible to Adam and human readers; the crux of Kafka's
short story is that the ape has become too humanized "by excellent men-
tors, good advice, applause, and orchestral music" to be able to describe
his former life. But my point is not to belabor the obvious—that humans
face great, perhaps insurmountable obstacles when they try to understand
what it would be like to be nonhuman. Rather, I am interested in why,
given the probable futility of the quest, systematic and sustained attempts
have nonetheless been made to escape anthropomorphism, to think one's
way into truly other minds. These attempts are admittedly rare, especially
if one abandons the realm of imaginative literature and restricts oneself to
inquiries based on argument and evidence. Yet such intellectual traditions
do exist; the two I shall focus upon here, of which the passages from Milton
and Kafka are emblematic, are medieval angelology and late-nineteenth-
and early-twentieth-century comparative psychology.[3]

My reasons for choosing these two particular examples, and especially
for treating them in tandem, may seem eccentric. They are remote from
one another in time, in intellectual and cultural context, in investigative
practices, in ultimate goals, and, above all, in subject matter—angels versus apes (or, more accurately, angels versus dogs).[4] Rational theology of
the sort pursued in thirteenth-century Paris by the likes of Bonaventure
and Thomas Aquinas contrasts starkly with the empirical science of animal behavior that Charles Darwin, George Romanes, Erich Wasmann,

Conwy Lloyd Morgan, and others labored to establish after the publication of Darwin's *Descent of Man, and Selection in Relation to Sex* in 1871. There are, however, parallels between the two traditions that are instructive for an investigation of anthropomorphism and its discontents. Both traditions regarded anthropomorphism as a formidable threat to their undertakings—recall that anthropomorphism was a theological sin long before it became a scientific one.[5] To apply human categories to God, and even to the separated intelligences commonly known as angels, was recognized by medieval theologians to be at once risky and inevitable—much the same predicament articulated by the post-Darwinian comparative psychologists. Both psychologists and theologians relied on analogy to bridge the unbridgeable—however different in other respects, a strictly hierarchical organization of divine creation, on the one hand, and evolutionary theory, on the other, both posit continua that underpin analogy. Moreover, both theologians and psychologists were centrally interested in two aspects of the human/nonhuman comparison: thought and feeling. Do angels feel sadness? Can they recognize individuals? Do animals have concepts? Are they bitten by remorse? In both cases, inquiries into the mental world of nonhumans served to sharpen and refine notions of human understanding and emotion.

It is at this point that the contrasts between the two traditions also become instructive: What exactly was understood under "understanding," be it angelic, animal, or human? Neither angelology nor comparative psychology aimed primarily at illuminating the nature of human mental life, but their endeavors to probe nonhuman minds involved them willy-nilly in contrasts and comparisons. Indeed, these inquiries into nonhuman minds might with some justice be regarded as among the most daring attempts ever made to fathom the nature and limits of the human mind.

My aim in juxtaposing these two traditions of inquiry into nonhuman minds is to suggest that the meaning of anthropomorphism has changed profoundly, along with notions of mental life. To this end, taking two disparate cases widely separated in time has its advantages. Contrasts are thrown into stark relief. What is it like to be a bat—or an angel, or a mouse? For the comparative psychologists, the answer to this question implied reconstructing the conscious experience of other life forms, which was in turn assumed to be powerfully shaped by sensory apparatus and bodily structure. The answer was, in short, the subjective experience of being that life form, which could only be inferred through a glass darkly, by observing its outward behavior. The writings of the comparative psychologists abounded with distinctions between the subjective and objective when they confronted the difficulties of animal minds (or for that matter, any minds other than one's own). We are still their heirs in this respect: when nowadays philosopher Thomas Nagel asks, "What is it like to be a bat?" he takes for granted that the answer ought to be about "conscious mental states . . . the subjective character of experience."[6]

This was not the kind of answer sought by the medieval theologians in their inquiries into angelology (although their methods otherwise bear a strong resemblance to those of modern analytic philosophers like Nagel). Not only were they innocent of the terms (and arguably of the concepts) "objective" and "subjective";[7] they were after something quite different, namely, the nature and workings of angelic understanding. Their efforts to analyze the angelic psyche were doubtless larded with as much anthropomorphism as those of the comparative psychologists keen to fathom the canine consciousness, but both the "anthropos" and the "morphos" in question were of quite different sorts. It is perhaps not so surprising that what is considered to be the sine qua non of the human shifts with historical and cultural context. It is perhaps more surprising that the shape of understanding the nonhuman—the "morphos" of anthropomorphism—also changes dramatically.

Perhaps the most dramatic of all these changes concerns the answer to this question: How does an angel—or an animal—think and feel? Since the mid-nineteenth century, investigators have automatically parsed that question into another one: What would it be like to be an angel or an animal? That is, they have assumed that the problem of studying nonhuman minds is the same as the problem of experiencing nonhuman subjectivities. To know how an ape thinks and feels is to imagine its consciousness, as a novelist might imagine the interior life of a character. But both the terminology and concepts of the objective and subjective, at least in their familiar sense, date only to the early decades of the nineteenth century.[8] Because the distinction between objectivity and subjectivity has become so fundamental to modern ways of thinking, it is hard to conceive of alternative ways of posing the question of how to understand nonhuman minds except in terms of objective behavior and subjective consciousness. Hence medieval angelology is useful as a kind of methodological thought experiment: If understanding other minds, both human and nonhuman, were not about probing alien subjectivities, that is, vicariously experiencing strange states of consciousness, what would it be about?

This essay, then, tries to put anthropomorphism to work: What can human projections onto the nonhuman, especially those acutely aware of the pitfalls of anthropomorphism, tell the historian about the most deeply rooted assumptions concerning the human mind and their mutability over time? What are the different ways in which knowledge of the nonhuman can be cast? What is it about nonhuman minds—be they angelic or animal, alien or robotic—that so irresistibly invites wistful speculations (wistful because almost certain to fail)? If the fact of anthropomorphism is undeniable, why is the yearning to transcend anthropomorphism so intense? Why, in short, are angels and animals good to think with, even if we never really succeed in thinking with them? And finally, why, despite this yearning, and despite methodological imperatives sternly repeated like commandments ("Thou shalt not commit anthropomorphism"), are the forbidden pleasures of imagining archangels or squirrels to be just like us, only attired in strange costumes and speaking unintelligible tongues, so sweet?

In the space of a brief essay, I can address these questions only schematically. In the next two sections on angelic and animal intelligences, I attempt a distillation of the views and practices of theologians and psychologists, respectively, on the problem of anthropomorphism and the best way to go about describing nonhuman mental life. I shall argue that there is a profound difference between modes of understanding nonhuman minds before and after the emergence of the modern objectivity/subjectivity distinction. In my conclusion, I return to the questions of why anthropomorphism is at once so encumbering and enchanting.

ANGELIC INTELLIGENCES

Among Milton's sources for his account of angelic life in *Paradise Lost* was almost certainly a Greek treatise, *On Celestial Hierarchies*, probably by an anonymous Syriac monk in the fifth century C.E., but long attributed in the Latin West to Dionysius the Aeropagite, the Athenian who converted to Christianity after hearing Saint Paul preach (Acts 17.34) and who by the second century C.E. had become identified as the first bishop of Athens. *On Celestial Hierarchies*, a work compounded of Jewish angel lore and Hellenistic Neoplatonism, was translated into Latin in the ninth century by Joannes Scotus Erigena, followed by new translations in the twelfth century. In the high Middle Ages, this text, especially its fifteenth chapter, became the principal fount for the western Christian theology, art, and literature of angels through the seventeenth century.[9] When, for example, Dante described the ranks of angels as flames and rehearsed the nine orders of "this hierarchy divine," he was relying on Pseudo-Dionysius, who had likened angels to the element of fire.[10] Along with passages in the Old and New Testaments mentioning angels, *On Celestial Hierarchies* (and the textbook tradition created by Peter Lombard's *Sententiae*) also guided the efforts of twelfth- and thirteenth-century theologians to reveal the nature of angels.[11]

There is, however, a pronounced shift in the angelology of Bonaventure and Thomas Aquinas from the earlier mystical and creedal reflections inspired by Pseudo-Dionysius. Pseudo-Dionysius's interchangeable use of the terms "angels" and "intelligences" encouraged thirteenth-century theologians to identify angels with the intelligences in Greek philosophy (especially in astronomy)[12] and more generally to embark upon an angelology less concerned with the symbolism and mission of angels than with their peculiar nature. Moreover, the rise of the dialectical methods of the *quaestio* at universities such as Paris (center of medieval angelology) promoted a logical and philosophical mode of analysis, honed to a sharp edge by the competitive rites of scholastic disputation and of masters vying for fee-paying students and ecclesiastical preferment. These intellectual and institutional conditions paved the way for the thirteenth-century efflorescence of what might be called rational angelology, self-consciously drawing more on reason than on revelation, until the Condemnations of 1277 issued by the Parisian bishop Etienne Tempier dampened this line of theological speculation.[13]

The rational theologians faced the challenge of imagining minds defined not only as different from but also superior to those of human beings; moreover, angelic minds were not joined to sensory organs[14]—a particularly knotty problem for scholastic psychology, which was based on the maxim that "nothing is in the mind which was not first in the senses." Descriptions of the divine mind, though of course infinitely removed from human minds, were in some ways a simpler matter: all perfections could simply be carried to their outermost limit. Angelic minds were, however, finite, even if superhuman, and the precarious bridges built out of materials drawn from scriptural passages, patristic teachings, and Aristotelian psychology and epistemology depended on delicate judgments of analogy and degree. Angelic thoughts and emotions had to be inferred from human thoughts and emotions, but with the full cautionary weight of a thoroughly different composition (predominantly or entirely spiritual as opposed to combined spiritual and corporeal), different ways of acquiring knowledge about the world (through intelligible forms rather than sensation), and different moral makeup (wills uncontaminated by sin and perfectly aligned to the will of God). In what follows, I shall try to give the flavor of these inferences, without entering into the many debates on specific issues. I shall concentrate on the views of Aquinas, which were arguably the culmination of scholastic angelology, shortly prior to the Condemnations of 1277. For my purposes, it is the form of the inference from the human to the nonhuman and its potential for generating novel psychological possibilities that is at issue.

How do angels know material things, according to Aquinas, given that they themselves are entirely immaterial and can neither see, hear, smell, taste, or feel? That they must know them follows from the hierarchical order of creation for Aquinas: if human minds can know material things, then a fortiori angels must know them, being higher in the order of being.[15] But angelic ways of knowing differ from both human and divine cognizance of the same objects. God knows all things, for they are merely emanations of the divine essence; humans know material objects by abstracting from sensations impressed upon their bodily organs. Angels in contrast converge to the same knowledge by intelligible species implanted in them by God at the creation.[16] In scholastic psychology, this is a more efficient way of knowing than abstraction from the senses, since what the latter achieves laboriously, the former attains directly, by an immediate intuition of the form (which in both cases is the proper object of knowledge). Moreover, angels manage to know many more things with fewer intelligible species. Similarly, higher orders of angels have more universal forms than lower ones, for example the Seraphim as compared to the Thrones or Archangels.

The knowledge of intelligible species is, however, not yet knowledge of individuals. Forms are individuated by their peculiar admixture of matter—in scholastic terminology, the potentiality of the matter has not been entirely perfected by the form. Hence the reason why this particular frog or crystal differs from its fellows is the recalcitrance of matter thwarting the species' form. Can angels, who are pure form, pick out individuals within a species? This is a question fraught with consequences for Christian devotion: guardian angels must be able to distinguish their wards from other human beings; archangels and angels properly so-called (that is, "messengers") are sent by God on missions to specific individuals—the archangel Gabriel, for example, must be competent to single out Mary, betrothed to Joseph of the House of David, from all of the other young women in Galilee in order to inform her that "her child will be called holy, the Son of God" (Luke 1.35). In short, for at least the lowest order of angels (Principalities, Archangels, Angels), being able to discriminate individuals is part of the job description.[17] Aquinas explains that whereas human minds know by analysis (*resolutio*), angelic minds identify individuals by synthesis (*compositio*), that is, by bringing together all of the intelligible forms in which the individual participates (imagine a kind of Venn diagram intersection of all the forms relevant to the individual in question).[18] Although painted with a human visage and eyes, Gabriel does not "see" Mary; he intuits her by a combination of intelligible species forms.[19]

As Milton has the archangel Raphael explain to Adam, angelic and human reason also differ generically from one another, the one intuitive and the other discursive. The discursive reasoning Raphael attributes to humans attains knowledge by enchained arguments, as in a mathematical demonstration; the intuitive knowledge of angels is, in contrast, immediate and self-evident. In keeping with the continuous movement of generation and corruption of all things in the sublunary sphere, human reason advances from one thing to another, through necessary and conjectural inference. Angels, too, must resort to this step-by-step discursive reasoning when they attempt to predict the future, which they can only do by inferences from causes to effects, or to divine the secret thoughts of humans, which again requires indirect inferences from outward bodily signs. (Only God knows immediately the future and the innermost thoughts and desires of human reason and will.) But angelic intelligence is primarily intuitive, knowing all the consequences of a premise immediately, in a flash of instantaneous and comprehensive cognition—as if one were to comprehend all of mathematics in a single illumination of self-evidence.[20] Yet there is a kind of movement, or at least progression, of states of understanding in the angelic mind. Angelic minds comprehend more with fewer intelligible forms than human minds do, but angels nonetheless require a number of such forms and must exercise their will to choose which form to contemplate, for even angels can understand only one thing at a time; God alone understands all things simultaneously.[21]

This is as close as Aquinas ever gets to speculating about the contents of angelic consciousness—to wondering, to pose a deeply anachronistic question, What is it like to be an angel? Medieval angelology also discussed angelic affections—angels know joy but not sadness; they are consumed by love—but it is the joy of beatitude and the ardent love of God, states glimpsed only by human saints, at least in this life.[22] Theologians based their claims about angelic minds on analogy, shuttling between the higher human faculties of intellect and reason and God's omniscience, and occasionally also on the hierarchy of creation: higher beings must understand all that lower beings understand and more; angelic understandings are as incorruptible as the pure aether in which they dwell. But there were almost no attempts to grasp angelic understanding empathetically, although Aquinas quoted Gregory the Great with approval: "man senses in common with the brutes, and understands with the angels."[23]

Hence the anthropomorphism of medieval angelology was of a structural, rather than a subjective sort. Thirteenth-century theologians were as acutely aware of the pitfalls of relying too heavily upon human models as the nineteenth-century comparative psychologists would be, although each advanced a principled (if different) rationale for the restricted use of human analogies. If anything, the challenge of investigating the nature of disembodied "intelligences existing apart" dwarfed that of understanding animal minds: dogs and monkeys at least have bodies and senses that resemble our own. No doubt the treatises of the angelologists were therefore at least as riddled with anthropomorphism as those of the post-Darwinian comparative psychologists; the same goes in spades for the literary and artistic depictions of angels based on these treatises. No carefree monkey ever frolicked as happily in the anecdotes of Darwin and Romanes as the ludic angels playing and dancing together in Dante's *Paradiso* or Fra Angelico's *Last Judgment*. But attempts to understand the angelic mind did not equate this undertaking with attempts to understand angelic consciousness. However anthropomorphic, medieval angelology was not about angelic subjectivity.

ANIMAL INTELLIGENCES

In *The Descent of Man* (1871), Darwin gingerly addressed the issue of the so-called higher faculties—abstraction, self-consciousness, individuality—in animals:

> No one supposes that one of the lower animals reflects whence he comes or whither he goes,—what is death, or what is life, and so forth. But can we feel sure that an old dog with an excellent memory and some power of imagination, as shewn by his dreams, never reflects on his past pleasures of the chase? and this would be a form of self-consciousness. . . . That animals retain their mental individuality is unquestionable.[24]

That dogs and other mammals possessed some form of consciousness, if not self-consciousness, was an almost universal assumption among evolutionists. Whether they possessed moral sense, intelligence, and even reason was more controversial,[25] but even these debates were informed by a general assumption that the qualities in question expressed themselves as a certain kind of conscious experience. Even the British comparative psychologist Lloyd Morgan, famously skeptical on the issue of animal reason (though not intelligence), framed the problem in terms of a certain kind of conscious experience (inevitably that of a dog): "When the dog sees a bone held above him by the kindly cook, just beyond his reach, he has not only a definite impression of the bone in the focus of his hungry consciousness, but he is aware also of much besides—the cook, the dresser, the kitchen-ceiling, and so forth, all of which is, indeed, of wholly subsidiary interest to him, but is none the less present to his consciousness. . . . There is a marked distinction between perceiving a distant object and perceiving the distance of the object."[26] Whether juicy bone in the concrete or distance thereto in the abstract, the mental capacities of Lloyd Morgan's dog boiled down to the contents of its consciousness.

My aim in this section is not to review the many-faceted debate over animal minds sparked by Darwinian evolutionary theory,[27] but rather to examine the role and nature of anthropomorphism in the efforts of comparative psychologists to adduce evidence for and against continuity between human and animal mental faculties. I shall argue that, in contrast to the inquiries of the medieval angelologists, those of the post-Darwinian comparative psychologists were stamped by a kind of anthropomorphism that was subjective in its aims and conception. I do not mean to assert thereby that the anthropomorphism practiced by the medieval angelologists was somehow "objective" (I believe it was neither subjective nor objective); my point is that the distinction between objective and subjective, barely older than Darwinism itself, recast the meaning and practice of anthropomorphism.[28] Instead of likening the structures and functions of human and nonhuman minds, as the angelologists had, the later practitioners of anthropomorphism drew analogies between the conscious experience of different species.

An exquisite awareness of the simultaneous necessity and dangers of anthropomorphism haunted the literature of comparative psychology from the appearance of *The Descent of Man* in 1871 until the triumph of behaviorism in the 1920s. Skeptics and true believers on the question of animal reasoning powers and moral judgment were united on this score. George Romanes, Darwin's adoring disciple and author of a compendious collection of stories about the alleged mental abilities of animals from protozoa to monkeys, and Margaret Washburn, advocate of new experimental methods in comparative psychology and sharp critic of Romanes's colorful anecdotes, agreed at least on this much. Romanes asserted the validity of the analogy from human to animal minds on evolutionary grounds, while at the same time admitting its inevitability—anthropomorphism was at once a virtue and a necessity: "If we observe an ant or a bee apparently exhibiting sympathy or rage, we must either conclude that some psychological state resembling that of sympathy or rage is present, or refuse to think about the subject at all; from the observable fact there is no other inference open."[29] Washburn, although she suspected evolutionists like Romanes of holding a brief for animal intelligence and deplored his "unscientific" observations, agreed with his diagnosis of the animal psychologist's predicament: "whether we will or no, we must be anthropomorphic in the notions we form of what takes place in the mind of an animal."[30] Even the American psychologist Edward Thorndike, a crusader for experiment in comparative psychology and a confessed infidel in the matter of animal intelligence, thought he would be able to discern deliberation in the cats he tested by looking at them, as well as by charting their learning curves.[31]

The anthropomorphism in question referred to the lived mental experiences of other animals. Romanes, who believed that he had gathered strong evidence for animal intelligence and reason, defined these higher faculties as implying "the conscious knowledge of the relation between means employed and ends attained."[32] Consciousness was in turn molded by the body and sensory apparatus of the particular animal; an invertebrate could not be expected to experience anger as a vertebrate did; the consciousness of dogs and deer would be dominated by olfactory sensations; animals lacking humans' "geometrical sense of touch" must form very different mental impressions.[33] German psychologist Wilhelm Wundt thought that there was in principle no difference between inferring conscious states of animal minds and unconscious states of human minds from observed behavior: in both cases "we must translate the processes that have led to the [observed] results into the language of our own consciousness."[34] Knowledge of the mind—one's own, those of other humans, and those of animals—was in this psychological tradition ipso facto knowledge of subjective consciousness. In his widely cited *Handbook of Psychology*, American psychologist James Mark Baldwin insisted that the "*most essential characteristic of mental states is their subjective nature,*" a consideration that to his mind in no way prejudiced the case for comparative psychology.[35] The question, What is it like to be an animal? had become unavoidable in the study of other minds.

Reservations about excessive anthropomorphism in comparative psychology did not necessarily unsettle the view that knowledge of animal minds was knowledge of animal consciousness. Lloyd Morgan's celebrated canon (he called it a "basal principle"), which continues to guide research in comparative psychology to this day,[36] dictates that "*in no case may we interpret an action as the outcome of the exercise of a higher psychical faculty, if it can be interpreted as the outcome of the exercise of one which stands lower in the psychological scale.*"[37] For Lloyd Morgan, the consistent application of this principle showed that animals were capable of great intelligence but not abstract reason; of sympathy but not justice—not even his own "favourite and clever dog."[38] Fond pet owners, cautioned Lloyd Morgan, compulsively projected their own concepts and standards of rectitude onto animals, conflating observed facts with the inferences drawn from them. If Mrs. Mann's dog Carlo apprehended the renegade dog Toby in the act of theft, it was not necessarily because of Carlo's sense of righteousness. If a friend's dog knew to set down the basket of eggs it was carrying before leaping the stile, it was not necessarily because the dog had reasoned that the eggs would otherwise break.[39] Yet Lloyd Morgan's ultimate grounds for denying these dogs abstract reason and morality (though not intelligence and sympathy) was subjective motive, not objective behavior. He did not, as later behaviorists would, refuse to speculate on the inaccessible contents of animal consciousness; rather, he insisted upon the gap between those subjective states and objective behavior that apparently betokened reason and moral sense, and he made subjectivity his ultimate criterion.[40] It was not enough to act rationally or justly; the proper states of mind must accompany these actions.

It is revealing to note which subjective states comparative psychologists read off from observed behavior with the greatest confidence—in which cases, in other words, they practiced anthropomorphism with the fewest reservations. Darwin was thoroughly convinced that dogs felt sympathy with their masters; so was Wundt.[41] So was Romanes, adducing the story of a Mrs. E. Picton, who persuaded her recalcitrant dog to allow itself to be bathed by giving it the cold shoulder for a week.[42] Even the cautious Lloyd Morgan cited the same story without demur, adding: "That dogs feel sympathy with man will scarcely be questioned by any one who has known the companionship of these four-footed friends. At times they seem instinctively to grasp our moods, to be silent with us when we are busy, to lay their shaggy heads on our knees when we are worried or sad, and to be quickened to fresh life when we are gay and glad—so keen are their perceptions."[43] Perhaps most telling of all was the response of those who believed that they had observed animal sympathy towards an injured conspecific. Romanes relates several stories of hunters who felt keen remorse for having killed or wounded monkeys—not because of the act of violence itself but because of the grief-stricken response of the other monkeys. Capacity for sympathy—recognized as such without hesitation by human observers—inducted the sensitive species into a moral community of sorts.[44] The human faculty that permitted inferences about animal emotions—the sympathetic imagination—was precisely the one that comparative psychologists were most certain they could discover in other species and also the one that elevated the animal highest in their moral estimation.

Drawing inferences about intellectual abilities of other species was a more vexed business, in part because the key terms "instinct," "intelligence," and "reason" were so variously defined by different authors. From the standpoint of the *longue durée* in the history of psychology, what is at least as striking as the convolutions of the definitional debates is the almost universal assumption that all three faculties varied among individuals within the same species, including the human species. Although it had been a commonplace since time immemorial that individuals differed from one another in tenacity of memory, vivacity of imagination, analytic penetration, wisdom, shrewdness of judgment, and a host of other intellectual competences, it was monolithic reason that defined the human species. Intelligence, as it came to be redefined in the latter half of the nineteenth century, was in contrast a general mental ability, applicable to any domain, and measurable as a continuous quality that ranked individuals as having more or less. In the work of Francis Galton, the foremost British exponent of the "enormous difference between the intellectual capacity of men," there was an obvious Darwinian component: individual variability provided the material upon which natural selection could work.[45] But even expositors of the new notion of intelligence who were indifferent to Darwinism, like Hippolyte Taine, emphasized the importance of studying individual differences (especially, in Taine's case, outright deviations).[46] The methods of discerning shades of difference in moral and intellectual endowment—phrenology, anthropometry, eventually intelligence and personality tests—reflected a new way of conceptualizing the mind. Minds were no longer qualitatively different from one another—rational from animal souls, male from female intelligences; instead, they differed only quantitatively and could be (at least in the case of intelligence) plotted as points along a continuum.[47]

Hence the investigation of animal minds became only a more far-flung case of figuring out how other human minds worked, the difficulties of understanding one's dog differing only in degree from those of making sense of a Frenchman. No doubt the "nature makes no leaps" doctrine of Darwinian evolution lent strong support to this view, but it also encompassed distinctions of class and education as well as race and species. Lloyd Morgan carefully marked the points along his own continuum of analogical inference about other minds:

> If he is an Englishman, of the same social grade as ourselves, of like tastes and habits of thought, educated in the same school system, the similarity will be fairly close, though even here there must be slight individual differences. But if he be a foreigner, of a different social grade from ours, differing from us in tastes and habits of thought, educated in other school systems than ours, there will be a wide margin of dissimilarity. We shall find no little difficulty in putting ourselves in his place, in understanding how with such and such facts staring him in the face he can hold the views he says he holds, and in conceiving how he could derive any pleasure from that which would bore us to death, or would set our aesthetic teeth on edge, or would

painfully shock our sensibility. In dealing with North Australians, or Maori or South Sea Islanders or Red Indians, our difficulties are proportionately increased.[48]

Even understanding one's own children was an exercise of analogical projection. Yet introspection remained the only vehicle for making progress along the continuum, from children to Frenchmen to Maori to other species; therefore, even biologists must be trained in the "psychological analysis" of their own minds.[49] Nor were the distinctions between these categories absolute: Lloyd Morgan defended himself against charges of anthropocentrism for rejecting the claim for abstract reason in animals by protesting that a good many humans, "excellent practical folk," acted intelligently but not rationally. Indeed, the intelligent inferences of some animals might well surpass "those of man, who is often distracted by many thoughts."[50]

This implied that individuals of other species must also be studied with an eye toward differences from their fellows. In his studies of the role of instinct and behavior of incubated chicks, Lloyd Morgan had no compunctions about singling out one, "Blackie," as especially venturesome and quick-witted.[51] He did more than merely relate how his dog Tony learned to lift the latch of the garden gate; he also chose to make a woodcut of the individualized Tony, in the act of lifting the latch with his head, the frontispiece of his book on *Animal Mind*.[52] Wundt thought that anthropocentrism was responsible for the assumption made by earlier naturalists that intraspecies homogeneity reigned in "psychic expressions"; a more enlightened science of animal behavior would detect individual heterogeneity.[53] Romanes suggested that there might be class differences among dogs as among people, dogs of the "aristocratic estate" being more sensitive to pain and showing greater "pride, sense of dignity, and self-respect" than their lowborn conspecifics.[54] The very method of prolonged observation of the same animals, as well as the narrative form of the anecdote or story, tended to individuate animal subjects. Experiments did not necessarily tug in the opposite direction—controlled experiments were and are conducted upon individual animals—but the methods of averaging results over many subjects did systematically substitute collectives ("thirteen cats") for individuals ("Spot"). As long, however, as both human and animal psychology were grounded in introspection and analogy, the individuation of mental experience seemed a natural corollary of using firsthand analyses of one's own mind to understand those of others.

Neither mental experience nor individuation marked the accounts of the medieval angelologists. They were keenly interested in the mental operations and affects of angels but did not attempt to imagine what it felt like to be one. And although angels were arguably superindividuated—each one a species unto itself or even, according to some authorities, a whole genus[55]—there was almost no speculation about how one differed from another, at least not within each of the nine orders. Yet the anthropomorphism practiced by the thirteenth-century theologians was as resolutely analogical as that pursued by the nineteenth-century comparative psychologists, and in both cases this was justified by strong assumptions of continuity in the scale of being. It is true that the theologians believed themselves to be reaching upward in that scale and the psychologists, downward, but this difference in direction did not alter either the method of analogy nor the assumption of finely graduated hierarchy.

But despite these common methods and assumptions, there was an irreducible contrast between the contents of the anthropomorphism practiced in the two cases: angelologists sought the structures of kinds; psychologists, the subjective experience of individuals. Underneath the smooth word "anthropomorphism" are hidden a multitude of *anthropoi*, of kinds of humanity—in this case, of kinds of mind—as well as the multitude of *morphoi*, of shapes of understanding other minds.

CONCLUSION: WHY SUBJECTIVITY?

This brisk canter through two episodes of concerted anthropomorphism has been more of a thought experiment than a genuine history of either. There is a great deal more that could be said about the varieties of anthropomorphism and their distinct uses and abuses: what might be called the "sociomorphism" of analogies between human and animal (especially insect) societies,[56] or the "cold" anthropomorphism of game theory applied to animal behavior, in contrast to the "hot" anthropomorphism of empathy (especially in primatology).[57] My aim here, however, is neither to taxonomize nor to criticize anthropomorphism nor to reveal (yet again) its ubiquity. I come neither to praise nor to blame, much less to bury, this venerable and variegated practice. Rather, I want to understand its fearsome repulsions and attractions, the methodological taboos that ban it as well as the intellectual ambitions that foster it. The inquiries of the medieval angelologists and post-Darwinian comparative psychologists serve this purpose well because in both cases their ambivalence was patent: they practiced anthropomorphism with a kind of desperation, aware of its risks and limits yet convinced that there was no other way to play the game and that the game was worth the candle.

What was that game, and why play? In contrast to the didactic anthropomorphism of Aesop's fables or the bestiary tradition or the reflexive anthropomorphism exploited by children's stories and Disney films, the anthropomorphism in these two cases was deliberate and investigative. It was the instrument of discovery, revealing the nature of other minds. This conviction that other minds exist, as well as the curiosity to investigate them, was and is by no means a universal phenomenon. Conviction and curiosity express a longing to transcend the limits of one's own intellect, emotions, and experience. The search for transcendence can pull in two opposing directions: on the one hand, toward the exoticism of certain brands of anthropology, history, and imaginative literature (especially science fiction), which revel in the astonishing variety of other minds; or, on the other hand, toward the distillations of philosophy, which seek the essence of reason or justice, independent of its particular manifestations. If the exoticist yearnings recall the comparative psychologists contemplating the life of ants, the universalist strivings suggest that there is still a great deal of covert angelology in the most relentlessly secularized philosophy. When Kant mused about whether the forms of the synthetic a priori bound all rational beings, not just humans,[58] or when, more recently, Thomas Nagel conjured up a "view from nowhere,"[59] one may wonder whether angels still inform these epistemological fantasies. But by calling them "fantasies," I by no means wish to impugn their philosophical utility: a rich imagination for the possibilities of other minds may be a precondition for creative epistemology, from Descartes's disembodied ego to Condillac's statue to Kant's shadowy "rational beings."

Both the exoticist and universalist approaches to transcendence share, at least in their modern form, a preoccupation with the language of perspective. The one aims for perspectival suppleness, the other for an escape from perspective altogether, but neither can do without the metaphor. That the metaphor of perspective to describe other minds should seem ineluctable is, however, a relatively recent phenomenon. Leibniz famously used it in his *Monadologie*, but to notably different ends: namely, to argue that because each monad's understanding was inherently limited and partial, a kind of panoramic integration of all the monads was necessary for complete knowledge.[60] The notion that the ability to assume other perspectives was both possible and salutary, and that a complete escape from perspective would be more salutary still, seems to have first emerged in force, complete with the metaphors of viewpoint and perspective, in the latter part of the eighteenth century, in what were then called the moral sciences—and in the company of the faculty of sympathy.[61] A full-dress history of sympathy has yet to be written, but even the fragments that are extant indicate how central it had become to both the theory and practice of social life by the end of the eighteenth century.[62] It is against this background that anthropomorphism became fatally linked to anthropocentrism, although there is no necessary link between the two: both were indicted as evidence of a narrow-minded, self-centered assumption that one's own perspective was in some way privileged.

The language of perspective carries with it weighty assumptions about what it means to understand other minds. Within the model of a world divided up into the objective and the subjective, and armed with the method of sympathetic projection, understanding another mind could only mean seeing with another's eyes (or smelling with another's nose or hearing with another's sonar, depending on the species)—"put yourself in his place," as Lloyd Morgan titled one of his chapters.[63] Understanding in the perspectival mode implied experience, and individualized experience at that. Here I can only hint at the several intellectual and cultural shifts that created the perspectival mode: the habits of interior observation cultivated by certain forms of piety; the increasingly refined language of individual subjectivity developed in the eighteenth- and nineteenth-century novel; the equation drawn between sensory experience and self by sensationalist psychology; political and economic individualism; the cult of sympathy, which expanded to embrace first children, then animals, and finally denizens of other times and places. Whatever the historical forces that forged it, the perspectival mode was most decidedly a creature of history. It is not simply another form of subjectivity; it is the apotheosis of subjectivity as the essence of mind. No medieval theologian would ever have recommended adopting the perspective of an angel in order to understand the angelic mind, any more than a specialist in artificial intelligence would attempt to adopt the computer's point of view. The very phrase "perspective of an angel" would probably have struck Aquinas as an oxymoron: angels have neither eyes to see nor fixed positions to see from.

The pleasures of anthropomorphism may be similarly of a distinctly historical sort. For us moderns, at least, they are guilty pleasures. We believe we ought to know better than to read the minds of dogs and beavers, much less those of bees and fish. Adults who indulge too obviously in these pleasures are suspected of childishness, here signifying ignorance rather than innocence. These responses closely parallel those of the trained historian to anachronism: it may be charming to imagine the ancient Greeks amusing themselves with hula hoops in the agora, but it is an uncomfortable charm. It will not do to obscure the otherness of other minds. This is not simply the reproach of narcissism, though it is also that. Nor is it a charge of perspectival rigidity: the precondition for finding, for example, a *Far Side* cartoon funny is being able to register the incongruity between perspectives—now and then, human and animal.[64]

Rather, the reproach is at root a moral indictment of sloth and insufficient empathy. To indulge the imagination with anthropomorphized beavers and anachronized Greeks, so the argument might run, is to rest content with what one already knows and feels, resisting the greater effort of empathic understanding of the truly alien. Empathy is in turn assumed to be the precondition for emotional and moral sympathy. Either we understand other minds subjectively or we do not understand them at all. Thinking and feeling like a beaver or an ancient Greek is perhaps impossible; yet anything else is, by this standard, a failure. The ineluctable conclusion of this argument seems to be that we are doomed to understand only our own kind because only in that circumscribed realm can empathetic and sympathetic understanding succeed (and even within these limits success is not guaranteed). It is paradoxical that empathy and sympathy, the glue of communities, should be invoked to contract communities to like minds, that is, to one's own species and contemporaries: to extend a neighborly gesture of recognition across centuries or species lines is to be suspected of overlooking the otherness of other subjectivities. Perhaps if we could formulate questions about understanding other minds in some other mode than "What is it like to a be an X?" we might partly redeem, both intellectually and morally, the pleasures of anthropomorphism.

NOTES

1. John Milton, *Paradise Lost* (1667), 5.470–90, in *The Complete Poetical Works of John Milton*, ed. William Vaughn Moody (Boston: Houghton Mifflin, 1924), 158–59.

2. Franz Kafka, "A Report to an Academy," trans. Willa and Edwin Muir, in *The Basic Kafka*, (New York: Washington Square Press, 1979), 248.

3. Cognitive ethology of recent decades offers a possible third case. For an overview of the issues and literature, see Donald R. Griffin, *Animal Minds* (Chicago: University of Chicago Press, 1992); for a sharp critique of this program, see J. S. Kennedy, *The New Anthropomorphism* (Cambridge: Cambridge University Press, 1992).

4. It would be more consistent with ordinary historical practice to compare views on angels and animals within the same period. The difficulty is that medieval bestiaries and encyclopedias take a rather flat and allegorical approach to animal minds; conversely, nineteenth-century angelology cannot compare with the sophistication and thoroughness of its thirteenth-century predecessor. For typical samples of each, see respectively *Physiologus latinus: Éditions préliminaires, versio B*, ed. F. J. Carmody (Paris: Librairie E. Droz, 1939); and Joseph Blackburn Leslie, *The Angels of God Viewed in Light of Philosophy and Scripture* (London: T. Woolmer, 1885).

5. On the theological ban against anthropomorphizing God in the Judaic and Christian traditions, see Charles T. Fritsch, *The Anti-Anthropomorphism of the Greek Pentateuch* (Princeton, N.J.: Princeton University Press, 1943); A. Marmor-

stein, *The Old Rabbinic Doctrine of God: Essays in Anthropomorphism* (London: Oxford University Press/Humphrey Milford, 1937); Klaus Heinrich, *Anthropomorphe: Zum Problem des Anthropomorphismus in der Religionsphilosophie* (Basel: Stroemfeld/Peter Stern, 1986).

6. Thomas Nagel, "What Is it Like to Be a Bat?" in his *Mortal Questions* (Cambridge: Cambridge University Press, 1979), 166.

7. On the history of the words and concepts "objective" and subjective" see Lorraine Daston, "Objectivity and the Escape from Perspective," *Social Studies of Science* 22 (1992): 597–618.

8. Lorraine Daston and Peter Galison, "The Image of Objectivity," *Representations* 40 (Fall 1992): 81–128.

9. *On Celestial Hierarchies*, as well as the other treatises attributed to Pseudo-Dionysius, can be found with Latin translations in J. Migne, ed., *Patrologia Graeca*, 161 vols. (Paris: Migne, 1857–66), vols. 3–4; in English translation, in *The Complete Works of Pseudo-Dionysius*, trans. Colin Luibhuid (New York: Paulist Press, 1987).

10. Dante Alighieri, *Paradiso* (comp. ca. 1315), canto 28, in *The Divine Comedy*, text with trans. by Geoffrey L. Bickersteth (Oxford: Basil Blackwell, 1965), 728–31. Pseudo-Dionysius arranged the nine orders (subdivided into three hierarchies), from top to bottom, as follows: Seraphim, Cherubim, Thrones; Dominions, Virtues, Powers; Principalities, Archangels, Angels.

11. On twelfth-century angelology, see Marcia Colish, "Early Scholastic Angelology," *Recherches de théologie ancienne et médiévale* 62 (1995): 80–109. Colish argues for a significant shift in the theology of angels with the introduction of Aristotelian natural philosophy, from angelic free will to angelic knowledge: see Colish, "Early Scholastic Angelology," 98–99.

12. J. A. Weisheipl, "The Celestial Movers in Medieval Physics," *The Thomist* 24 (1961): 286–326. On angels as the subject of thought experiments in medieval physics and metaphysics, see Wolfgang Breidert, "Naturphilosophische Argumente in der Engelslehre," in *Mensch und Natur im Mittelalter*, ed. Albert Zimmermann and Andreas Speer, 1. Halbband (Berlin: Walter de Gruyter, 1991), 468–77.

13. David Keck, *Angels and Angelology in the Middle Ages* (New York: Oxford University Press, 1998), 73–90. Keck notes that almost one-seventh of the propositions condemned in 1277 related to angelology (including some positions advanced by Aquinas, such as the immateriality of angels) and documents the chilling effect of the decree on subsequent theological activity in this area: see 112–14. Dante also has rather harsh things to say about scholastic angelology: *Paradiso*, canto 39, ll. 70–75, in *Divine Comedy*, trans. Bickersteth, 734.

14. Whether angels were a mixture of form and matter (as Bonaventure maintained) or pure form (Aquinas) was a hotly debated issue, with devotional consequences: see O. Lottin, "La composition hylemorphique des substances spirituelles: Les debuts de la controverse," *Revue néo-scholastique de philosophie* 34 (1932): 21–41; Keck, *Angels*, 93–99.

15. Thomas Aquinas, *Summa theologia* (Taurini: P. Marietti, 1922), 4 vols., part 1, qu. 57, art. 2, vol. 1, 330–31; cp., Aquinas, *Summa contra Gentiles. Summa gegen die Heiden*, ed. and trans. Karl Albert and Paulus Engelhardt (Darmstaft: Wussenschaftliche Buchgesellschaft, 1992), 5 vols., bk. 2, qu. 99, vol. 2, 504–6.

16. Aquinas, *Summa theologica*, part 1, qu. 55, art. 2, vol. 1, 362–63; cp., Aquinas, *Summa contra Gentiles*, bk. 2, qus. 91, 96, vol. 2, 464–69, 486–90.

17. There was some controversy as to whether the higher orders of angels were sent on missions. See Colish, "Angelology," 93 and passim.

18. Aquinas, *Summa contra Gentiles*, bk. 2, qu. 100. According to a controversial position taken by Aquinas, angels cannot be individuated by matter, being pure form, and must therefore each be of different species, the multiplication of species being nobler than the multiplication of individuals within the species: *Summa contra Gentiles*, bk. 2, qu. 92; cp., Aquinas, *Summa theologica*, part 1, qu. 57, concerning the necessity that angels be able to recognize individuals in order to execute their ministries.

19. On the subsequent fate of the cognition of individuals in late scholasticism, see Sebastian J. Day, O.F.M., *Intuitive Cognition: A Key to the Significance of the Later Scholastics* (St. Bonaventure, N.Y.: Franciscan Institute, 1947); Amos Funkenstein, *Theology and the Scientific Imagination from the Middle Ages to the Seventeenth Century* (Princeton, N.J.: Princeton University Press, 1986), 137–39, 294–95.

20. Aquinas, *Summa theologica*, part 1, qu. 58, art. 3; qu. 57, arts. 3–4.

21. Aquinas, *Summa contra Gentiles*, bk. 2, qu. 101.

22. Keck, *Angels*, 105–9.

23. Aquinas, *Summa theologica*, part 1, qu. 54, art. 5.

24. Charles Darwin, *The Descent of Man, and Selection in Relation to Sex* (1871; reprint, Princeton, N.J.: Princeton University Press, 1981), 62–63.

25. Darwin, after providing several stories to illustrate the reasoning powers of animals, thought the point too patent to dwell upon, at least for dog owners: "Any one who is not convinced by such facts as these, and by what he may observe with his own dogs, that animals can reason, would not be convinced by anything that I could add." Darwin, *The Descent of Man*, 47.

26. Conwy Lloyd Morgan, "The Limits of Animal Intelligence," *The Fortnightly Review* 60 (1893): 232.

27. See the excellent account in Robert J. Richards, *Darwin and the Emergence of Evolutionary Theories of Mind and Behavior* (Chicago: University of Chicago Press, 1987), esp. 190–234, 375–404.

28. On the impact of the subjective/objective distinction on nineteenth-century science, see Lorraine Daston, "Objectivity Versus Truth," in *Wissenschaft als kulturelle Praxis, 1750–1900*, ed. Hans Erich Boedecker, Peter Reill, and Jürgen Schlumbohm (Göttingen: Vandenhoek und Ruprecht, 1999), 17–32.

29. George J. Romanes, *Animal Intelligence* (London: Kegan Paul, Tench, & Co., 1882), 9.

30. Margaret Floy Washburn, *The Animal Mind: A Text-Book of Comparative Psychology*, (1907) 3rd rev. ed. (New York: Macmillan, 1926), 12.

31. "Each of the twelve cats was tried in a number of different boxes, and in no case did I see anything that even looked like thoughtful contemplation of the situation or deliberation over possible ways of winning freedom." E.L. Thorndike, "Do Animals Reason?" *Popular Science Monthly* 55 (1899): 482.

32. Romanes, *Animal Intelligence*, 17.

33. Washburn, *Animal Mind*, 3; C. Lloyd Morgan, *Animal Life and Intelligence* (London: Edward Arnold, 1890–91), 333, 338.

34. Wilhelm Wundt, *Vorlesungen über die Menschen- und Thierseele*, ed. Wolfgang Nitsche, 2 vols. (1863; reprint, Berlin: Springer-Verlag, 1990), 1:443.

35. James Mark Baldwin, *Handbook of Psychology: Senses and Intellect*, 2nd ed. (New York: Henry Holt, 1896), 5, 15.

36. See Elliott Sober's essay in this volume.

37. C. Lloyd Morgan, *An Introduction to Comparative Psychology* (London: Walter Scott, 1895), 53.

38. Lloyd Morgan, *Animal Life*, 350.

39. Lloyd Morgan, *Animal Life*, 406, 367.

40. Lloyd Morgan, *Animal Life*, 400.

41. Darwin, *Descent of Man*, 77. Wundt, *Vorlesungen*, 1:456.

42. Romanes, *Animal Intelligence*, 440–41.

43. Lloyd Morgan, *Animal Life*, 398–99.

44. Romanes, *Animal Intelligence*, 472–76. On the cultivation of sympathetic responses to animals in Victorian England, see Harriet Ritvo, *The Animal Estate: The English and Other Creatures in the Victorian Age*, (Cambridge, Mass.: Harvard University Press, 1987), 125–66. See also Gregg Mitman's essay in this volume.

45. Francis Galton, *Hereditary Genius. An Inquiry into its Laws and Consequences* (1869) (2nd ed., 1892; reprint, Gloucester, Mass.: Peter Smith, 1972), 58.

46. Hippolyte Taine, *De l'Intelligence* (1870), 2 vols., 5th ed. (Paris: Hachette, 1888), 1:16.

47. On the case of male and female intelligence, see Lorraine Daston, "Die Quantifizierung der weiblichen Intelligenz," in *Aller Männerkultur zum Trotz*, ed. Renate Tobies (Frankfurt: Campus, 1997), 69–82.

48. Lloyd Morgan, *Comparative Psychology*, 41–42.

49. Lloyd Morgan, *Comparative Psychology*, 52.

50. Lloyd Morgan, *Animal Life*, 377.

51. Lloyd Morgan, "Limits," 226 and passim.

52. C. Lloyd Morgan, *The Animal Mind* (London: Edward Arnold, 1930), 5–7.

53. Wundt, *Vorlesungen*, 444.

54. Romanes, *Animal Intelligence*, 439. See Paul White's essay in this volume.

55. Anselm of Canterbury, for example, argued (*pace* Origen's view that even Lucifer and the other rebel angels were capable of rehabilitation) that since each angel is a genus unto itself, if Christ had assumed the nature of an angel in order to redeem the fallen angels, only that one angel would be saved, the sacrifice not being transferable across genera. Colish, "Angelology," 87.

56. See, for example, Jean-Marc Drouin, "L'image des sociétés d'insectes à l'époque de la Révolution," *Revue de Synthèse* 113 (1992): 333–46; Jeffrey Merrick, "Royal Bees: The Gender Politics of the Beehive in Early Modern Europe," *Studies in Eighteenth-Century Culture* 18 (1988): 7–37.

57. For an example of "cold" anthropomorphism, see John Maynard Smith, *Evolution and the Theory of Games* (New York: Cambridge University Press, 1982); for "hot" anthropomorphism, see Franz de Waals, *Peacemaking Among Primates* (Cambridge, Mass.: Harvard University Press, 1989).

58. Immanuel Kant, *Kritik der reinen Vernunft* (1781/1787), ed. Raymund Schmidt (Hamburg: Felix Meiner, 1976), B72, 92–93.

59. Thomas Nagel, *The View from Nowhere* (New York: Oxford University Press, 1986), 3–12.

60. Gottfried Wilhelm Leibniz, *Discours de métaphysique et monadologie* (comp. 1714) (Paris: J. Vrin, 1974), secs. 56–58.

61. Adam Smith, *The Theory of Moral Sentiments* (1759), ed. D. D. Raphael and A. L. Macfie (Oxford: Oxford University Press, 1976), 135 and passim; Johann Martin Chladenius, *Allgemeine Geschichtswissenschaft* (Leipzig: Friederich Lanckerischeus Erben, 1752), 95–96.

62. The most suggestive attempts so far have come from literary historians: see, for example, D. Marshall, *The Surprising Effects of Sympathy* (Chicago: University of Chicago Press, 1982); Glenn Hendler, *Public Sentiments: Structures of Feeling in Nineteenth-Century American Literature* (Chapel Hill: University of North Carolina Press, 2001), and Amit S. Rai, *Rule of Sympathy: Sentiment, Race, and Power, 1750–1850* (New York: Palgrave, 2002).

63. Lloyd Morgan, *Animal Mind*, chap. 2, 21–39.

64. Charles D. Minahen, "Humanimals and Anihumans in Gary Larson's Gallery of the Absurd," in *Animal Acts: Configuring the Human in Western History*, ed. Jennifer Ham and Matthew Senior (New York: Routledge, 1997), 231–51.

• • •

CHAPTER 3

The Experimental Animal in Victorian Britain

• • •

Paul S. White

> *As we are just now looking with scientific seriousness at our animals, we will discard all anthropomorphic interpretations.*
> —GEORGE LEWES, *Sea-side Studies* (1858)

During the Victorian age, a greater variety of animals peopled Britain than perhaps at any period before or since. Zoos and menageries, formerly the possession of private societies and estates, began to open in the 1830s, enabling the populace to view exotic species that had previously been seen only in print.[1] Animal husbandry and breeding, a preoccupation of great landowners in the Georgian period, became a consuming passion for large networks of collectors and fanciers. Pet ownership, confined largely to the upper classes before the nineteenth century, became a widespread middle-class phenomenon.[2] Work animals were as prominent in the streets of new urban centers as in the fields of rural Britain, and sporting animals, whether steed, retriever, or game, continued to inspire devotees of the hunting set.[3] A rich array of anthropomorphic depictions were drawn from each of these settings. Ferocious, extravagantly adorned, tirelessly industrious, or selflessly devoted, caged lions, prize pigeons, cart horses, and lap dogs, respectively, could serve as emblems of imperial conquest and class distinction or as servants and family friends.

The Victorian period also saw the appearance in large numbers of another kind of animal, whose emergence is linked to the advent of biology and physiology as professional disciplines and the rise of the laboratory as the site of knowledge production in the life sciences. Although there were continuities with older traditions of comparative anatomy and zoology, the new laboratory-based disciplines aped the experimental ethos and exactitude of sciences such as physics and sought independence from the institutional structure of museums, where whole families of animals were displayed for taxonomic purposes and, increasingly, for public instruction and amusement. Within the highly regulated and enclosed environment of the laboratory, all manner of creatures, from single-celled organisms to mammals, resided together with a growing array of instruments of observation, manipulation, and measurement.[4]

On the surface, the experimental animal would not appear to be an anthropomorphic entity. The discipline that one undertook as a student and observer of nature, wrought in the practice of experiment and the use of instruments which assisted the operator's hand and eye, was designed to minimize or eliminate the distorting influences of human attribution. As the physiologist and man of letters George Lewes remarked, the ascription of human qualities to other creatures, however pervasive in popular literature, was inappropriate in scientific study. In contrast to authors who routinely attributed sagacity to fish and astonishment to anemones, Lewes counseled his readers to avoid construing animals "according to the analogies of our own structure." Anthropomorphism derived from an ignorance of inner organization and function and was best avoided by observing nature "with patient zeal," that is, with the discipline of comparative physiology.[5]

The strong tendency to anthropomorphize, and its inimicality to science, were extensively theorized in the period. In his *Principles of Sociology* (1876) and other works, Herbert Spencer described how notions of deity and supernatural agency had arisen through the simple idealization and extension of the human personality to natural objects and phenomena otherwise incomprehensible. Animism, the belief in ghosts, spirits, and gods, afforded a measure of comprehension and control to primitive peoples incapable of grasping the true nature of material causes.[6] Darwin traced the tendency back to animal ancestry, comparing the "rapid and unconscious" reasoning of the savage, who imagined natural objects animated by spiritual essences, to that of the dog who growled at a parasol blown by the breeze.[7] Anthropomorphism for these commentators was a deeply rooted instinct, ascendant at an early stage in the development of the human race and gradually receding before the conceptions of orderly action and of universal, impersonal forces that characterized modern science. But it was also an inclination that persisted in the childhood of every individual and in persons unschooled in scientific knowledge and methods. Indeed, among a substantial and influential portion of Victorian society, anthropomorphism was rife, resistant, and even hostile to the science that would displace it. From the mid-1870s, it formed the basis of a notorious critique of experimenters, especially those whose research involved operations on living animals.

This view of anthropomorphism and its relations to science fits well with historian Keith Thomas's virtually canonical account of a shift in sensibility toward animals among urban populations in the modern period. As a result of new modes of acquiring and applying knowledge in the "Enlightenment," according to Thomas, Europeans were able to appropriate powers hitherto associated with nature. No longer conceived as a fearful antagonist, nature became instead an object of human affection and manipulation.[8] Thomas's thesis is evoked in Harriet Ritvo's masterful study of animals in Victorian society to explain the simultaneous rise of sentimentality characteristic of middle-class pet keeping and the unprecedented exploitation of animals in sport, the marketplace, and the laboratory. Those remote from the harsh utilitarian use of animals could transfer their tender feelings to lesser creatures, while others, not so removed, could exercise their mastery unimpeded by sympathy.[9] Drawing on a *longue durée* history of Enlightenment science, technology, and sentiment, Ritvo's account reinforces the view presented in all the major studies of the antivivisection movement, namely, that anthropomorphism was a force *outside* the laboratories of Victorian Britain, not within them. Anthropomorphism reared its sentimental head among members of the Victorian "lay" public who, for better or worse, applied their tender feelings for household pets to experimental subjects.[10]

A different picture emerges, however, if we look first to the multitude of experimental animals, rather than to the routines and controversies of animal experiment, for patterns of anthropomorphism. Dramatically diverse perspectives on animal life emerged depending on the creature chosen for scientific investigation, with correspondingly different views of human nature drawn from the animal under study. In laboratories of the new reflex physiology, frogs became indistinguishable from machines, while the instruments constructed to monitor their movements grew increasingly animate. Research on the circulatory and respiratory systems and on the "higher" functions of the brain, typically performed on domestic animals and anthropoid apes, raised questions about the nature of feelings, volition, and rational action, both within animal subjects and human operators. The experimental animal could, of course, also be human. In researches on the automatic functions of the nervous system, unconscious cerebration, instinct, and emotional expression, lower vertebrates appeared remarkably like asylum inmates, infants, and patients undergoing a hypnotic trance.

Evolutionary theories of development, degeneration, and atavism made for a two-way traffic between "man and brute." If some experimenters ranked the apes the highest because their natural inquisitiveness made them "scientific animals," practitioners could themselves undergo reversion in the laboratory, as bestial instincts were unleashed through the repeated and prolonged infliction of pain on helpless creatures. Finally, the performance of experiments in various settings became a showcase for the human virtues associated with the scientific life and, as such, was an exhibition of another breed of animal—the experimenter *himself*. In the public debates and controversies that surrounded these researches, the meaning of anthropomorphism was highly contested, but in the laboratory, too, the boundaries between the animal and the human could be destabilized by the very experiments designed to clarify them.

THE APPARATUS OF REFLEX PHYSIOLOGY

In his 1870 work *The Common Frog*, the naturalist St. George Mivart described how the creature began its life with the organization of a fish and underwent a remarkable metamorphosis, attaining the condition of an air-breathing quadruped, capable of rapid terrestrial motion (see figure 1).[11] Yet despite these extraordinary features, no great frog collectors or specialists were spawned in the Victorian period. The creature was studied instead as a generic animal, a representative vertebrate, and even, despite its taxonomy, as a surrogate mammal.[12] "Though cold-blooded," Darwin remarked, "their passions are strong," and females occasionally expired from suffocation as three or four males competed for her partnership in the mating process.[13] Once in sexual congress, a male was so persistent that it continued its grasp long after it had been decapitated.[14] The frog was clearly a creature driven from below. Its ability to perform without limbs, without its head, or indeed to be practically decomposable into parts was a central feature in physiological experiments throughout the nineteenth century and long before.

The laboratory life of the frog has been reverently sketched by the historian Frederick Holmes in his article "The Old Martyr of Science."[15] Holmes drew his title from the German physiologist and physicist Hermann Helmholtz, who performed his classic experiments on muscular movement almost exclusively on frogs. The heroic sacrifices of the creature in the face of repeated poisonings, chokings, and mutilations moved the French physiologist Claude Bernard, who had studied the action of curare on frogs, to dub the creature "the Job of physiology." Following Luigi Galvani's experi-

3.1 *Rana temporania*. From St. George Mivart, *The Common Frog* (London: Macmillan, 1874), frontispiece. By permission of the Syndics of Cambridge University Library.

ments in the 1790s, frogs became the preferred subject of inquiries into animal electricity in the nineteenth century. Such experiments were typically performed on the frog's isolated muscles, which were readily stimulated by irritating a segment of the adherent nerve, and which could continue to function for upwards of thirty hours after being detached from the body.

Developed first in Germany and France, such instruments were gradually introduced into Britain in the 1860s by practitioners like John Burdon-Sanderson, who had trained in laboratories abroad.[16] Burdon-Sanderson's most important contribution to this effort was the *Handbook of the Physiological Laboratory*, which he produced in conjunction with colleagues at the Brown Sanitary Institution and University College, London.[17] The *Handbook* was a comprehensive manual for the performance of experiments in physiology and histology and described hundreds of animal experiments. One feature of the work that was noted by readers outside the research community was that the descriptions, centered as they were on the functioning and manipulation of instruments, virtually erased the animal subjects from the scene of experiment. Yet frogs did feature in these accounts in at least one crucial way: they were deconstituted and reassembled as components of scientific instruments. Indeed, in the works of experimental physiologists in France and Germany, the frog rarely appeared as an animal unto itself. Instead, segments of the creature formed part of an instrumental ensemble, as in the muscle telegraph of Emile du Bois-Reymond or in the myograph used by Helmholtz to measure muscular action in the thigh-muscle (see figure 2). Once removed from the creature and fastened in a vice within the glass case, the muscle became part of a stimulus-response mechanism, set going by the finger of the operator and functioning like "clockwork"

3.2   THE MYOGRAPH OF HELMHOLTZ. FROM I. ROSENTHAL, *GENERAL PHYSIOLOGY OF THE MUSCLES AND NERVES* (LONDON: KEGAN PAUL, 1881), 52. BY PERMISSION OF THE SYNDICS OF CAMBRIDGE UNIVERSITY LIBRARY.

until stopped.[18] Irritation was administered by the machine itself, and the muscle then contracted, raising a pencil that inscribed a vertical line on a rotating cylinder, producing a well-defined curve. These much-vaunted self-recording instruments not only transformed physiological functions into paper and ink, they transmuted animal subjects into working parts of the experimental apparatus.

The muscles and nerves of the frog, placed in functional relationships with an array of graphic recording instruments, formed the basis for reflex physiology and spawned a large literature in which the operations of the generic vertebrate, their lower drives and instincts, their habitual acts, even their emotional and intellectual life were extrapolated up the chain of being to humans. On the continent, the links between experimental physiology and its instruments and human automata were explicit, as in the work of Etienne-Jules Marey, whose research on animal mechanics fed directly into state-sponsored projects for the measurement of human energy and the maximizing of its force for industrial and military use.[19] Although the factory system was more extensive in Britain, relations between science and the state were more tenuous, and much work, particularly in the natural-historical and life sciences, continued to operate within a culture of individualism. No elaborate mechanical aesthetic or factory discipline was drawn from experimental physiology.[20] Instead, the frog became a touchstone for considerations of moral character, self-consciousness, and freedom of the will.

In 1870, one of Britain's leading physiologists, Thomas Huxley, delivered a paper at the Metaphysical Society in London entitled "Has a Frog a Soul."[21] Huxley recounted the eighteenth-century debate between the physicians Albrecht von Haller and Robert Whytt, whose experiments with frogs were designed to determine the locus of the soul. Huxley also described the recent experiments by Eduard Pflüger and others in which acid was applied to the thigh of a frog whose head had been severed just above the medulla oblongata. The headless frog tried to wipe off the irritant with the dorsal surface of its foot. When its foot was cut off, it tried with its leg; and eventually, after a pause, with the foot of the other leg. It then remained motionless for hours until a new stimulus was given. Huxley proposed a further experiment in which the decapitated head and trunk were sent one hundred miles in opposite directions. Each part, he maintained, would continue to perform equally purposive, though quite distinct actions, adapting means to ends in a manner usually deemed rational. The debate over the seat of the soul, whether it resided in both the head and spinal cord or materially extended over a distance of 200 miles, was itself a platform for the question of automatism, namely, whether purposive, coordinated activity was the result of nervous constitution or consciousness.

The question, with its clear implications for the moral nature of humans, was taken up in earnest at one of the next meetings of the society by Archbishop Henry Manning, who argued that automatic functions of the body and the brain were guided by a moral agent, the will, which acted on the brain through the operation of attention.[22] By fixing the mind or the sense organs on particular ideas or objects, the will could determine the course of action in a definite direction. The reflex action of the nervomuscular apparatus and the automatic and instinctual action of the cerebrum were in fact instruments of the will. They could be regulated by a succession of thoughts and emotions, themselves directed by selective attention. What indicated that the exercise of attention was an act of will, rather than purely automatic, was the presence of effort. Attention was the result of a struggle in the mind and was thus preeminently a moral function, mobilized in the overcoming of temptation or in altering a course of habit.

In support of his arguments, the archbishop referred to the work of William Carpenter, whose influential writings on comparative and mental physiology contained extensive accounts of animal and human automatism, unconscious cerebration, and the operation of the will through selective attention. Carpenter proposed a scale of physiological functions, mapped onto a scale of being, with the will as the seat of government, presiding over a contest between the lower drives of animal nature.[23] In an address to the Sunday Lecture Society in London in 1875, Carpenter compared the behavior of headless frogs to sleeping humans, referring to actual experiments in which sleeping subjects were tickled under the nose while first one hand then the other was restrained from scratching.[24] Experiments analogous to those of Helmholtz and others on frogs were widely performed on hypnotic patients and asylum inmates, who behaved precisely like will-less automata. Analogous instruments were designed for such subjects, whose arm and leg muscles displayed frog-like characteristics of extreme irritability. A slight stimulus, such as a stroking of the skin or a cutaneous irritation of the leg could produce contraction for prolonged periods in hypnotic and hysterical subjects.[25] The analogy was completed with reference to a wide range of cases of animal hypnosis, including frogs that had been rendered paralytic by gently scratching their backs.

Carpenter, together with Huxley and others, led a campaign to reinterpret the phenomena of animal magnetism, mesmerism, and nervous illness in the terms of reflex physiology.[26] In the process, hypnotic subjects, asylum patients, and other sufferers of nervous disease became in effect experimental animals, losing their will (or their soul), so that medical science, underpinned by experimental physiology and its laboratory-based technologies, could restore it. For the healthy to remain healthy, for the "common man" to avoid degeneration into the state of the common frog, the constant exercise of self-control was required, duly strengthened by education and good breeding.[27] As one Edinburgh lecturer on mental diseases counseled his students, the best means of resisting animal gratification was to subject passion itself to analysis, or scientific education. For "young men entering on the threshold of manhood," he recommended the calm and earnest direction of attention to certain facts about the reproduction of the species, an exercise to be undertaken in physiological laboratories.[28] One of the truly reflexive features of reflex physiology was that scientific activity, the performance of experiments in particular, was itself a discipline of self-mastery—a means of strengthening the power of the will, as manifest in the faculty of attention, over the bodily functions, appetites, and emotional drives. Physiological experiments performed in laboratories, teaching hospitals, and public demonstrations could display the experimenter as a masterful manipulator of mechanical forces—respiratory movements, circulation, locomotion, sensation, pain: the physical and emotional bases of life itself.

A DOG'S LIFE

Following the tradition established by popular demonstrators in mechanics' institutes, provincial literary and philosophical societies, and fashionable London venues such as the Royal Institution, physiological experiments were occasionally reenacted in various public settings for the purposes of instruction and "rational entertainment."[29] For experiments performed before nonspecialist audiences, frogs were the creatures of choice, in part because they evoked little sympathy. For all of its acknowledged suffering, the frog inspired little pity. The use of other experimental subjects, especially domestic animals, outside of the enclosed space of the laboratory was more risky, however. One demonstration, made at the meeting of the British Medical Association in 1874, prompted a trial of the demonstrators by the Royal Society for the Prevention of Cruelty to Animals. The operation involved the injection of various alcoholic substances into the thigh of a dog, which had been brought into the room strapped to a board, struggling to free itself from its fetters.[30] The experiment was performed in order to observe the animal's convulsions, thus demonstrating the physiological effects of alcoholism, widely regarded in the medical literature of the period as a nervous disease arising from a weakness of the will. When a royal commission was convened in the same year to inquire into the practice of vivisection, there was considerable debate about the use of domestic animals.

dogs

One of the members of the commission, the editor of the *Spectator*, R. H. Hutton, issued a separate report calling for the exemption of dogs and cats from experiment because they were in fact members of the human family or household.[31] Hutton claimed that in the course of domestication, such animals had acquired the same heightened sensitivities that distinguished civilized men from barbarous tribes. It was treacherous and insensitive to commit such animals, who had been bred and trained up so as to place their confidence in humans to scientific use.

As family friends and devoted servants, dogs embodied Victorian values more fully and consistently than did any other creature. Despite the claims of a few naturalists, one of whom had spent long hours teaching his pet rudimentary mathematics, dogs were ranked among the highest of animals because of their moral nature, not their intellect.[32] A large devotional literature, composed in natural-historical and ethological mode, attested to the loyalty, courage, and obedience of the dog. Drawing partly on his own experience, Darwin described the moral virtues of the dog in his 1872 work *On the Expression of the Emotions in Animals and Man*. The tenderness and sympathy of the creature toward its master was a marked trait, according to Darwin, and was always mutual (see figure 3).[33] In his edition of his father's letters, Francis Darwin dwelled at some length on the great naturalist's love for dogs, especially the "delightfully tender" Polly and a half-bred retriever, Bob, whose abrupt change of demeanor from cheerfulness to dejection at the end of his walks was featured in *Expression*.[34]

According to some, the freely flowing exuberance and affection of dogs made them more humane than man. As the philanthropist and moral writer Frances Power Cobbe described it: "Their eagerness . . . joyousness [and] transparent little wiles, are to me more winning . . . more really and intensely human . . . than the artificial, cold and selfish characters one meets too often in the guise of ladies and gentlemen."[35] Possessed of limited thought but unlimited love, dogs were creatures whose humble devotion could heal the wounds of disappointed or betrayed affection and by silent sympathy bring cheer and comfort to the old, poor, or lonely whom the rest of the world had abandoned. Cobbe favored an evolutionary theory of the sentiments that ranked the spontaneous impulse of sympathy first among the mental faculties. Following the moral philosopher William Lecky she presented the history of European morals as a progressive development in which affections were extended first to one's immediate family then to one's class, one's nation, all nations, and finally to the animal world. The bond of sympathy between humans and their domestic animals, particularly dogs, thus

3.3 CARESSING ITS MASTER. FROM CHARLES DARWIN, *ON THE EXPRESSION OF THE EMOTIONS IN ANIMALS AND MAN* (LONDON: MURRAY, 1872), 55. BY PERMISSION OF THE SYNDICS OF CAMBRIDGE UNIVERSITY LIBRARY.

represented the highest achievement of moral progress.[36] Darwin gave a similar account in *The Descent of Man, and Selection in Relation to Sex* (1871), arguing that social instincts such as sympathy and pity evolved through the operation of natural selection on the level of the group, gradually becoming more tender and diffused and finally embracing the lower animals.[37]

Unlike Darwin, however, Cobbe and others used this evolutionary vantage point to launch a critique of experimental physiology. Henry Salt, an early advocate of "animal rights," founded a broad campaign against vivisection, blood sports, meat eating, and millinery on the doctrine of evolutionary kinship, citing examples from Darwin's *Descent* of the possession of emotions, memory, curiosity, and reason by animals. Though modern scientific methods had led to a recognition of the close relationship between humans and other creatures, Salt claimed, these same methods had had the sinister effect of leading practitioners to neglect the anima of their subjects. Salt attributed cruelty to vivisectors, who believed that animals were mere automata, devoid of spirit and individual character: "They are caught and impelled by the overmastering passion of knowledge; and, as a handy subject for the gratification of this passion, they see before them the helpless race of animals." "The cure for cruelty is therefore to induce men to cultivate a sympathetic imagination."[38] In order to rouse public opposition to vivisection, critics often gave graphic descriptions of experiments, describing the cries and shrieks of the animals under the knife and the various devices used to restrain their movements. In *The Modern Rack*, Cobbe took plates from Bernard's *Physiologie opératoire* in order to display what Burdon-Sanderson's *Handbook* effectively erased, the subjection of animals to science (see figure 4).[39] Unlike their French and German counterparts, English textbooks in physiology virtually never portrayed whole animals undergoing experimentation. The lavish volume of plates that accompanied Burdon-Sanderson's work, for example, showed only various recording instruments, graphic displays, individual organs, and microscopic sections. Many critics argued that the performance and witnessing of vivisection, increasingly common in medical education by the 1870s, eroded human sympathy and unleashed brutal passions, with practitioners undergoing a process of zoomorphism in the laboratory as bestial instincts were unleashed through the repeated and prolonged infliction of pain on helpless creatures. It would be easier, Cobbe remarked, to imagine such operators as ignorant or hunger-driven or drunk than as men at the "intellectual summit of our social system, [the] calm, cool, deliberate . . . and (it is said) the otherwise kindly-disposed and genial men of science."[40]

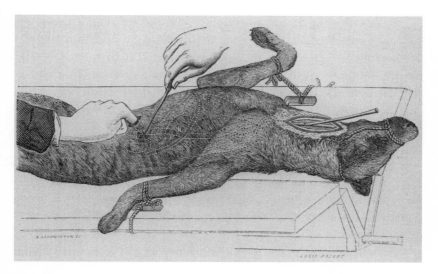

3.4   CATHETERIZATION OF THE HEART. FROM CLAUDE BERNARD, *LEÇONS DE PHYSIOLOGIE OPERATOIRE* (PARIS: J. B. BAILLIÈRE ET FILS, 1879), 282. BY PERMISSION OF THE SYNDICS OF CAMBRIDGE UNIVERSITY LIBRARY.

MONKEY GRIP

This severing of head and heart, of mind and morality, was typified in another animal, completely undomesticated, yet by contemporary accounts remarkably human and increasingly utilized in experiments in neurophysiology in the last quarter of the nineteenth century. Begun in rooms at the West Riding Lunatic Asylum in conjunction with the work of John Hughlings Jackson and James Crichton-Browne on epilepsy and other nervous diseases, David Ferrier's research on cerebral localization eventually made large use of monkeys, whom he argued were essential in the examination of higher mental functions.[41] Ferrier's findings were publicly challenged at the International Medical Congress in 1881 by the Strasbourg physiologist Friedrich Goltz, who performed tricks before the distinguished assembly with his constant companion, a lobotomized dog. Press accounts gave Ferrier the victory, however, when he produced monkeys whose brains had been systematically lesioned weeks before and who were unable to carry out routine stimulus-response exercises, let alone the supposedly purposeful behavior exhibited by Goltz's dog.[42] Ferrier's experiments seemed to confirm the natural-historical accounts of Darwin and others in which the full range of expressions, displayed so pathetically by dogs, were really automatic mechanisms, materially based, and evolved through natural and sexual selection.

As described by traveling naturalists and armchair ethologists, monkeys and apes, in comparison with dogs, seemed fundamentally amoral. Commentators agreed that they possessed maternal devotion in a high degree, yet their violence and disobedience were so pronounced that they were deemed useless for all purposes of labor, made very mischievous pets, and were most often likened to human children.[43] In a series of experiments on infants several weeks old, Dr. Louis Robinson showed the human hand to possess a surprising grasping power at birth, far in excess of its requirements and yet precisely in proportion to that of young monkeys, who needed to grip the hair of their mothers when in motion. Robinson took photographs of the infants, suspended for up to two minutes from a horizontal bar, which was later transformed into a tree branch by the artist of this woodcut (see figure 5).[44]

On learning that his disciple George Romanes had received a standing ovation for a talk on mental evolution at the British Association meeting in 1878, Darwin advised him to keep a young monkey in order to observe its mind.[45] Romanes secured the loan of a macaque from the Zoological Gardens and had it chained in the bedroom of his invalid mother, where its behavior was regularly recorded in his sister Charlotte's diary. After observing the creature absorbed for hours in screwing and unscrewing the handle of the hearth brush until the task was perfected, the sister noted: "The desire to accomplish a chosen task seems sufficient inducement to lead him to take any amount of trouble. This seems a very human feeling, such as is not shown, I believe, by any other animal . . . he never rests nor allows his attention to be distracted until it is done." The most distinctive feature of the creature's psychology was its "tireless spirit of investigation [and] keen satisfaction . . . in making any little discovery . . . repeating the results over and over again . . . when a monkey behaves like this," Charlotte concluded, "it is no wonder that man is a scientific animal!"[46]

That scientific enterprise should be nascent exclusively in a creature renowned for its destructiveness and lack of moral feeling does not seem to have troubled the writers on animal behavior. Romanes was a founding member of the Physiological Society, formed in 1876 for the protection of vivisection for scientific purposes following the recent government measure for licensing and inspection of animal-research facilities.[47] The identification of monkeys with human infants gave a childlike innocence to scientific curiosity that was in marked contrast to the image of the experimenter as masterful moral agent that emerged from reflex physiology. And yet the scientific animal, the medical researcher, for example, was to be a kind of evolutionary amalgam of the strengths and virtues of all these experimental creatures. In the frontispiece to *Mental Evolution in Animals*, Romanes

3.5 Infant, six weeks old. From G. J. Romanes, *Darwin and After Darwin* (London: Longmans, Green, 1892), 81. By permission of the Syndics of Cambridge University Library.

placed an ethological tree in which various mental faculties branched off from the trunk of reflex action and volition. Reflection and self-conscious thought appear on one side, moral expressions, on the other.[48] Beside the tree are a series of corresponding scales for emotional and intellectual development. Anthropoid apes are ranked alongside dogs at the highest level of animal evolution, having reached that point from opposite sides, as it were, of the same tree. The scale furthest to the right, the "psychogenesis of man," shows how ontogeny recapitulates phylogeny in behavioral terms, with the characteristic features of each organism, from protoplasm to batrachia (frogs) to mammals, acquired in the development of every human individual.

In some of the apologetic literature of medical researchers that was generated during the vivisection controversy, the experimenter appears as a divided self, struggling to overcome instinctual sympathies for other creatures in order to fulfill commitments to a higher good.[49] Fondness for dogs and other animals was often attested to by animal experimenters, including Ferrier himself, and featured in their evidence given before the commission on vivisection.[50] That experimenters were dog owners and dog lovers, that they possessed sympathy and tenderness and yet were able, on entering the laboratory, to mobilize their curiosity, stem the tide of sentiment, and perform like well-tuned instruments for the pursuit of truth and medical mercy was a crucial part of their self-legitimization; it asserted their preeminent position on the physiological and moral scale of being, ahead of their critics, who, like the lower creatures they advocated, were slaves to their sentimental affections. As the consulting surgeon to Queen's Hospital, Birmingham, wrote,

> Some persons fear that scientific experiments on living animals may brutalize, by hardening the experimenter. . . . They would think otherwise, if they knew more of physiology and psychology. . . . The subjugation of emotion by reason, of instinct by volition, is one of the most signal triumphs of intellectual culture. . . . Is it not possible to lavish too much sympathy on Magdalenes, murderers, and fools, and to forget the special trials of men and women endowed with aspiring intellects and racking passions, with nerves strung, and hearts thumping, to the utmost of physical endurance?[51]

CONCLUSION

In his book *Lords of the Fly*, Robert Kohler depicts the genetics laboratories of the mid-twentieth century as ecosystems, in which *Drosophila* is an "active player," living in "symbiotic relationship" with its human operators, its life cycle suiting an academic calendar.[52] The experimental animals of the Victorian period, likewise, were more than just passive material for science. But while laboratory practices and instruments were indeed adapted to the bodies and temperaments of frogs, dogs, and monkeys, it would not seem that the creatures flourished like the fruit fly or achieved "commensuality" with their experimenters. In Victorian terms, this would indeed have been remarkable, since the very practice of laboratory science involved a disciplined disregard for the feelings or perspective of the animal under study.

An identity was forged between laboratory animals and human *patients*, particularly in the sphere of bacteriology, where animal bodies were in notable instances a successful proving ground for human cures. Such links were important in the promotion of laboratory diagnostics and procedures in medicine. But achievement in the laboratory, and more arguably the sick-room, seemed to require that practitioners perform in the manner of precision instruments. The mechanization and automation of scientific practice and the instrumental use of animals (and human subjects) remained highly controversial through the end of the nineteenth century.[53] The connection between animals and humans claimed by medical science was severed by arguments that portrayed the discipline and routines of laboratory life as cruel, and therefore inhumane. Because of the primacy of the will in Victorian accounts of mind and behavior, a human automaton was potentially a beast, driven by lower instincts and passions it could not control. Evolutionary continuities between humans and animals, useful in underwriting practices like vivisection and ethology, could also facilitate claims about the degeneration of "gentlemen of science" whose natural sympathies for their human and animal fellows had been deadened by the abstract pursuit of truth.

Some of the arguments advanced today in defense of animal experiments are based on distinctions that were drawn in the Victorian period: for example, humans have wills, animals do not.[54] On the other hand, those in support of animal rights have sought a common ground for all species through appeals to the theory of evolutionary kinship put forward by Darwin.[55] Highly controversial experiments on domestic animals and primates continue to be performed with a view to grounding human/animal distinctions in laboratory science. Classic extrapolations from the fruit fly notwithstanding, debate about the representativeness of experimental animals is ongoing.[56] At the same time, the humane treatment of such animals has become a discipline unto itself, offering assessments of "well-being" from the animals' point of view and a psychology of the laboratory technician as a highly sympathetic subject.[57] The questions, What is human? and What is animal? are thus inextricably twined with issues of which procedures have legitimacy in this defining process and which groups set the terms and fix the boundaries of anthropomorphism. Definitions of the animal and human easily fall prey to nature/culture distinctions that, in turn, authorize academic discourses both in the sciences and humanities.[58] In the Victorian period, the stakes (in human terms) were the authority of laboratory practices and scientific medicine and the role of people outside of these professions to intervene in debates about their natures, their bodies, and the care of the animals who gave significance to their world.

NOTES

1. On the wide range of animals and their diverse roles in Victorian society, see especially Harriet Ritvo, *The Animal Estate: The English and Other Creatures in the Victorian Age* (Cambridge, Mass.: Harvard University Press, 1987). On zoos and menageries, see R. J. Hoage and William Deiss, eds., *New Worlds, New Animals: From Menagerie to Zoological Park in the Nineteenth Century* (Baltimore: Johns Hopkins University Press, 1996); Clinton H. Keeling, "Zoological Gardens of Great Britain" in *Zoo and Aquarium History: Ancient Animal Collections to Zoological Gardens*, ed. Vernon Kisling (Boca Raton, Fla.: CRC Press, 2001), 49–74; and Sofia Åkerberg, *Knowledge and Pleasure at Regent's Park: The Gardens of the Zoological Society of London During the Nineteenth Century* (Umeå, Sweden: Umeå Univeritets tryckeri, 2001).

2. On breeders and breeding, see James Secord, "Nature's Fancy: Charles Darwin and the Breeding of Pigeons," *Isis* 72 (1981): 163–86, and "Darwin and the Breeders: A Social History," in *The Darwinian Heritage*, ed. David Kohn (Princeton, N.J.: Princeton University Press, 1985), 519–42; and Judy Urquhart, *Animals on the Farm: Their History from the Earliest Times to the Present Day* (London: MacDonald, 1983). On pets, see Harriet Ritvo, "The Emergence of Modern Pet-Keeping," in *Animals and People Sharing the World*, ed. A. N. Rowen (Hanover, N.H.: University Press of New England, 1988), 13–31.

3. On the livestock trade and work animals, see Richard Perren, *The Meat Trade in Britain, 1840–1914* (London: Routledge and Kegan Paul, 1978), 16–25, 32–33; and Keith Chivers, "The Supply of Horses in Great Britain in the Nineteenth Century," in *Horses in European Economic History: A Preliminary Canter*, ed. F. M. L. Thompson (Reading: British Agricultural History Society, 1983), 31–49; and F. M. L. Thompson, "Horse and Hay in Britain, 1830–1918," in *Horses in European Economic History: A Preliminary Canter*, ed. F. M. L. Thompson (Reading: British Agricultural History Society, 1983), 50–72. On hunting and other blood sports, see Robert Malcolmson, *Popular Recreations in English Society, 1700–1850* (Cambridge: Cambridge University Press, 1973), 45–50, 118–38; and John MacKenzie, *The Empire of Nature: Hunting, Conservation and British Imperialism* (New York: Manchester University Press, 1998), 26–53.

4. On the rise of the life-science laboratory, see Andrew Cunningham and Perry Williams, eds., *The Laboratory Revolution in Medicine* (Cambridge: Cambridge University Press, 1992). The relations between new life sciences and older natural-historical and museum-based traditions are explored in John Pickstone, "Museological Science? The Place of the Analytical/Comparative in Nineteenth-Century

Science, Technology, and Medicine," *History of Science* 32 (1994): 111–38; and Lynn Nyhart, "Natural History and the 'New' Biology," in *Cultures of Natural History*, ed. N. Jardine, J. Secord, and E. Spary (Cambridge: Cambridge University Press, 1996), 426–43. On the central role of instrumentation in the professionalization of physiology and scientific medicine, see R. G. Frank Jr., "The Tell-Tale Heart: Physiological Instruments, Graphic Methods, and Clinical Hopes, 1854–1914," in *The Investigative Enterprise: Experimental Physiology in Nineteenth-Century Medicine*, ed. William Coleman and Frederick Holmes (Berkeley: University of California Press, 1988), 211–90; and Soraya de Chadarevian, "Graphical Method and Discipline: Self-Recording Instruments in Nineteenth-Century Physiology," *Studies in History and Philosophy of Science* 24 (1993): 267–91.

5. George Lewes, *Sea-side Studies* (London: Blackwood and Sons, 1858), 365–69.

6. Herbert Spencer, *The Principles of Sociology* (London: Williams and Norgate, 1876), 1:414–15, 440–53. See also, Spencer, "The Use of Anthropomorphism," *The Leader*, 5 November 1853; and *First Principles*, 6th ed. (London: Williams and Norgate, 1900), 12–15, 24, 37–39. On the derivation of anthropomorphism from anthropocentrism, see also Lorraine Daston, "How Nature Became the Other: Anthropomorphism and Anthropocentrism in Early Modern Natural Philosophy," in *Biology as Society, Society as Biology: Metaphors*, ed. Sabine Maasen et al. (Dordrecht: Kluwer Academic, 1995), 37–56.

7. Charles Darwin, *The Descent of Man, and Selection in Relation to Sex*, 2 vols. (London: John Murray, 1871), 1:67.

8. Keith Thomas, *Man and the Natural World* (London: Allen Lane, 1983); see, for example, 300–03. Links between Thomas's account and Norbert Elias's celebrated description of a "new emotional climate" in the modern period have been noted; see Joanna Swabe, *Animals, Disease, and Human Society: Human-Animal Relations and the Rise of Veterinary Medicine* (London: Routledge, 1999).

9. Ritvo, *The Animal Estate*, 2–3. Thomas's arguments similarly provide an explanatory framework in James Serpell, *In the Company of Animals: A Study of Human-Animal Relationships* (Oxford: Basil Blackwell, 1986), 160–64, 170. MacKenzie, *The Empire of Nature*, 26–28, provides a partial critique of Thomas's argument, underscoring the importance of a romantic view of nature as wild and violent in the culture of Victorian hunting.

10. Ritvo, *The Animal Estate*, 157–66. On the antivivisection movement, see Richard French, *Antivivisection and Medical Science in Victorian Society* (Princeton, N.J.: Princeton University Press, 1975); James Turner, *Reckoning with the Beast: Animals, Pain, and Humanity in the Victorian Mind* (Baltimore: John's Hopkins University Press, 1980); and Nicolaas Rupke, ed., *Vivisection in Historical Perspective* (London: Croom Helm, 1987).

11. St. George Mivart, *The Common Frog* (London: Macmillan, 1874), 4.

12. See, for example, A. Milnes Marshall. *The Frog: An Introduction to Anatomy, Histology, and Embryology* (London: Smith, Elder and Co., 1882), which ran through ten editions by 1909.

13. Darwin, *The Descent of Man*, 2:26.

14. Henry Maudsley, *Physiology of Mind* (New York: Appleton, 1877), 147–48.

15. Frederick Holmes, "The Old Martyr of Science: The Frog in Experimental Physiology," *Journal of the History of Biology* 26 (1993): 311–28.

16. On the introduction and early use of these instruments in Britain, see "Physicians and Physicists," *Lancet* (25 November 1865), 599; and Christopher Lawrence, "Physiological Apparatus in the Wellcome Museum: 1. The Marey Sphygmograph," *Medical History* 22 (1978): 196–200.

17. John Burdon-Sanderson et al., eds., *Handbook for the Physiological Laboratory*, 2 vols. (London: J. & A. Churchill, 1873). For relevant discussions of the *Handbook*, see Stewart Richards, "Drawing the Life-Blood of Physiology: Vivisection and the Physiologists' Dilemma, 1870–1900," *Annals of Science* 43 (1986) 27–56, and "Vicarious Suffering, Necessary Pain: Physiological Method in Late Nineteenth-century Britain," in Nicolaas Rupke, ed., *Vivisection in Historical Perspective* (London: Croom Helm, 1987), 125–48.

18. These instruments are described in I. Rosenthal, *General Physiology of the Muscles and Nerves* (London: Kegan Paul, 1881).

19. Etienne-Jules Marey, *Animal Mechanism: A Treatise on Terrestrial and Aerial Locomotion*, 2nd ed. (London. Henry S. King, 1874). On the industrial and military application of graphic technologies on the continent, see Marta Braun, *Picturing Time: The Work of Etienne-Jules Marey* (Chicago: University of Chicago Press, 1992), 320–48; Robert M. Brain and M. Norton Wise, "Muscles and Engines: Indicator Diagrams and Helmholtz's Graphical Methods," in *Universalgenie Helmholtz: Rückblick nach 100 Jahren*, ed. Lorenz Krueger (Berlin: Akademie Verlag, 1995), 124–45; and Robert M. Brain, "The Graphic Method," Ph.D. diss., University of California, Los Angeles, 1996. On Marey and the industrial aesthetic, see François Dagognet, *Etienne-Jules Marey: A Passion for the Trace*, trans. Robert Galeta with Jeanine Herman (New York: Zone, 1992), 165–73.

20. Jack Morrell, "Individualism and the Structure of British Science in 1830," *Historical Studies in the Physical Sciences* 3 (1971): 183–204; Peter Alter, *The Reluctant Patron: Science and the State in Britain, 1850–1920* (Oxford: Berg, 1987). On the industrial factory as a model for production in certain physical sciences, see Simon Schaffer, "Late Victorian Metrology and Its Instrumentation: A Manufactory of Ohms," in *Invisible Connections: Instruments, Institutions, and Science*, ed. R. Bud and S. Cozzens (Bellingham, Wash.: SPIE Optical Engineering Press, 1992), 23–56.

21. Thomas Huxley, "Has a Frog a Soul; and of What Nature Is That Soul, Supposing It to Exist?" in *Papers Read at the Meetings of the Metaphysical Society*, ed. Arthur Russell (Edinburgh: n.p., 1896).

22. H. E. Manning, "The Relation of the Will to Thought," *Contemporary Review* 16 (1871): 468–79.

23. William Carpenter, *Principles of Human Physiology*, 5th ed. (London: Churchill, 1855), 590–92, 618–33.

24. William Carpenter, *The Doctrine of Human Automatism* (London: Sunday Lecture Society, 1875).

25. Detailed experiments are described in Alfred Binet and Charles Féré, *Animal Magnetism* (London: Kegan Paul, Trench, 1887); and Rudolf Heidenhain, *Animal Magnetism: Physiological Observations* (London: Kegan Paul, 1880).

26. See Alison Winter, *Mesmerized: States of Mind in Victorian Britain* (Chicago: University of Chicago Press, 1998).

27. William Carpenter, *Principles of Mental Physiology*, 5th ed. (London: Kegan Paul, 1879), 330–36. Also see Andrew Combe, *The Management of Infancy, Physiological and Moral: Intended Chiefly for the Use of Parents* (Edinburgh: Maclachan and Stewart, 1871).

28. T. S. Clouston, *Science and Self-Control* (Edinburgh: n.p., 1886), 2.

29. On public demonstrations and scientific showmanship, see Iwan Morus, Simon Schaffer, and James Secord, "Scientific London," in *London: World City, 1800–1840*, ed. C. Fox (New Haven: Yale University Press, 1992), 129–42.

30. *Vivisection Prosecution: Report of a Prosecution of Physiologists by the R. S. P. C. A., at the Town Hall, Norwich, for Alleged Cruelty to Two Dogs* (London: Robert Hardwicke, 1875).

31. *Report of the Royal Commission on the Practice of Subjecting Live Animals to Experiments for Scientific Purposes; with Minutes of Evidence and Appendix. Presented to both Houses of Parliament by Command of her Majesty* (London: George Eyre and William Spottiswoode, 1876), xxii–xxiii.

32. The author's efforts with his black poodle, "Van," are described in John Lubbock, *On the Senses, Instincts, and Intelligence of Animals with Special Reference to Insects*, 2nd ed. (London: Kegan Paul, Trench, 1889), 272–85.

33. Darwin, *The Descent of Man*, 1:77; Charles Darwin, *The Expression of the Emotions in Man and Animals* (London: Murray, 1872), 57–58.

34. Francis Darwin, ed., *Life and letters of Charles Darwin*, 3 vols. (London: Murray, 1888), 1:113–15.

35. Francis Power Cobbe, *Life of Francis Power Cobbe as Told by Herself*, 2 vols. (London: Richard Bentley and Son, 1894), 2:241–42.

36. Francis Power Cobbe, *Darwinism in Morals, and Other Essays* (London: Williams and Norgate, 1872). Also see the discussion of animal sympathy as a recent development in the progress of moral sentiments in William Lecky, *History of European Morals* (London: Longmans, Green, 1865), 182–88.

37. Darwin, *The Descent of Man*, 1:103.

38. Henry S. Salt, *Animals' Rights Considered in Relation to Social Progress* (London: Macmillan, 1894), 12, 72–74, and *Humanitarianism: Its General Principles and Progress* (London: William Reeves, 1891), 18–19. The use of evolutionary theory by Salt and other animal protectionists is discussed in Chien-Hui Li, "Mobilizing Traditions in the Animal Defence Movement in Britain, 1820–1920," Ph.D. diss., University of Cambridge, 2002, 170–204.

39. Francis Power Cobbe, *The Modern Rack: Papers on Vivisection* (London: Swan and Sonnenschein, 1889); Claude Bernard, *Leçons de Physiologie Operatoire* (Paris: J. B. Baillière et fils, 1879).

40. Cobbe, *Life*, 2:290.

41. On these early researches in neurophysiology, see J. Hughlings Jackson, "Observations on the Localisation of Movements in the Cerebral Hemispheres, as Revealed by Cases of Convulsion, Chorea and Aphasia," *West Riding Lunatic Asylum Medical Reports* 3 (1873): 175–95; David Ferrier, "Experimental Researches in

Cerebral Physiology and Pathology," *West Riding Lunatic Asylum Medical Reports* 3 (1873): 30–96; David Ferrier, *The Functions of the Brain* (London: Smith, Elder, 1876); James Crichton-Browne, *The Doctor Remembers* (London: Duckworth, 1938); and Robert M. Young, *Mind, Brain, and Adaptation in the Nineteenth Century: Cerebral Localization and its Biological Context from Gall to Ferrier* (New York: Oxford University Press, 1990).

42. For accounts of the Ferrier-Goltz exchange, see *International Medical Congress, 7th Session Held in London, August 2–9, 1881, Transactions* (London, 1881); "The International Medical Congress," *British Medical Journal* (8 October 1881), 588–89; and Jurgen Thorwald, *The Triumph of Surgery*, trans. Richard and Clara Winston (London: Thames and Hudson, 1960), 13–39.

43. On maternal affection in monkeys and apes, see Darwin, *The Descent of Man*, 1:40–41. On their thievery and mischievousness, see Henry Walter Bates, *The Naturalist on the River Amazons*, 2 vols. (London: Murray, 1863), 1:247, 323, 2:309–11; and George Romanes, *Animal Intelligence* (London: Kegan Paul, Trench, 1882), 471–76. See also Ritvo, *The Animal Estate*, 30–39.

44. George Romanes, *Darwin and After Darwin: An Exposition of the Darwinian Theory and a Discussion of Post-Darwinian Questions* (London: Longmans, Green, 1892), 81.

45. Charles Darwin to George Romanes, 20 and 28 August 1878 and 2 September 1878, Charles Darwin Papers, American Philosophical Society, nn. 546 and 547.

46. Romanes, *Animal Intelligence,* 491–98.

47. Edward Sharpey-Schafer, *History of the Physiological Society During its First Fifty Years, 1876–1926* (Cambridge: Cambridge University Press, 1927).

48. George Romanes. *Mental Evolution in Animals* (London: Kegan Paul, Trench, 1883).

49. See, for example, Elie de Cyon, "The Anti-Vivisection Agitation," *Contemporary Review* 43 (1883): 506.

50. *Report of the Royal Commission*, Q. 2346 (Michael Foster), Q. 3249–50 (David Ferrier).

51. Sampson Gamgee, *The Influence of Vivisection on Human Surgery*, 2nd ed. (London: J. and A. Churchill, 1882), 27–28.

52. Robert Kohler, *Lords of the Fly: Drosophila, Genetics, and the Experimental Life* (Chicago: University of Chicago Press, 1994); and "Drosophila: A Life in the Laboratory," *Journal of the History of Biology* 26 (1993): 281–310.

53. On controversies within the medical community over new diagnostic technologies, see Christopher Lawrence, "Incommunicable Knowledge: Science, Technology, and the Clinical Art in Britain, 1850–1914," *Journal of Contemporary History* 20 (1985): 503–20. On human patients as experimental material, see Coral Lansbury, "Gynaecology, Pornography, and the Anti-vivisection Movement," *Victorian Studies* 28 (1985): 413–37.

54. Michael Allen Fox, *The Case for Animal Experimentation: An Evolutionary and Ethical Perspective* (Berkeley: University of California Press, 1986), 13–17, 44–46.

55. See, for example, Peter Singer, ed., *In Defence of Animals* (London: Basil Blackwell, 1985), 9.

56. Ilana Lowy, "The Experimental Body," in *Medicine in the Twentieth Century*, ed. R. Cooter and J. Pickstone (Amsterdam: Harwood, 2000), 435–49.

57. See, for example, Lynette Hart, ed., *Responsible Conduct with Animals in Research* (Oxford: Oxford University Press, 1998).

58. On the discourse of anthropology in this regard, see Tim Ingold, "The Animal in the Study of Humanity," in *What Is an Animal?* ed. Tim Ingold (London: Unwin Hyman, 1988), 84–99; and "From Trust to Domination: An Alternative History of Human-Animal Relations," in *Animals and Human Society: Changing Perspectives*, ed. Aubrey Manning and James Serpell (London: Routledge 1994), 1–22.

PART II

THINKING WITH ANIMALS
IN EVOLUTIONARY BIOLOGY

• • • •

CHAPTER 4

Comparative Psychology Meets Evolutionary Biology
Morgan's Canon and Cladistic Parsimony

• • • •

Elliott Sober

For many scientists, "anthropomorphism" is the name of a factual mistake and an intellectual failing. Anthropomorphism is often defined as the error of attributing human mental characteristics to nonhuman organisms; people are said to fall into this error because they are sentimental and uncritical. It is a revealing fact about current scientific culture that the opposite mistake—of mistakenly refusing to attribute human mental characteristics to nonhuman organisms—does not even have a ready name. The ethologist Frans De Waal has suggested the somewhat ungainly phrase "anthropodenial" to label this second type of error.[1] Will this phrase take hold as an equal partner of "anthropomorphism," or will one idea remain vivid while the other at best lurks in the shadows?

Although "anthropomorphism" is often defined as an error, it need not be, and the same goes for "anthropodenial." The hypothesis that a nonhuman organism has a psychological trait that human beings possess may or may not be correct, and the same goes for the hypothesis that the organism lacks some trait that human beings have. Suppose that O is a nonhuman organism and we are considering whether O has or lacks a mental characteristic M that we know attaches to human beings. There are two possible states of the world and two possible views we could take concerning whether O has M, thus generating the four possible outcomes depicted in the accompanying table. Mistakenly accepting that O has M is called a "type-1 error"; mistakenly denying that O has M is a "type-2 error." Scientists often take pains to avoid the type-1 error of mistaken anthropomorphism, but they often seem less concerned about avoiding the type-2 error of mistaken anthropodenial. Why?

This question can be posed both sociologically and logically. The former construal of the question would lead us to consider the cultural factors that have produced this unequal emphasis in scientific thinking. A full discussion of the historical development of science's wariness about anthropomorphism is a project much larger than I can undertake here. However, I do want to note that the type-1 error of mistaken anthropomorphism is often taken to reflect a kind of tenderheartedness, whereas the type-2 error of mistaken anthropodenial is supposed to reveal a kind of tough-mindedness. Supposedly, it is mere sentimentality to think that your pet has mental states, but it is a sign of strength, not weakness, to resist this temptation. Emphasis on the error of anthropomorphism and a relative lack of attention to the opposite error is part of a more general pattern in scientific culture in which tough-mindedness is valued.[2]

In this essay, I want to discuss an important episode in the development of science's asymmetric attitude towards anthropomorphism and anthropodenial. My approach will be both historical and conceptual. Psychologists have for a long time guarded against the risk of anthropomorphism by invoking a methodological principle that the nineteenth century comparative psychologist C. Lloyd Morgan stated and defended in his *Introduction to Comparative Psychology*: "In no case may we interpret an action as the outcome of the exercise of a higher psychical faculty, if it can be interpreted as the outcome of the exercise of one which stands lower in the psychological scale."[3] Morgan called this his "canon," and the name has stuck. Morgan gave an interesting defense of his principle, which I'll describe and evaluate.

		Possible states of the world	
		O lacks M	*O has M*
Possible conclusions one might draw	*Deny that O has M*	valid anthropodenial	type-2 error
	Accept that O has M	type-1 error	valid anthropomorphism

TABLE 4.1

To understand Morgan's canon historically, we must understand what Morgan was reacting *against*. Darwin had argued for the mental continuity of human and nonhuman organisms. His chosen successor, George Romanes, continued to emphasize this idea. Darwin's objective was to show that evolutionary ideas apply to mental characteristics no less than they apply to morphological and physiological traits. If all living things are related genealogically, we can locate the emergence of novelties in the interior branches of phylogenetic trees in which the tips represent current species and interior nodes represent common ancestors. Given the fact of common ancestry and the gradualism that was part of Darwin's conception of natural selection, contemporary species should exhibit similarities.[4] Bringing this evolutionary point of view to bear on mental phenomena therefore meant that psychological continuities had to be found between human beings and the rest of nature.

Darwin and Romanes developed this point about psychological evolution by relating anecdotes about animal behavior that were saturated with anthropomorphism.[5] For example, in chapter 2 of *The Descent of Man*, Darwin tells stories about animal behavior to support the claim that language, self-consciousness, an aesthetic sense, and belief in God are qualitatively similar (though not identical) with mental faculties found in nonhuman organisms. Here is a characteristic passage:

> The tendency in savages to imagine that natural objects and agencies are animated by spiritual or living essences, is perhaps illustrated by a little fact which I once noticed: my dog, a full-grown and very sensible animal, was lying on the lawn during a hot and still day; but at a little distance a slight breeze occasionally moved an open parasol, which would have been wholly disregarded by the dog, had any one stood near it. As it was, every time that the parasol slightly moved, the dog growled fiercely and barked. He must, I think, have reasoned to himself in a rapid and unconscious manner, that movement without any apparent cause indicated the presence of some strange living agent, and no stranger had a right to be on his territory.[6]

Morgan also wished to uphold the evolutionary hypothesis that all life is genealogically related, but he saw that the case for evolution does not require one to gloss over the differences that separate human beings and the rest of nature. One branch of a phylogenetic tree can develop novelties that do not emerge in others; a shared genealogy does not require that there be no qualitative differences among the traits exhibited by related species.[7]

Although this insight of Morgan's accords well with a modern evolutionary point of view, there is something decidedly *un*modern about

Morgan's ideas on the foundations of psychology. Like many psychologists writing at the time, Morgan maintained that attributing mental states to others depends on an introspective examination of one's self. When I raise a cup to my lips, this is because I believe that the cup contains a palatable liquid that I desire to drink. When I see another human being perform the same action, I infer a similar mental cause. Morgan saw that this pattern of inference extends across species boundaries. What Morgan termed the "double inductive method" leads one to interpret the behavior of organisms in other species as stemming from the same causes that move human beings to action. However, Morgan did not conclude that this induction *justifies* anthropomorphism—on the contrary, he thought it gives rise to a *bias*—the bias of anthropomorphism.

This bias requires a counterbalance, and that was the role that the canon played in Morgan's thought.[8] Morgan believed that the *simplest* hypothesis would be that other organisms are just like us. If I drink water because I believe that water is thirst quenching and want to stop being thirsty, then the simplest inference is that other organisms drink water for the very same reason.[9] It is Morgan's canon that leads one to ask whether drinking behavior in other species can be explained by a psychological mechanism that is "lower" than the beliefs and desires that animate human beings. If the behavior *can* be so explained, then it *should* be so explained. We should conclude that other organisms are *not* like us psychologically. The proximate mechanism that causes drinking in human beings differs from the mechanisms at work in other organisms.

Seen in this historical context, it is evident that Morgan's canon served a useful function; it provided a needed corrective to naive anthropomorphism. The effect of using the canon is that the chance of type-1 error is reduced. However, this point is not enough to justify the canon. After all, type-2 error is error too. Although the canon helps one avoid the bias of anthropomorphism, the question needs to be asked as to whether the canon introduces an opposite bias of its own. If nonhuman organisms really *are* like us in certain respects, the canon may lead us to miss this fact about nature. The canon would not make sense if it merely avoided one bias by falling prey to another.[10]

Morgan did not claim that the canon is justified simply because it reduces the chance of type-1 error. Rather, he argues that the canon has a specifically evolutionary justification. He formulates the problem of justification by asking the reader to consider three "divergently ascending grades of organisms." Species *a*, which represents man, has ascended to a higher level than *b*, which represents dogs, and *b* has risen higher than some other species, *c*. Each of these organisms may exhibit to some degree each of three "ascending faculties or stadia in mental development," numbered 1, 2, and 3. For example, 2 might be sense perception, and 3 might be the ability to reason abstractly. How much will these three faculties be developed in the three species? Morgan describes three possible patterns by which psychological faculties might be distributed across the three species; he called each distribution pattern a "method." I've reproduced his graphical representation (Morgan, *An Introduction to Comparative Psychology*, 56) of the problem in figure 1.

Morgan calls the first possibility the "Method of Levels." Here, "the faculties or stadia are of constant value. In the diagram, *b* has not quite

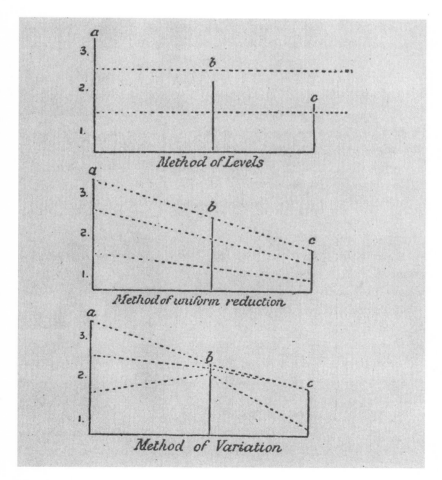

4.1 THE THREE "METHODS" THAT MORGAN DISCUSSES WHEREBY THREE MENTAL FACULTIES (1, 2, 3) MIGHT BE DISTRIBUTED AMONG THREE SPECIES (A, B, C).

reached the level of the beginning of the third or highest faculty, while *c* has only just entered upon the second stadium" (57). The method of levels apparently says that an organism must attain a certain level of development of a lower faculty before it can have any trace whatever of a higher faculty. The second alternative Morgan dubs the "Method of Uniform Reduction." In this arrangement, "in both *b* and *c* we have all three faculties represented in the same ratio as in *a*, but all uniformly reduced" (57). The idea here is that a lower organism has all the faculties that a higher organism possesses but has them developed to a lesser extent. The third alternative is the "Method of Variation," "according to which any one of the faculties 1, 2, or 3, may in *b* and *c* be either increased or reduced relative to its development in *a*" (57). This pattern seems to be the least constraining of the three; evidently, the method of variation is the method of *anything goes*. Morgan summarizes how these methods differ by asking us to suppose that

> *b* represents the psychic stature of a dog. Then, according to the interpretation on the method of levels, he possesses the lowest faculty (1) in the same degree as man; in faculty (2) he somewhat falls short of man; while in the highest faculty (3) he is altogether wanting. According to the interpretation on the method of uniform reduction he possesses all the faculties of man but in reduced degree. And according to the interpretation on the method of variation he excels man in the lowest faculty, while the other two faculties are both reduced but in different degrees. (57)

Morgan then asserts that the process of evolution by natural selection entails that "it is the third method . . . which we should expect *a priori* to accord most nearly with observed facts." He notes that "in the diagram by which the Method of Variation is illustrated, the highest faculty 3 is in *c* reduced to zero;" the total absence of higher faculties in lower organisms is entirely possible. This point allows him to bring his argument for the canon to its conclusion. If the method of variation is correct, then "any animal may be at a stage where certain higher faculties have not yet been evolved from their lower precursors; and hence we are logically bound not to assume the existence of these higher faculties until good reasons shall have been shown for such existence" (59). It is here that we can see the slippage in Morgan's logic. The method of variation does say that it is possible for an organism to have lower but not higher faculties. However, the method also allows for the possibility that an organism will have a higher faculty but not a lower one and also for the possibility that it will have both. Given that Morgan's canon instructs us to take an *asymmetric* attitude towards anthropomorphism and anthropodenial, the principle cannot be justified by the method of variation, which postulates *no asymmetry at all* in the evolutionary process.

Notice the exact wording that Morgan chooses; he says that "we are logically bound *not to assume the existence* of these higher faculties" without evidence for their existence. But what he needs to show is that we are logically bound to assume the nonexistence of these higher faculties if we lack evidence for their existence. Not assuming the existence of something (agnosticism) is a different matter from assuming its nonexistence (atheism). The wording that Morgan chooses is unobjectionable if we interpret it carefully; indeed, it is just an instance of the general claim that we should not assume the existence of *anything* unless we have evidence. However, this wording does not entail an asymmetry between higher and lower; it would be equally correct to say that "we are logically bound not to assume the existence of *lower* faculties" in a nonhuman organism without evidence for their existence. Modern comparative psychologists sometimes put this point by saying that absence of evidence is not the same as evidence of absence.

In addition to this gap in Morgan's reasoning, it also is unclear what Morgan means by "lower" and "higher." He applies these predicates both to species and to mental faculties. Human beings are "higher" than dogs, and abstract reasoning is a "higher" faculty than sense perception. Morgan's graphical representations give the impression that the "highness" of a species is the sum of the degrees of development of its separate faculties; however, Morgan never describes how these faculties can be rendered commensurable and then summed. If human beings have a greater ability in abstract reasoning than dogs, while dogs have greater sensory acuity than human beings, which species is "higher" overall?

Given that Morgan thought of himself as bringing Darwinian considerations to bear on comparative psychology, one might hope to find some help on this problem in Darwinian theory itself. However, here it is worth reflecting on the fact that Darwin once wrote himself a memo to never say "higher" and "lower."[11] This was no mere passing scribble; it characterized a deep and enduring implication of the hypotheses that Darwin developed. The theory of evolution by natural selection undermines the idea of a linear scale of nature in which each stage is higher or lower than every other. Darwin replaced the ladder with the tree; lineages diverge from each other and develop different adaptations that suit them to their peculiar conditions of life. In this framework, it makes no sense to ask whether one contemporary species is higher or lower than another.[12]

Morgan was very much in the grip of the Spencerian doctrine that evolution always marches from simple to complex.[13] To the degree that the canon depends on this claim of directionality, the canon is in trouble. Although life started simple and thus had to show a net increase in complexity (it had nowhere to go but up), the history of life is peppered with cases of evolutionary simplification. For example, the evolution of parasites typically involves a transition from complex to simple as the parasite loses features found in its free-living ancestor. And even if we assume that evolution always moves from simpler to more complex traits, it still is unclear why human beings are "higher" than dogs. After all, we are not descended from present-day canines; rather, we and they have a common ancestor. The Spencerian idea guarantees only that descendants are "higher" (that is, more complex) than their ancestors.

Perhaps the closest that modern Darwinian theory comes to the distinction between "higher" and "lower" is the distinction between derived and ancestral character states. A lineage begins with a certain suite of characters, which we can call "the ancestral condition." When novelties evolve, we say that the new forms introduced into the lineage are "derived." It is left entirely open whether the derived form of a character is more complex than the ancestral form. In fact, the distinction between ancestral and derived characters is always relative to the portion of a lineage that one is considering. For example, consider a lineage in which species X is ancestral to species Y and Y is ancestral to species Z. Suppose that X lacks wings, Y has wings, and Z has no wings. If we are considering the portion of this lineage that goes from X to Y, winglessness is the ancestral condition; however, if we wish to talk about the part that goes from Y to Z, then wings are ancestral and winglessness is derived. Although it is easy to take on board the idea that the ancestral/derived distinction depends on which lineage one is discussing, it is perhaps less than intuitive to say that the lower/higher distinction has this sort of relativity. Given this, it is perhaps not surprising that "lower" and "higher" have largely lapsed from the language of evolutionary biology.

The question I now wish to explore is whether Morgan's canon makes sense when "higher" and "lower" are replaced with "derived" and "ancestral." What is the status of the following "modernized" version of Morgan's canon:

> In no case may we interpret an action as the outcome of the exercise
> of a derived psychical faculty, if it can be interpreted as the outcome
> of the exercise of an ancestral faculty.

Let's begin exploring this question by considering the problem depicted in figure 2. Here we see human beings and dogs as two tip species in a phylogenetic tree. We assume that the species at the root of the tree has the ancestral state A and that human beings have the derived form D of the character. Our question is whether we should attribute D or A to dogs. This problem can be analyzed by using a standard idea in evolutionary biology—that the plausibility of rival hypotheses can be evaluated by considering how parsimonious they are. In this context, parsimony is measured by seeing how many changes in character state would have to occur under each of the competing hypotheses.[14] This way of thinking about parsimony is sometimes called "cladistic parsimony," to indicate that it is a principle that is specifically about phylogenetic trees ("clade" comes from the Greek word for "branch"); its connection with the broader and vaguer principle of parsimony (aka "Ockham's razor") is a matter of continuing discussion.

The point to notice about figure 2 is that the two possible assignments of character state to dogs are equally parsimonious. Whether we say that dogs have D (figure 2a) or that they have A (figure 2b), at least one change in character state must have occurred in the branches of the evolutionary tree. The location of this change is indicated by a "slash" through the relevant branch in the phylogenetic tree. In the problem we are considering, the modernized formulation of Morgan's canon is false—assigning dogs the ancestral character state is neither more nor less plausible than assigning them the derived state.

The analysis gets a little more complicated if we have additional information about the characteristics of species other than human beings. For example, in the three problems depicted in figure 3, we begin with information about the characteristics of human beings and other species, and we

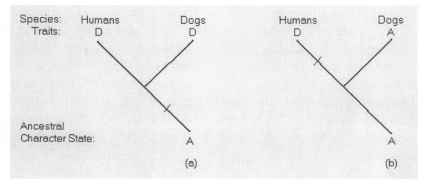

4.2   Given just that human beings have the derived character state D, (a) assigning the derived character state D to dogs and (b) assigning the ancestral character state A to dogs are equally parsimonious. Cladistic parsimony does not discriminate between anthropomorphism and anthropodenial in this instance.

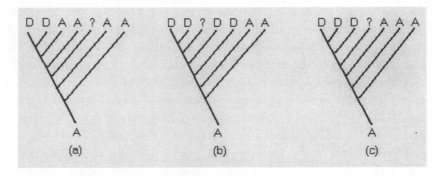

4.3   Assuming that human beings (the left-most tip species in each tree) have the derived character state D, different assignments of character states to dogs—the species indicated by the question mark—can sometimes differ in parsimoniousness if one has additional knowledge of the character states of other, related species. See the text for details.

wish to use parsimony to assign a character state to dogs. In figure 3a, it is more parsimonious to hypothesize that dogs have the ancestral character state. In figure 3b, parsimony favors assigning the derived character state to dogs. In figure 3c, the two possible assignments are equally parsimonious. However, the inferences represented in figures 3a and 3b are not available in the problem we have been considering. In that problem, we are supposed to begin with just one "observation"—that human beings have the derived character state.[15] As we saw in figure 2, that single datum provides no help in deciding which character state to attribute to dogs.

All is not lost, however, in that cladistic parsimony *does* provide advice about a slightly different problem, which is depicted in figure 4.[16] Let's suppose that human beings and dogs are both observed to exhibit some derived *behavior* B. This means that the root of the tree is in the state not-B. Parsimony favors regarding B as a homology (figure 4a) rather than as a homoplasy (figure 4b). A homology is a similarity inherited from a common ancestor; a homoplasy is a similarity that is the result of two or more independent derivations of the trait. So far we have said nothing about the proximate mechanisms (psychological or otherwise) that might be causing dogs and humans to produce this behavior. Let's call the psychological mechanism that human beings use to produce the behavior M, and let's suppose that an alternative mechanism, A, also could produce the behavior. Our question is whether we should attribute M or A to dogs. The two possibilities are depicted in figures 4c and 4d. Since the root of the tree is assumed to lack the behavior B, it follows that neither M nor A is present

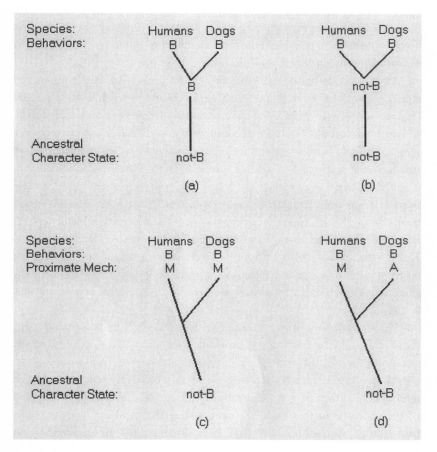

4.4 IF HUMAN BEINGS AND DOGS BOTH EXHIBIT A DERIVED BEHAVIOR B, THEN IT IS MORE PARSIMONIOUS (A) TO VIEW THE SHARED BEHAVIOR AS A HOMOLOGY THAN (B) TO HYPOTHESIZE THAT IT EVOLVED INDEPENDENT-LY IN THE TWO LINEAGES. IN ADDITION, IT IS MORE PARSIMONIOUS (C) TO CONJECTURE THAT HUMAN BEINGS AND DOGS PRODUCE THE BEHAVIOR BY USING THE SAME PROXIMATE MECHANISM M THAN (D) TO CLAIM THAT HUMAN BEINGS AND DOGS DEPLOY DIFFERENT PROXIMATE MECHANISMS.

ancestrally. Given all this, it turns out that assigning M to dogs (4c) is more parsimonious than assigning A to dogs (4d). Parsimony, in this instance, favors anthropomorphism, just as Morgan claimed.

It is important to understand this conclusion in the right way. Cladistic parsimony does not provide a blanket justification for attributing human characteristics to nonhuman organisms. This is the lesson of figure 2. How-ever, figure 4 represents a more specific problem in which parsimony does favor anthropomorphism over anthropodenial. *If two derived behaviors are homologous, then the hypothesis that they are produced by the same proximate mechanism is more parsimonious than the hypothesis that they are produced by different proximate mechanisms.*

An interesting feature of Morgan's canon is that it accords no special status to psychological characteristics. For Morgan, mental traits can be "higher" or "lower," but so too can features of respiration and digestion. Morgan's canon is a principle of comparative *biology*, not just of comparative *psychology*. In this sense, the cladistic analysis I have described is very much in the spirit of Morgan's approach. The principle of cladistic parsimony applies to any trait that evolves—to traits about the mind no less than to traits about digestion and respiration. However, once Morgan's terms "lower" and "higher" are replaced with the more scientifically coherent concepts of "ancestral" and "derived," the argument leads to a conclusion that differs from Morgan's. There is no presumption in favor of treating human beings as different from the rest of nature; on the contrary, there is a circumstance in which the presumption is precisely in the opposite direction.

Morgan's canon, in the modernized formulation I have supplied, conflicts with cladistic parsimony, but that does not settle whether cladistic parsimony is a valid principle of evolutionary reasoning. As noted, it is a principle that is widely used in evolutionary biology, though it must be added that its status is at present a matter of scientific debate. But regardless of the outcome of that debate, it seems clear that nothing like the reformulation of Morgan's canon that I have discussed will find a justification in evolutionary theory. There is no evolutionary presumption in favor of assuming that nonhuman organisms differ from human beings, either in terms of their mental or their nonmental characteristics.

Even though evolutionary theory offers no justification of Morgan's canon, it is possible that something like his principle can be given a non-evolutionary justification. Contemporary ethologists often invoke a "principle of conservatism," according to which we should prefer attributing "less sophisticated" abilities to nonhuman organisms over "more sophisticated" abilities when both would suffice to explain the behavior we observe.[17] Whether this principle discards Morgan's categories of "higher" and "lower" or merely supplies them with new labels is a question worth asking. Although it is not clear what "degrees of sophistication" means here, the use that ethologists make of the principle renders two of its elements unambiguous. The first is that attributing a nonmental faculty to an organism is supposed to be preferable to attributing a mental faculty when both are consistent with the observed behavior. And within the category of mentalistic explanation, attributing fewer mental abilities to an organism is supposed to be preferable to attributing more. Contemporary ethologists, unlike Morgan, do not attempt to provide an evolutionary justification of their principle. In fact, they usually do not discuss what justifies it at all; they merely rely on its being intuitive.

Morgan's canon (both in Morgan's own formulation and in the one that uses the evolutionary concepts of derived and ancestral characters) and the principle of conservatism are maxims of "default reasoning." They say that some hypotheses should be presumed innocent until proven guilty, while others should be regarded as having precisely the opposite status. Perhaps these default principles deserve to be swept from the field and replaced by a much simpler idea—that we should not indulge in anthropomorphism *or* in anthropodenial until we can point to observations that discriminate between these two hypotheses. It is desirable that we avoid the type-1 error of mistaken anthropomorphism, but it also is desirable that we avoid the type-2 error of mistaken anthropodenial. However, the best way to minimize the risk of *both* types of error is not to embrace an a priori prejudice. The only prophylactic we need is empiricism.[18]

NOTES

1. F. De Waal, "Anthropomorphism and Anthropodenial: Consistency in our Thinking About Humans and Other Animals," *Philosophical Topics* 27 (1999): 255–80.

2. Another application of the distinction between tough-mindedness and tendermindedness in science that William James drew in his book *Pragmatism* may be found in the ongoing debate in evolutionary biology concerning group selection. Those sympathetic to group selection are often portrayed by their critics as naive sentimentalists who see nature through rose-colored glasses; those same critics congratulate themselves on their willingness to stare nature's dark side full in the face. For discussion, see E. Sober and D. Wilson, *Unto Others: The Evolution and Psychology of Unselfish Behavior* (Cambridge, Mass.: Harvard University Press, 1999).

3. C. Lloyd Morgan, *An Introduction to Comparative Psychology*, 1st ed. (London: Walter Scott, 1894), 53. In the book's second edition Morgan rephrases the canon and then adds an important clarification; C. Lloyd Morgan, *An Introduction to Comparative Psychology*, 2nd edition, (London: Walter Scott, 1903): "To this, however, it should be added, lest the range of the principle be misunderstood, that the canon by no means excludes the interpretation of a particular activity in terms of the higher processes if we already have independent evidence of the occurrence of these higher processes in the animal under observation."

4. For a more detailed examination of how the ideas of common ancestry and natural selection interact in evolutionary theory, see E. Sober and S. Orzack,

"Common Ancestry and Natural Selection," *Britsh Journal for the Philosophy of Science* 54 (2003): 423–37.

5. R. Richards, *Darwin and the Emergence of Evolutionary Theories of Mind and Behavior* (Chicago: University of Chicago Press, 1987).

6. Darwin, *The Descent of Man, and Selection in Relation to Sex* (1871; reprint, Princeton, N.J.: Princeton University Press, 1981), 1:67.

7. G. Gottlieb, "Comparative Psychology and Ethology," in *The First Century of Experimental Psychology*, ed. E. Hearst (Hilldale, N.J.: Lawrence Erlbaum, 1979), 150.

8. G. Burghardt, "Animal Awareness: Current Perceptions and Historical Perspective," *American Psychologist* 40 (1985): 912.

9. Even though Morgan thought that his canon *conflicted* with the principle of parsimony, his successors took precisely the opposite position, usually without even pointing out that their understanding of the canon differed from Morgan's. For example, B. Skinner, *The Behavior of Organisms* (New York: Appleton Crofts, 1938), 4, says "Darwin, insisting upon the continuity of mind, attributed mental faculties to subhuman species. Lloyd Morgan, with his law of parsimony, dispensed with them in a reasonably successful attempt to account for characteristic animal behavior without them." E. Boring, *History of Experimental Psychology* (New York: Appleton Century Crofts, 1950), 474, also says that the canon is a version of the razor but denies that the principle of parsimony is legitimate when the problem is to infer the mental capacities of nonhuman organisms. "Nature is notoriously prodigal," according to Boring, so "why should we interpret it only parsimoniously?" It is an interesting historical problem why Morgan's canon was transformed from a specifically Darwinian principle to a general methodological maxim and an interesting epistemological question whether this reformulation allows the principle to be justified.

10. Consider, for example, a principle that is the mirror image of Morgan's canon—that we should attribute higher mental faculties rather than lower ones, when both would account for the data. This maxim reduces the chance of type-2 error.

11. M. Ghiselin, *The Triumph of the Darwinian Method* (Berkeley: University of California Press, 1969), 70.

12. This is not to say that Darwin disavowed the idea of evolutionary progress; see D. Ospovat, *The Development of Darwin's Theory* (Cambridge: Cambridge University Press, 1981), chapter 9. Sober discusses modern evolutionary theory's attitude towards this concept; see E. Sober, "Progress and Direction in Evolution," in *Progressive Evolution?* ed. J. Campell (Boston: Jones and Bartlett, 1994), 19–33; see also the essays in Matthew H. Nitecki, ed. *Evolutionary Progress* (Chicago: University of Chicago Press, 1988).

13. Gottlieb, "Comparative Psychology," 150; Boakes, *From Darwin to Behaviorism: Psychology and the Minds of Animals* (Cambridge: Cambridge University Press, 1984), 40.

14. For discussion, see E. Sober, *Reconstructing the Past: Parsimony, Evolution, and Inference* (Cambridge, Mass.: MIT Press, 1988); and E. Sober, "Reconstructing the Character States of Ancestors: A Likelihood Perspective on Cladistic Parsimony," *The Monist* 85 (2002): 156–76.

15. None of us "observes" that *all* human beings have a given mental trait. The problem of why we are entitled to extrapolate across species boundaries also applies within our own species, as Morgan recognized; this is the setting of the traditional philosophical problem of other minds; see E. Sober, "Evolution and the Problem of Other Minds." *Journal of Philosophy* 97 (2000): 365–86.

16. This argument is presented in F. De Waal, "Complementary Methods and Convergent Evidence in the Study of Primate Social Cognition" *Behaviour* 118 (1991): 297–320, and is further discussed in E. Sober, "Evolution and the Problem of Other Minds."

17. See, for example, D. Cheney and R. Seffarth, *How Monkeys See the World* (Chicago: University of Chicago Press, 1990).

18. E. Sober, "The Principle of Conservatism in Cognitive Ethology," In *Naturalism, Evolution, and Mind*, ed. D. Walsh (Cambridge; Cambridge University Press, 2001), 225–38.

CHAPTER 5

· · · · ·

Anthropomorphism and Cross-Species Modeling

· · · · ·

Sandra D. Mitchell

INTRODUCTION

"Anthropomorphism" has long been considered a bad word in science.[1] It carries the stale dust of nineteenth-century anecdotal evidence for the continuity of humans with nonhuman animals. Darwin claims that "there can, I think, be no doubt that a dog feels shame . . . and something very like modesty when begging too often for food."[2] But anthropomorphism is neither prima facie bad or necessarily nonscientific. It can be both, but it need not be either.

There has been a recent resurgence of interest in anthropomorphism, attributable to two developments—the rise of cognitive ethology and the requirements of various forms of expanded, environmental ethics. The first, the investigation into the mental life and behavior of animals, has a history clearly traceable from Darwin through the nineteenth-century British evolutionist George Romanes and twentieth-century European ethologists Niko Tinbergen and Konrad Lorenz to contemporary biologists.[3] This is a straightforward trajectory of scientific theories and experiments designed to provide a comprehensive framework for studying the functions, evolution, and development of behavior and its physiological bases. In the 1970s, cognitive ethology arose with a new emphasis on the mental experiences of animals, particularly in their natural environment, in the course of their daily lives.[4] The move to attributing explanatory mental states to nonhuman animals has been controversial since its beginnings.[5] In part the dispute has been conceptual, in part methodological. What does it mean to say that an animal has conscious awareness of its own thoughts, and how could one experimentally access the truth or falsity of such a claim?

Some of the most interesting and relevant work in this area has been directed at explaining the behavior of chimpanzees. Since it is generally agreed that the chimp is our phylogenetically closest relative, it makes evolutionary sense that the features of that species are more likely to be similar to features of our species than those of species whose connection is more attenuated. Darwin's and our love of dogs notwithstanding, it is in primate research that the most plausible anthropomorphic theses are to be found. Or, as Daniel Povinelli claims in *Folk Physics for Apes*, "if the argument by analogy cannot be sustained when it comes to behaviors that we share in common with our nearest living relatives, it can hardly be expected to survive more general scrutiny."[6] Indeed, as I will report later, Povinelli argues just this—that a strong version of anthropomorphism cannot be sustained in explaining even some chimpanzee behaviors.

A strong version of anthropomorphism found in some advocates of cognitive ethology aims to explain behaviors of nonhumans by appeal to mental states similar to the ones we take to explain our own behavior. Of particular interest is the thesis that chimps have a "theory of mind," that is, beliefs about the beliefs of others. Such second-order beliefs are invoked to make sense of behavioral variation. For example, a human would respond differently to two actors on the basis of beliefs about what those actors could see. If one of them had a clear view of a source of food, while the other's view of the food was blocked by a barrier, then it would make sense to follow any indication of food given by the one whom you believe can see the food and hence will know where it is. Do chimps do the same thing? Do they do it for the same reasons? As I will discuss below, arguments from analogy and experimental results are brought to bear on answering this type of question.

The second source of interest in the similarities of humans and nonhuman animals arises from the animal rights and environmental ethics movements, which have sought to transform the criteria by which we determine what beings merit moral consideration. Animal welfare and animal rights ethical positions make the nature of nonhuman experience determinate of who and what we must count in judging the moral correctness of our actions. The utilitarian version of animal welfare advocated by Peter Singer (1991) designates sentience or the ability to feel pain as sufficient for having interests that must be considered. The deontological animal rights position, like that of Tom Regan (1983) grants inherent value and moral rights to any being that has "emotion, memory, belief, desire, the use of general concepts, intentional action, a sense of the future, and some degree of self-awareness."[7] Thus, the existence of feelings and cognitive states of non-human organisms is no longer just an academic question of whether or not the Rumbaugh's Kansi has language[8] or dolphins can recognize themselves in a mirror[9] but is rather a set of facts about the world that we need to know to ethically decide what to eat and what to wear. Thus, the manner and degree to which nonhuman animals are similar to human beings becomes an even more pressing scientific problem in a context in which the very morality of our actions depends on the answer.

At its basis, anthropomorphism involves claims about the similarity of nonhuman objects or beings to humans and the centrality of human concepts and abilities to classify behaviors across ontological categories. Strong anthropomorphism asserts that some description of a feature of human beings applies in the same way to a feature of a nonhuman animal. Critics of anthropomorphism often attack the presumptive character of such claims, like Darwin's *lack of doubt* of the internal nature of a dog's experience. Observers have been too willing to characterize nonhumans using descriptive language that has humans as its primary referent. By describing a dog as feeling shame when it walks away with its tail between its legs, one is not gathering neutral data with which to test the myriad of theories about the nature of dogs but rather is assuming in that very description that dogs have mental or emotional states like human mental and emotional states. But what is at fault here? Is it the presumptiveness or the anthropomorphism?

After all, similarity between humans and nonhuman animals is just what we should expect on the basis of an evolutionary account of the origin and diversification of life on the planet—but not any willy-nilly similarity. As a scientific claim about the facts of the world, any specific similarity between human immune systems, say, and mouse immune systems, or be-tween human beliefs and chimp beliefs, must be grounded in more than a general truth of the continuum of life and backed by more than an imposi-tion of the same descriptive language.

In what follows I will evaluate the arguments and evidence for a range of stances toward anthropomorphism from global rejections to specific models. The bumper sticker version of this essay could be: Science made too easy is bound to be wrong. In the end I will argue that specific anthropo-morphic theses are supported or not supported by the same rigorous ex-perimental and logical reasoning as any other scientific model. However, even though anthropomorphic models can be treated as science as usual, unique problems for these models still will remain. These problems have to do with the way in which language descriptive of our experiences travels back and forth between scientific and social domains.

I will first consider some global objections to anthropomorphism. These attack the logical or conceptual transgressions that the act of describing nonhumans in human terms is supposed to commit. I will then look at empirical arguments for and against specific instances of the anthropomorphism ascribed to nonhuman primates. Finally I will consider some social contextual concerns that arise from the scientific anthropomorphic models.

LOGICAL OBJECTIONS

A. Anthropomorphism entails a category mistake. To speak of dogs with feelings of shame is like referring to a Bach partita as being purple. This objection is easily dismissed as a relic of the view that humans are a separate and unique species, either created to be such or so far evolved that no predicates true of us could be true of other organisms. Surely the evolution of life on the planet tells against this being a logical claim. For a Cartesian who holds that animals are just complicated machines that lack the souls that make humans human, it might hold sway, but we are centuries beyond that.[10]

B. Anthropomorphism is defined as the *overestimation* of the similarity of humans and nonhumans and hence by definition could not yield accurate accounts.[11] But this is humpty-dumptyism. "When *I* use a word," Humpty Dumpty said, in rather a scornful tone, "it means just what I choose it to mean—neither more nor less."[12]

If we choose to let "anthropomorphism" be so defined, then we merely shift the question to be, *When* is it anthropomorphism, and *when* is it possibly a legitimate similarity? That is, when does a relevant similarity hold such that describing a cognitive state like "believing Sue cannot see the banana" could be equally true of an adult human, a human infant, and a chimpanzee? Such substantive questions cannot be reduced to mere matters of definition.

C. Anthropomorphism is *necessary* or *unavoidable*, since there is no amorphism or neutral language with which to describe behavior. If we do not use the predicates that describe our own human behavior, such as " believing X, wanting Y, deceiving Z" for describing nonhuman animals, then we have to use language appropriate for machines, like "moving toward the object, picking up the banana, looking toward the gate."

This position makes two mistakes. The first is that it presupposes a conceptual and linguistic impoverishment that is not justified. It underestimates our ability to discriminate and refer to multiple states of a system or many-valued parameters. As recent research has suggested, we may end up thinking that chimpanzees do not have the same kind of mental representations that we have but nevertheless think they have mental representations that mediate their behavior. They are not input-output machines but cogitating organisms. They just may not do it the way we do.[13] The second mistake is to confuse anthropocentrism with anthropomorphism. It is true that the descriptions we apply to anything are created *by* us, but they need not be *of* us. That is, we are the source of the terms and predicates, but they need not be terms and predicates that apply principally to our behaviors.

If anthropomorphism is not bad for *logical* reasons, then the extent of the acceptability of claims of similarity must be empirically grounded. This indeed is the conclusion that many recent commentators on anthropomorphism have reached.[14] Do chimpanzees have language, like us? Do they have beliefs about the beliefs of other chimps or of humans? Testing for the presence or absence of mental states, representations internal to the cognizing agent and presumably causally relevant to the behaviors we can observe is no easy matter. I will now turn to the two main types of observational evidence that are used to justify anthropomorphism; the argument by analogy and experimentation.

EMPIRICAL QUESTIONS

ARGUMENT BY ANALOGY

An *argument by analogy* is invoked to support a claim about the unobserved features of one system—the "target" of the analogy—based on the presence of that feature in another system—the "model system." The relevant similarities between the two systems are what justify the inference. Traditional analyses of analogical arguments render them fairly weak.

TRADITIONAL ACCOUNT OF ANALOGICAL ARGUMENT STRUCTURE.

Premise 1: System M is observed to have features a, b, c.
Premise 2: System T is observed to have features a, b, c.
Premise 3: System M is observed also to have feature d.

Conclusion: Therefore, system T must have feature d.

This inductive argument structure is supposed to capture everyday reasoning. For example, suppose two students in a class have the same study habits and the same grades on the midterm exam. I observe that student M gets an A on the final exam. Suppose student T has not yet taken the exam. On the basis of the observed similarities, I can infer that student T will also get an A. This is clearly not deductively valid, as student T might be ill or fail to study in the manner she studied in the past or might have lost her book or for any number of reasons not perform the way I expect on the basis of her similarity to student M. Thus there is no deductive guarantee that the conclusion, "Student T will get an A on the exam" is true. Nevertheless, the analogy permits inductive support for the inference. Certainly I would have more reason to believe student T would get an A than I would of other students who bear no similarities to student M.

The strength of an analogy is sometimes rendered in terms of the number of similarities between the two systems. The more features in common, the more likely the target system will have the ascribed unobserved feature. But quantifying over similarities is notoriously difficult and, quite frankly, beside the point. The sheer number of similar features does not immediately warrant the relevance of the similarities for the presence or absence of the feature of interest. Humans and mice have a large number of differences, and yet we are comfortable using the results of drug tests on mice to infer the consequences of those drugs on human biochemistry.

A more sophisticated rendering of the logic of analogical arguments, developed by Weitzenfeld[15] and related to structure-based accounts given in the cognitive sciences,[16] suggests that the inference of the presence of the unobserved feature in the target system is based on assumptions about the relations within each of the two analogous structures, rather than just their unstructured sets of properties. For example, according to Weitzenfeld's account, a claim that a human being will have an adverse reaction to saccharine based on experimental studies on mice is entailed by an assumption of the isomorphism obtaining between the causal structures governing mouse and human biochemistry. Thus, when using information about the model system to draw conclusions about the target system, for example, mice to human inferences or, as we shall see, human beliefs in anthropomorphic inferences to chimp beliefs, what establishes the relevant similarities will be the causal or determining structures in those two systems. If they have isomorphic structures, then the inference is sound. If not, then the conclusions are not supported.

There are two important components to this account of analogy. The first is that it is structural isomorphism between the model and target that deductively guarantees an inference from the observed feature of the model to the unobserved feature of the target. However, isomorphism is a rather weak relationship between two structures, since the reason the mapping works may be accidental. Think of the mapping from stellar constellations as seen from earth such as Orion or Ursa Major to the spatial configurations of hunters and bears. For analogical arguments to be informative, the reason the relations in the model structure—for example, mouse ingestion of large quantities of saccharine inducing mouse production of tumors—maps onto the relations in the target structure—that is, human ingestion of saccharine in diet foods and subsequent cancers—must be nonaccidental, that is, governed by a rule or causal law. This is all rather abstract philosophy. The main point of the structural approach to analogical arguments is to focus attention on to the relationships between the variables in the each system as well as the relationships between the two systems, rather than on simply the number of features shared by the two systems. Let's bring it back to the case at hand.

A clear reconstruction of the analogical argument for inferring that chimps are like us is provided by Povinelli:

P1: I exhibit bodily behaviors of type B (i.e., those normally thought to be caused by second-order mental states).
P2: Chimps exhibit bodily behaviors of type B.
P3: My own bodily behaviors of type B are usually caused by my second-order mental states of type A.

C: Therefore bodily behaviors of type B exhibited by chimps are caused by their second-order mental states of type A, and so a fortiori chimps have second-order mental states of type A.

Povinelli, *Folk Physics for Apes*, 13.

In the traditional philosophical analysis of analogical arguments, the number of similarities between humans and chimpanzees would determine the strength of support for the conclusion. Phylogenetic proximity is brought to bear to suggest that we have more similarities with chimps than other species since we are historically closer to them. Divergence occurred more recently from chimpanzees than from other species and hence we expect them to be more like us than would be toads or amoebae. But notice how weak this support actually is. Divergence is presumed, and distinction is required for humans and chimps *not* to be the same species. Many features may be shared, but just the ones we are interested in, second-order mental states for example, may be the ones that constitute the break in the lineage. So evolutionary proximity may entail more similar features but not necessarily the relevant features.[17]

The more sophisticated analysis of analogical inference suggests a different understanding of the argument. Here, what makes human experience relevant to conclusions about chimp experience is not the number of similarities but the presence of isomorphic causal structures. What causes a human behavior B is, supposedly, a human second-order mental state A. But is this the same causal structure found in chimpanzees? If it is, then even though we cannot ask the chimp what belief motivated its behavior, we can be justified in thinking that if the human and chimp behaviors are the same or similar, then the beliefs that cause them are the same are similar. However, this shifts the question of the legitimacy of analogical reasoning to the determination of whether the causal structures generating behaviors in humans and in chimpanzees are isomorphic. That is the subject of the second type of empirical evidence that I will discuss below.

To summarize so far, anthropomorphic theses can be seen as instances of analogical inferences. We ascribe to other organisms the features we take to be true of us. Phylogenetic relatedness seems to render weak support for the conclusion of such inferences, so weak that they can only garner some modest plausibility for the conclusions. However, a stronger analogical inference is supported when there is justification for isomorphism of causal structures in the two systems generating the features we are interested in. On this account the analogy requires a different type of evidence than evolutionary history alone. Statistical and experimental data are required to support the premises that would entail the inference. So how can empirical evidence help?

Argument from Experimental Data

Advocates of cognitive ethology cry foul when their opponents reject the enterprise from the beginning just for being anthropmorphic. They would rather let the facts decide. But this is not as easy as it might sound. The controversial anthropomorphic theses ascribe to nonhumans just those sorts of features that are not directly accessible to observation. Allen and Hauser want to know whether apes have a concept of death.[18] Premack and Woodruff explore whether apes have a "theory of mind" that is invoked in generating behaviors that appear to be acts of deception.[19] It is obvious that we cannot just look at a chimpanzee, or another human being for that matter, and see its internal mental state. As Romanes put it,

> if I contemplate my own mind, I have an immediate cognizance of a certain flow of thoughts or feelings, which are the more ultimate things—and indeed the only things—of what I am cognizant. But if I contemplate Mind in other persons or organisms, I can have no such immediate cognizance of their thoughts and feelings; I can only *infer* the existence of such thoughts and feelings from the activities of the persons or organisms which appear to exhibit them.[20]

We cannot ask a chimpanzee to report to us the content of its cognition. We have access experimentally and observationally only to the very behaviors we take as the effects of the ascribed mental causes. So how can observation and experiment help decide this issue?

It is worth noting that the reason one suggests that concepts and second-order beliefs might be the causes of nonhuman behaviors is because we believe that they are the causes of our own behaviors. This view assumes there is a causal structure or mechanism that we can investigate that generates behaviors as the effect of beliefs.[21] When I think my husband is joking about where the car keys are, but a friend who is with us is telling the truth, then I do not walk in the direction of the place mentioned by my husband to find my keys. Rather I go to the location cited by my friend. I hear the utterances of each of them, and my behavior is caused not just by those utterances but also by my beliefs about the beliefs of the speakers.

How do I know this? It is introspection or personal self-knowledge that gives me insight into the causal structure that underlies my actions. What if a third party, say, a neighbor, is standing next to me when both my husband and my friend pronounce on the location of the keys? Furthermore, when asked to get the keys, while I go to the location mentioned by my friend, the neighbor goes the other way, to the location cited by my husband. What do I think caused the neighbor's behavior? I don't have the kind of subjective access to his internal mental states that I have to my own. I can reason only by analogy that the causes of his behavior are the same kind of things that cause my behavior. I do not think the neighbor is a machine, I do not think he is being physically pulled in the direction he is moving, and so on. I think that he must think that my husband was being serious and not joking and that this belief is a contributing cause of the neighbor's behavior.

This is the same type of argument by analogy outlined above, only applied to humans rather than to chimpanzees. If the evidence for beliefs being the cause of behavior is solely the subjective experience of the believer/actor, then I need to ascribe to other human beings the possession of an unobservable mental cause to explain their reasoned behaviors. This is the well-known philosophical problem of "other minds." But the ascription of unobservable mental causes to humans seems to be very much like the ascription to nonhuman beings. Why should it be sanctioned in the case of other humans and not sanctioned in the case of, say, honeybees? And where does that leave the inference when directed toward chimpanzee behavior?

There are two places to look for answers to these questions: background assumptions about the nature of intra- and interspecific similarity and behavioral experiments. I will first consider the background assumptions.

There are good grounds to assume that basic causal structures or mechanisms are the same for different members of the same species of organism. Although different individual organisms are spatiotemporally distinct and harbor all sorts of variation in particular features, the basic biological mechanisms most directly connected to surviving and reproducing are most likely to be the same. The reason is that these are the features upon which evolution by natural selection will have been quickest and strongest to act. Variations that have relatively negative effects on survival and reproduction are not kept around. That is how evolution by natural selection works. Even with the caveat of recognizing the continual generation of variation within a species, it nevertheless is a safe assumption that there will be little variation in the basic functioning of organisms within a species. The species is the correct boundary for this degree of similarity because it is the potentially interbreeding population that is the receptacle for the consequences of natural selection.

As I remarked above, a cause/effect relationship observed in one system (my subjective access to the beliefs that cause my action) can be inferred to apply to another system (seeing the neighbor's actions and inferring his mental cause) if I have grounds to think the two systems are causally isomorphic. Species membership, for the biological reasons given above, gives us the grounds for that inference. Not only are the causal structures in me and my neighbor isomorphic, we have reasons to think they are homeomorphic. That is, there is just one type of causal structure operating in human beings, instantiated in each individual. In addition, there are other observable physical similarities that we take to also substantiate the homeomorphism of the psychological causal system among individuals of our species. These include the neurophysiological substrate of psychological causation, that is, the structure of the brain and nervous systems, the sensory apparatus that detect features of the world that are then represented in beliefs, and so on. In addition, the indirect access to internal mental states by the verbal reports of actors gives us additional grounds to think that causal isomorphism holds. This is still no guarantee.[22] Indeed, even the self-report of why one acts the way one does can be challenged.[23] Nevertheless, there are good, if fallible grounds for believing that other human beings have the same sort of second-order beliefs that are causally relevant to their actions since we have grounds for believing that the same causal mechanisms are at work in all members of the species.

What is the objection to extending this inference from humans to nonhumans? First of all, we have fewer types of supporting evidence than in the case of human-to-human inference. There is no self-reporting to be acquired from the chimp about the reasons for its actions. There is no shared species membership from which to support causal isomorphism. However, we can look to the similarity or dissimilarity of neurophysiological structure, sensory apparatus, and so on. And, importantly, we can look to behavioral observations and experimentation (see table 5.1).

The experimental data on whether or not chimpanzees have second-order beliefs, unfortunately, permits of multiple interpretations. Povinelli's *Folk Physics for Apes* reports a number of experiments done on captive chimpanzees over a five-year period to investigate how they conceive of the physics that underlies their use of tools in particular or, more generally, to "elucidate the nature of the mental representations that guide this behavior" (1). In service to this goal, Povinelli provides evidence against the strong argument by analogy. A series of experiments were done to determine whether chimpanzees have the concept that others "see." This is a basic second-order belief. I look at another human being and have a visual experience of that person. I look at their eyes and notice that they are directed at the door. I form a belief that the person sees the door, that is, a belief about her internal visual representation. I can then act on the basis of what I believe that she does or does not see. Povinelli's group studied whether chimpanzees engage in the same kind of cognitive process.

Povinelli dissects forming a belief that another organism sees a particular object into a number of components. The organism must notice the eyes of the other and then follow the gaze of the other toward the object under perception. Interest in eyes and gaze direction are present in a wide range of species, and these abilities may well have emerged as adaptations to predation and social interactions. But how much like humans are the

TABLE 5.1	GROUNDS FOR ATTRIBUTING CAUSAL ISOMORPHISM			
	Evolutionary relatedness	Self-reporting	Neurophysiological and other physical features	Behavioral statistics
Human-to-Human inference	Strong support	Strong support	Strong support	Strong support
Human-to-chimpanzee inference	Weak support	N/a	Some support	Mixed support

internal states of other organisms that engage in these behaviors? Povinelli puts the point as follows:

> Some researchers interpret the mutual gaze that occurs between infants and adults, as well as among great apes during complex social interactions as *prima facie* evidence of an understanding of the attentional aspect of seeing. And admittedly, there is a certain allure to the idea that, because mutual gaze in adult humans is often attended by representations of the mental states of others, comparable behavior in human infants (or other species) is probably attended by similar representations. But is mutual gaze in apes (for example) really attended by the same psychological representations as in human adults, or is this just a projection of our own way of thinking onto other species? (22)

In short, is this just wishful anthropomorphism, or can we get evidence that apes have the same or similar cognitive state as humans?

The first step in Povinelli's study was to establish whether chimpanzees had the same behavioral abilities, that is, gaze following, as do human infants and human adults. For the analogical argument to work, the effects—behaviors in this case—expressed in the two systems have to be the same, and then one infers that the causes of these effects are also the same. Experiments show that chimps and one-and-one-half-year-old human infants similarly responded to head movement, eye movement, left/right specificity, gaze following outside of visual field, and so on. So he concluded that chimps and humans engage in similar responses to a series of eye movement stimuli presented to them. Behaviors are the same. But what more is going on?

Povinelli devised ingenious experiments to try to test if chimp's gaze-following behavior indicated the possession of second-order mental states. He entertained two possible explanations, a low-level and high-level account. The low-level account interprets the chimp's gaze-following behavior to express cognition about behavioral propensities of the person whose gaze they followed, where the high-level account claims chimps form concepts about the internal mental states of the person whose gaze they are following. That is, the low-level model is akin to what happens when a human visually follows the path of a billiard ball being hit by a cue ball. We see the ball being hit and its initial motion and develop expectations of its behavior at a subsequent time. It initially moves towards the corner pocket, hence it will continue to move in a straight line toward the pocket. The high-level model is akin to a human watching another human looking in the direction of the billiard ball. In this case the perceived eye motion induces beliefs about what the observer *sees*. The human's eyes move following the ball, hence the human sees the ball's motion. The Povinelli group hypothesized that the high- and low-level accounts would make different predictions in cases where the observed individual's gaze was obstructed by an opaque barrier. If the low-level account were right, the observing chimp would just scan a line from the eyes of the observed being until something was noticed. This is based on eyes looking right indicating something is right, and a barrier would be irrelevant. If the high-level account were right, the observing chimp would walk around the barrier to see what was being seen. This would be based on eyes looking right indicating there must be something that is seen that is on the other side of the barrier. The results of an opaque-barrier test were unambiguously in support of the high-level model. The chimps walked around the barrier to see what the person in the experiment was looking at. The conclusion naturally drawn was that chimps understand what it is for someone else to see or represent the world; hence they have second-order beliefs just like humans.

However, a dozen other experiments involving seeing supported the low-level model of cognition. In these experiments, the chimps were presented with two humans displaying different capacities to see them, and it was observed whether the chimps responded differently to the two humans. The test response was begging behavior, and the question was did the chimps beg significantly more to the human who did not have his gaze obstructed? The obstruction conditions of the humans in the test included being blindfolded, having a bucket over one's head, having hands over one's eyes, and facing backward in relation to the observing chimpanzee.

In three of the four conditions, the chimps were as likely to gesture to the person who could *not* see them as to the person who could. However, in the front-facing-versus-back-facing case they did beg more to the human with his front facing the chimp. So the low-level account captured three of the experimental conditions, whereas the high-level account was supported by one of the experimental conditions. To try to distinguish whether it was the seeing that mattered or the front position, Povinelli introduced a fifth experimental set up. This time, both humans had their backs to the observing chimp, but one was looking over her shoulder at the chimp, the other was not. "To our surprise and in full support of the low-level model, on the looking-over-the-shoulder trials the apes did not prefer to gesture to the person who could see them" (*Folk Physics*, 34).

Povinelli's group continued to introduce new seeing/not seeing experimental conditions to the chimps using screens and eyes-open/eyes-shut conditions to try to figure out what was going on. In the end, Povinelli rejected the high-level, second-order belief model and suggested that through trial and error the apes learned a set of procedural rules about successful gesturing (1. gesture to person whose front is facing forward; 2. if both fronts present or absent, gesture to person whose face is visible; and 3. if both faces visible or occluded, gesture to person whose eyes are visible). The chimpanzees do not appear to be using a concept of seeing to help them decide to whom to gesture. Instead, the chimpanzees after lots of trial and error behaved "as if" they had our concept of seeing. Important for Povinelli's conclusion is the fact that the behavior at the end of the study was different from the chimps' behavior at the beginning of the study. They learned something, namely, how to gesture to the person *we* would say could see them. In contrast, three-year-old human children compared in these experiments were shown to have the behaviors appropriate to understanding a concept of seeing from the beginning; no variation in behavior occurred for the humans.

Do these experiments tell us whether the similarity of chimp and human behavior indicates a similarity of internal mental cognition? Povinelli concludes that it is still open to interpretation. Indeed, he postulates three different ways to account for the behaviors of the chimps in the experiments. First, they could have entered the test without a concept of seeing but through the testing came to construct the concept. Second, they could have entered the test with a general conception of attention and constructed a notion of visual attention. And third, they could have neither entered nor exited the tests with an understanding of the mental state of visual attention (*Folk Physics*, 42). Rather, they constructed an "as-if" understanding of seeing-as-attention. The third option is like the familiar case of Clever Hans, the horse who appeared to be able to do arithmetic.[24]

An anomaly for Povinelli's preferred low-level interpretation is that the opaque-barrier tests did support the high-level model of cognition for the chimps. Povinelli takes the preponderance of evidence to suggest that the low-level model is much better supported and gives a reinterpretation of the opaque-barrier test that would account for this contrary bit of evidence. On the way, he points out that if we walk into the laboratory with an anthropomorphic attitude, we are much more likely to continually refine and retest experimental results that support the low-level model and accept on its face the results of tests like the opaque barrier test that support an anthropomorphic high-level model.

What conclusion should we draw from these experiments on chimpanzees? Does the fact that their behavior and our behavior are sometimes indistinguishable indicate that the causes of those behaviors in us and in them are also the same? Does the fact that their behavior and our behavior are sometimes different indicate that the causes of their behaviors are not the same as ours? The experimental results are, at best, ambiguous and, according to Povinelli, lean toward a rejection of strong anthropomorphism. Indeed, as you will recall, he said that if the similarity of human and nonhuman behaviors does not license the analogical inference to same causes for chimpanzees, then it can hardly be credible for other species. At least it should be clear how difficult it is to get unambiguous experimental results for anthropomorphic models. There is no consensus in the scientific community about the significance of the Povinelli experiments, with criticisms often focused on the possible crucial dissimilarity between captive chimps, the subjects of Povinelli's studies, and chimps in the wild.[25]

CONCLUSION

What is the fate of anthropomorphism in contemporary science? I have argued that the global arguments against anthropomorphism cannot be maintained in a post-Darwinian scientific world. Given that humans *are* biologically related to other species, the ascription of concepts whose natural home is in describing human features and behaviors may very well apply to nonhumans. That being said, there is also no global support for the cavalier exportation of human descriptive concepts to nonhumans. Rather, I have suggested that a piecemeal evaluation of the credibility of specific claims of similarity, based on a causal-isomorphism model of analogical reasoning, must be undertaken. There are a variety of types of evidential support for grounding specific anthropomorphic models, and so judgments of its legitimacy in different cases may well vary.

In short, anthropomorphic models are specific, scientifically accessible claims of similarity between humans and nonhumans. As such, they must be substantiated by evidence that there are similar causal mechanisms responsible for generating the apparently similar behaviors that are observed. If experimental and background theoretical support do provide that evidence, then there should be no objection to using the same descriptive language for both humans and nonhumans. If that evidence is not provided, then using the same predicate for a full-fledged human behavior to refer to an "as-if" nonhuman behavior will be misleading and inaccurate.

With respect to the issue of cognitive similarities, the current scientific debates indicate that it is difficult to get definitive evidence either way for even the simplest second-order belief that "A sees X." It would appear to get progressively more difficult when the descriptions carry not just causal assumptions but also social and moral baggage. Let's return for a moment to Darwin's dogs: "There can, I think, be no doubt that a dog feels shame ... and something very like modesty when begging too often for food." What would count as evidence that the behavior was an instance of shame? What is it for us to act out of a feeling of shame? It is not just that we have a belief about the physical world, such as, "there is a rock two meters in front of me, thus I will move in a way to avoid colliding with the rock." It is not just that we have a belief about another or my own belief, such as, "there is a person two meters in front of me who sees an object that is blocked from my view." But shame must include something like an internal set of norms of appropriate behavior to which I compare my current behavior and find it wanting. For that to be accessible to behavioral experiments seems a long shot.

Not surprisingly, the most controversial and consequential claims about the similarity between humans and nonhuman animals are the most difficult to substantiate. And yet it is these claims that play a fundamental role in the growing field of cognitive ethology. Perhaps the most telling insights that will be gleaned from careful study of the nature of the cognitive similarity or dissimilarity between humans and nonhumans will be reflexive. That is, characterizing the ways in which nonhuman cognition differs from human cognition may force a reevaluation of our account of human cognition itself.

The same may be true for the advocates of expanding the domain of moral consideration to nonhumans. A deeper understanding of the lives of other animals may shift the focus from the anthropocentric question of whether other beings are sufficiently like humans to warrant the same moral rights as humans to a more generalized analysis of what capacities, whether found in humans or not, ought to be the basis of moral consideration.

NOTES

This paper was presented at the Max Planck Society for the History of Science Conference on Thinking with Animals and the Pittsburgh-London Consortium in the Philosophy of Biology and Neuroscience. I wish to thank lively discussions at both those conferences and especially comments by Joel Smith, Lorraine Daston, Elliott Sober, and John Dupré.

1. See J. B. Kennedy, *The New Anthropomorphism* (Cambridge: Cambridge University Press, 1992), for an account of the behaviorist attack on anthropomorphism; Stewart Elliott Guthrie, "Anthropomorphism: A Definition and a Theory," in *Anthropomorphism, Anecdotes, and Animals: The Emperor's New Clothes?* ed. R.W. Mitchell, N.S. Thompson, and H.L. Miles (New York: SUNY Press, 1996), 501, cites criticisms of anthropomorphism back to Bacon, Spinoza, and Hume.

2. Charles Darwin, *The Descent of Man, and Selection in Relation to Sex* (1871; reprint, Princeton, N.J.: Princeton University Press, 1981), 42; quoted in Elizabeth Knoll, "Dogs, Darwinism, and English Sensibilities," in *Anthropomorphism, Anecdotes, and Animals: The Emperor's New Clothes?* ed. R. W. Mitchell, N. S. Thompson, and H. L. Miles (New York: SUNY Press, 1996), 14.

3. See especially George Romanes, *Animal Intelligence* (New York: D. Appleton, 1883); Niko Tinbergen, *The Study of Instinct* (Oxford: Clarendon Press, 1951); Konrad Lorenz, *Studies in Animal and Human Behavior*, vols. 1 and 2 (Cambridge, Mass.: Harvard University Press, 1970, 1971). See also R. A. Hinde, *Ethology: Its Nature and Relations with Other Sciences* (New York: Oxford University Press, 1982); and John Alcock, *Animal Behavior: An Evolutionary Approach* (Sunderland, Mass.: Sinauer, 1997), for modern examples.

4. Donald R. Griffin, *The Question of Animal Awareness: Evolutionary Continuity of Mental Experience* (New York: Rockefeller University Press, 1976).

5. See W. Mason, "Windows on Other Minds," review of *The Question of Animal Awareness*, by Donald R. Griffin, *Science* 194 (1976): 930–31.

6. Daniel J. Povinelli, *Folk Physics for Apes* (Oxford: Oxford University Press, 2000), 9.

7. Mary Anne Warren, "A Critique of Regan's Animal Rights Theory," in *Between the Species*, ed. Louis P. Pojman (Stamford, Conn.: Wadsworth, 2001), 46, presents this summary of Regan's view.

8. Sue Savage-Rumbaugh, Stuart G. Shanker and Talbot J. Taylor, *Apes, Language and the Human Mind* (New York: Oxford University Press, 1998). Kansi is a bonobo chimpanzee who can manipulate physical symbols in a way that looks very much like human language.

9. Mark Derr, "Brainy Dolphins Pass the Human 'Mirror' Test," *New York Times*, 1 May 2001.

10. See Emanuela Cenami Spada, "Amorphism, Mechanomorphism, and Anthropomorphism," in *Anthropomorphism, Anecdotes, and Animals: The Emperor's New Clothes?* ed. R. W. Mitchell, N. S. Thompson, and H. L. Miles (New York: SUNY Press, 1996), 37–50.

11. See Guthrie, "Anthropomorphism: A Definition," 53; and Hugh Lehman, "Anthropomorphism and Scientific Evidence for Animal Mental States," in *Anthropomorphism, Anecdotes, and Animals: The Emperor's New Clothes?* ed. R. W. Mitchell, N. S. Thompson, and H. L. Miles (New York: SUNY Press, 1996), 105.

12. Lewis Carroll, *Through the Looking Glass* (New York: Putnam, 1972), chapter 6.

13. See Povinelli, *Folk Physics.*

14. See Marc Beckoff, Colin Allen, and Gordon M. Burghardt, eds., *Cognitive Animal: Empirical and Theoretical Perspectives on Animal Cognition* (Cambridge, Mass.: MIT Press, 2002); and Povinelli, *Folk Physics.*

15. Julian S. Weitzenfeld, "Valid Reasoning by Analogy," *Philosophy of Science* 51 (1984): 137–49.

16. See J. R. Hayes and H. A. Simon, "Understanding Tasks Stated in Natural Language," in *Speech Recognition*, ed. D. R. Reddy. (New York: Academic Press, 1975); and M. L. Gick and K. J. Holyoak, "Schema Induction and Analogical Transfer," *Cognitive Psychology* 15 (1983): 1–38.

17. See Christopher Lang, Elliott Sober, and Karen Strier, "Are Human Beings Part of the Rest of Nature?" *Biology and Philosophy* 17 (2002): 661–71, for a detailed assessment of the import of phylogenetic proximity for causal similarity.

18. Colin Allen and Marc Hauser, "Concept Attribution in Nonhuman Animals: Theoretical and Methodological Problems in Ascribing Complex Mental Processes," *Philosophy of Science* 58 (1991): 221–40.

19. D. Premack and G. Woodruff, "Does the Chimpanzee Have a Theory of Mind?" *Behavioral Brain Sciences* 1 (1978): 515–26.

20. Romanes, *Animal Intelligence*, 15.

21. Of course, there is a debate on whether the folk notion of belief is a part of a scientific account of behavior; alternatives include epiphenomenalism with respect to beliefs as well as eliminativism in favor of physical neural structures. See Owen J. Flanagan, *Science of the Mind*, 2nd ed. (Cambridge, Mass.: MIT Press, 1991), for an overview of the various positions.

22. Numerous arguments about color perception, inverted spectra, and so on will attest that even when a human being says, "I believe the apple is red," there is no proof that their subjective experience of red is the same as any other individual who when looking at the same object utters the same sentence. See D. J. Chalmers, *The Conscious Mind* (Oxford: Oxford University Press, 1996).

23. See Alison Gopnik, "How We Know Our Own Minds: The Illusion of First-Person Knowledge of Intentionality," *Behavioral and Brain Sciences* 16, no. 1 (1993): 1–14.

24. Clever Hans was a horse who lived in Berlin at the beginning of the twentieth century who allegedly could do arithmetic, indicating sums by the number of times he tapped his hoof to the ground. Of course, he failed to display this ability when his trainer, from whom he presumably was getting cues for foot tapping, was absent from the scene. See Oskar Pfungst, *Clever Hans (the Horse of Mr. Von Osten)* (Bristol, UK: Thoemmes Press, 1911).

25. See M. D. Hauser, "Elementary, My Dear Chimpanzee," *Science* 291 (2001): 440–41; A. Whiten, "Tool Tests Challenge Chimpanzees," *Nature* 409 (2001): 133; and Colin Allen, "A Skeptic's Progress," *Biology and Philosophy* 17 (2002): 695–702.

PART III

THINKING WITH ANIMALS
IN DAILY LIFE

· · · · · ·

CHAPTER 6

People in Disguise
Anthropomorphism and the Human-Pet Relationship

· · · · · ·

James A. Serpell

> *One of the most remarkable features of our domesticated races*
> *is that we see in them adaptation, not indeed to the animal's or*
> *plant's own good, but to man's use or fancy.*
> —CHARLES DARWIN, *The Origin of Species*

Sometime ago, I received an e-mail message from a middle-aged woman (whom I shall call Alice) living in Philadelphia with her elderly mother, and a Maltese terrier (whom I shall call Sweetpea):

Dear Dr. Serpell, I have a 4 year-old Maltese Terrier who knows things no dog knows. She knows all of the letters of the alphabet. When I put the letters in front of her, she will show me with her paw any letter I ask for. She knows the letters in order from A to Z, and she will pick them out even if they are upside down. She knows numbers in order up to at least 20. She will answer correctly addition, subtraction and multiplication problems. She knows 5 shapes, 6 colors, the suits in a card deck, 4 clock faces, and the appropriate pile of buttons when asked to find a pile with a certain number of buttons. She knew all of this the first time she was asked. . . . You have to see her to believe her. She was featured on NBC 10 News three weeks ago. Don Lemon of NBC 10 and the cameraman were stunned by what she does. They said they get a lot of calls about dogs, and they have seen a lot of dogs, but they have never seen a dog do what she does. You are welcome to come and see this amazing animal. She also says "I love you."

I arranged to visit Alice and Sweetpea and observed both of them carefully as the latter, a somewhat overweight lapdog, performed her surprising routine. First she was asked to identify numbers, letters, and various objects arranged on the floor in front of her. She did this by walking forward and placing her right paw on each chosen item. Problems of mental arithmetic were also answered with alacrity, and little cardboard clock faces, each bearing a different time, were selected without hesitation. Most of the time, Sweetpea gave correct responses and received in return small morsels of steamed asparagus—her favorite treat. Sometimes she even began moving in the right direction before her mistress had finished speaking. When, on occasion, she made mistakes, Alice would repeat the question rather sternly until Sweetpea corrected herself. Throughout this demonstration, it was striking to observe how Sweetpea almost never looked at the objects she was being asked to select from. Instead, she stared fixedly at her owner's face and upraised hand bearing the desirable asparagus treat.

After about twenty minutes of this, Alice asked me for my opinion of Sweetpea's abilities. As diplomatically as I could, I explained that Sweetpea appeared to be a "Clever Hans," or the canine equivalent of Wilhelm von Osten's famous "counting horse" at the turn of the last century, whose uncanny abilities, it turned out, had been shaped by the subtle nonverbal signals provided unwittingly by his owner.[1] Alice regarded me skeptically and said that this was not possible since she never gave Sweetpea any signals, nonverbal or otherwise. "Then," I said, half sarcastically, "she must be reading your mind." "Oh, no," said Alice, "she gets the right answers even if I keep my mind completely blank." It turns out that Alice and her mother have developed an entirely different theory to explain the dog's unusual talents. Sweetpea, they believe, is the reincarnation of Alice's recently deceased grandmother. They reached this startling conclusion based on a shared proclivity for steamed asparagus and by providing the dog with the letters of the alphabet and then asking her to spell out her identity like a sort of canine Ouija board. Ten times in succession Sweetpea had spelled out the letters *M-O-M*—the grandmother's nickname.

Alice's interpretation of Sweetpea's behavior represents an unusually extreme form of anthropomorphism—that is, *the attribution of human mental states (thoughts, feelings, motivations, and beliefs) to nonhumans*. Not only does Alice view Sweetpea as human in a general sense, her belief in the dog's humanity is disconcertingly specific. At the same time, neither Alice nor her mother are especially peculiar or eccentric in other ways, at least by Philadelphia standards, and their behavior is really only an exaggerated expression of a trait that is almost universal among pet owners. People throughout the world feed their pets on human food, give them human names, celebrate their birthdays, take them to specialist doctors when they become ill, mourn them when they die, and bury them in pet cemeteries with all the ritual trappings of a human burial.[2] In the United States, people even dress their pets in designer-label fashions,[3] enroll them in daycare,[4] and provide them with renal transplant surgery at a cost of approximately $6,500 per kidney.[5] Surveys have shown that 75 percent of pet owners consider their animals akin to children, and nearly half of the women in one survey said that they relied more on their dogs and cats for affection than on their husbands or their children.[6]

Most previous discussions of anthropomorphism in the scientific literature have tended to dwell on its validity (or lack thereof) as a technique for describing and interpreting animal behavior.[7] In this paper I intend, as far as possible, to avoid the whole question of whether anthropomorphism is a useful, appropriate, or accurate method for interpreting animals and their behavior and concentrate instead on the ways in which it explains, in evolutionary terms, both the benefits and the harms of pet ownership. Viewed from this perspective, anthropomorphism emerges as a powerful transformative force that has not only molded the behavior and morphology of our animal companions in unprecedented ways but also, through them, enhanced our own health and well-being.

THE ORIGIN OF ANTHROPOMORPHISM

Anthropomorphism appears to have its roots in the human capacity for so-called reflexive consciousness—that is, the ability to use self-knowledge, knowledge of what it is like to be a person, to understand and anticipate the behavior of others. As far as is known, other animals (with the possible exception of some of the great apes and, perhaps, dolphins) lack a "theory of mind," or the capacity to attribute mental states to others. Humans, in contrast, have been described as "natural psychologists," with the power to penetrate and explore other minds by the light of their own subjective mental experiences.[8] Quite when this exceptional ability expanded outward to encompass nonhumans is anybody's guess, although the archaeologist Steven Mithen has claimed that anthropomorphism is one of the defining characteristics of anatomically modern humans (*Homo sapiens sapiens*) and that it probably evolved no more than 40,000 years ago.[9]

Whatever its ultimate origins, anthropomorphism has had far-reaching consequences. By enabling our ancestors to attribute human thoughts, feelings, motivations, and beliefs to other species, it opened the door to the incorporation of some animals into the human social milieu, first as pets and ultimately as domestic dependents.[10] In fact, according to Mithen, without anthropomorphic thinking neither pet keeping nor animal domestication would ever have been possible.[11]

PETS AS SOURCES OF SOCIAL SUPPORT

Of course, merely stating that anthropomorphism made pet keeping possible does not help to explain why this practice has persisted for at least 14,000 years and possibly far longer. From a purely evolutionary standpoint, pet keeping is an anomalous activity.[12] It is easy to explain, for example, why people keep chickens, pigs, or sheep: these animals are worth at least their own weight in eggs, meat, hide, or fiber. But what could possibly be the adaptive value of keeping Siamese cats or miniature schnauzers? Natural selection, we know, favors individuals who behave in ways likely to maximize their own survival and reproductive success and/or that of their own close relatives.[13] Even the theory of reciprocal altruism, developed by Robert Trivers in 1970, requires that we should only help other unrelated individuals when there is a reasonable likelihood of that help being reciprocated at some point in the future.[14] Since pets do not even belong to the same species, much less the same kin group, and are surely incapable of remembering and returning past favors, it is difficult to imagine how pet keeping evolved or why it persists. Pet keeping, moreover, is expensive. About 800,000 people require medical treatment for dog bites each year in the United States,[15] and, according to recent estimates, Americans spend around \$11.6 billion per year on prepared pet foods (more than they spend on baby food), and \$11 billion per year on pet health care.[16]

A common response to this evolutionary puzzle, and one that keeps being regurgitated in the literature, is the idea that pets are simply social parasites who have perfected the art of releasing and exploiting our innate parental instincts—the so-called "cute response."[17] Parallels are sometimes drawn with the phenomenon of brood parasitism in birds, in which the parasite's nestling seems to exaggerate many of the care-soliciting aspects of the host's, thus insuring that it is fed assiduously to the detriment of its foster parents and siblings. The superficially infantile appearance of some lapdogs lends support to this idea, but it should be emphasized that a key difference between people and songbirds is that the latter are presumably unaware that they are feeding and caring for a nonconspecific intruder. People may indeed find puppies or pug dogs cute, but they are certainly never in any doubt concerning their true provenance.[18] Another long-standing and denigrating view of pet owners portrays them as akin to users of pornography—that is, individuals who are either unable or unwilling to form "normal" relationships with fellow human beings and who resort to pets as counterfeit substitutes for unattainable reality. Accepting this notion, however, would require us to believe that more than half of all American householders (and about a third of European ones) are either severely misanthropic or socially handicapped.[19]

Fortunately, there is also a third, less disparaging theory of pet ownership according to which people keep animals for companionship for essentially the same reasons that people wear overcoats to keep out the cold: because by doing so they enhance their own health and quality of life. Research on the putative health benefits of pet ownership is still at a relatively early stage of development, but already it has yielded a variety of interesting findings. Pet owners, for instance, have been shown to possess fewer physiological risk factors (high blood pressure and serum triglycerides and cholesterol levels) for cardiovascular disease than nonowners, and they also exhibit improved survival and longevity following heart attacks.[20] They also appear to be more resistant to the stressful effects of negative life events, resulting in fewer health problems and fewer visits to doctors for treatment.[21] The acquisition of a new pet has also been associated with improvements in owners' mental and physical health and with sustained reductions in their tendency to overreact to stressful situations.[22] Significantly, pet owners who report being very attached to their pets tend to benefit more from pet ownership than those who are less attached, and dog owners tend to do better than cat owners, perhaps because the attachment for dogs, on average, is stronger.[23] Interpreting such findings is often difficult, but most authorities now agree that these are the kinds of results one would expect if pets were serving as a form of social support.[24]

Cobb defined social support as "information leading the subject to believe that he is cared for and loved, esteemed, and a member of a network of mutual obligations."[25] More recent authors have tended to distinguish between "perceived social support" and "social network" characteristics. The former represents a largely qualitative description of a person's level of satisfaction with the support he or she receives from particular social relationships, while the latter is a more quantitative measure incorporating the number, frequency, and type of a person's overall social interactions.[26] In practice, both kinds of social support tend to be broken down into different components. These include (a) *emotional support*: the sense of being able to turn to others for comfort in times of stress; the feeling of being cared for by others; (b) *social integration*: the feeling of being an accepted part of an established group or social network; (c) *esteem support*: the sense of receiving positive, self-affirming feedback from others regarding one's value, competence, abilities, or worth; (d) *practical, instrumental, or informational support*: the knowledge that others will provide financial, practical, or informational assistance when needed; and (e) *opportunities for nurturance and protection*: the sense of being needed or depended upon by others.[27]

However we choose to define it, the importance of social support to human well-being has been acknowledged implicitly throughout history, and, within the last ten years, an extensive medical literature has emerged confirming a strong, positive link between social support and improved human health and survival. In particular, social support has been shown to protect against cardiovascular disease and strokes, rheumatic fever, diabetes, nephritis, pneumonia, and most forms of cancer, as well as depression and suicide.[28] The precise mechanisms underlying these life-saving effects of social support are still the subject of some debate, but most experts seem to agree that the principal benefits arise from the capacity of supportive social relationships to buffer or ameliorate the deleterious health effects of prolonged or chronic life stress.[29] In theory, this salutary effect of social support should apply to any positive social relationship, any relationship in which a person *believes* that he or she is cared for and loved, esteemed, and a member of a network of mutual obligations. The socially supportive potential of pets, assuming it exists, should therefore hinge on their ability to produce similar effects by behaving in ways that make their owners *believe* that the animal cares for and loves them, holds them in high esteem, and depends on them for care and protection.

What evidence exists that pets actually fulfill this type of role? Surprisingly, few of the many studies that have investigated the health effects of pet ownership during the last twenty years have considered the behavior of the pet, or the owner's perception of the behavior of the pet, as an important factor in all of this. Rather, pets have been treated as a sort of uniform therapeutic intervention that is either present or absent, as if all pets were equivalent in their effects regardless of species, breed, temperament, or behavior. But if pet ownership can be usefully conceptualized as another kind of social relationship, analogous to marriage or friendship, then clearly these relationships should be studied as dyadic interactions in which both participants—human and animal—play important parts.[30] Only a handful of studies have attempted this, and their findings are revealing.

In a small study conducted in England some years ago, it was found that people's professed attachments to their pets were strongly influenced by their evaluations of the animal's behavior. These pet owners, in general, had a good sense of the kinds of behavior they did and did not want from their pets, and they appeared to respond to a good match between what they wanted and what they got from the animal by becoming more attached to it.[31] More recently, researchers in New Zealand investigated whether the degree of behavioral matching, or "compatibility," between the pet and owner affected the owner's health. They found that owners who reported a high degree of behavioral compatibility between their pets and themselves were not only more attached to their animals but also experienced better overall mental health, enhanced feelings of well-being, less distress, more positive affect, less anxiety, and fewer physical symptoms of ill-health than those with less compatible pets.[32]

To examine the kinds of human-animal interactions involved in these assessments, Sheila Bonas and colleagues at Warwick University in England recently used a survey instrument called the "Network of Relationships Inventory" as a means of getting people to describe and evaluate the different kinds of social support they derive from both their human and nonhuman relationships.[33] She found that although human relationships scored higher overall in terms of aggregate social support, pet dogs actually scored higher than humans on a number of specific social or "relational provisions": specifically, "reliable alliance," "nurturance," and "companionship."[34] Cats ranked lower than dogs and higher than other pets, overall, although even cats rivaled humans in terms of their ability to provide "reliable alliance" and "nurturance." Humans only perform substantially better than dogs for "instrumental aid" and "intimacy," both of which depend to a greater extent on either higher cognitive capacities or language.[35] Bonas's subjects also reported far less conflict in their relationships with pets compared with other people. Again, the pet's lack of linguistic ability was probably an important consideration. Because they are unable to talk, pet animals are also unable to judge or criticize their owners, lie to them, or betray their trust.

Bonas's study clearly suggests that her subjects had no difficulty describing and evaluating their nonhuman companions using precisely the same relational parameters as those developed and used to describe relationships with humans. By implication, then, these people must have interpreted and evaluated the various behavioral signals of social support they received from their pets *as if* they were coming from fellow human beings. In other words, anthropomorphism—the ability, in this case, to attribute human social motivations to nonhumans—is what ultimately enables people to benefit socially, emotionally, and physically from their relationships with companion animals. Most pet owners believe that their animals genuinely "love" or "admire" them, "miss" them when they are away, feel "joy" at their return, and are "jealous" when they show affection for a third party.[36] One could, of course, argue that these people are simply deluding themselves and that the feelings and emotions they impute to their animals are entirely fictitious. Be that as it may; the fact remains that without such beliefs, relationships with pets would be far less meaningful. Anthropomorphism rules because, for most people, any other interpretation of the animal's behavior—any suggestion that it might be motivated by other than human feelings and desires—would instantly devalue these relationships and place them on a more superficial and less rewarding footing. It is not, of course, impossible for a person to identify with and appreciate the "dog-ness" of dogs or the "cat-ness" of cats, but in most cases these are special skills that need to be learned. Anthropomorphism, in contrast, tends to come naturally.

ANTHROPOMORPHIC SELECTION—BEYOND THE "CUTE RESPONSE"

While anthropomorphism would appear to be responsible for many of the benefits people derive from the company of pet animals, its effects on the animals are more equivocal. In purely numerical terms, of course, most companion animal species now vastly outnumber their wild ancestors. Due to habitat loss and persecution by humans, the wolf (*Canis lupus*), the presumed ancestor of the domestic dog, is now extinct or endangered throughout much of its former range, while the African wild cat (*Felis silvestris libyca*), the progenitor of the domestic cat, is much less common now than it used to be. The genetic integrity of many of these isolated populations of wolves and wild cats is also increasingly threatened by interbreeding with their free-roaming, domestic descendents.[37] In contrast, domestic dogs and cats now occur on virtually every island and continent where there are people (apart from Antarctica), and worldwide populations have exploded to the point where it is almost impossible to provide an accurate estimate of their numbers. According to recent figures from the United States alone, there may be as many as 58 million pet dogs in America and nearly 73 million pet cats,[38] although some would argue that the latter figure should be increased by between 30 and 60 per cent to accommodate unowned strays and feral animals.[39] Clearly, if evolutionary success is judged entirely on the basis of numbers, anthropomorphism has been a tremendous boon to these animals.

From an animal welfare perspective, however, the effects of anthropomorphism are far less benign. Anthropomorphic selection[40]—that is, *selec-*

tion in favor of physical and behavioral traits that facilitate the attribution of human mental states to animals—imposes unusual and unique pressures on the objects of its attentions, in much the same way that the phenomenon of "female choice" does in sexual selection. The extravagant plumes, crests, combs, wattles, and displays used by the males of many polygamous bird species to intimidate their rivals and impress prospective mates are thought to be runaway products of arbitrary female preferences for grotesque or elaborate physical adornments and behavior.[41] Some of these excrescences may be aesthetically appealing to the human eye, but for the males who carry them they can become potentially serious handicaps, imposing severe energy costs and both attracting the attention of predators and impairing the bearer's ability to escape from them.[42] Similarly, many companion-animal breeds have become effectively crippled or handicapped by selection for traits that appeal to our anthropomorphic perceptions.

Perhaps the most extreme example of this process can be found in the English bulldog, once a powerful, athletic animal and now recently described as the canine equivalent of a train wreck. With its severely brachycephalic head, prognathous upcurved mandible, distorted ears and tail, stunted limbs, and ungainly movements, the bulldog more closely resembles a "veterinary rehabilitation project than a proud symbol of athletic strength or national resolve."[43] In addition to their physical deformities, most bulldogs must now be born by caesarian section, and the breed is crippled by multiple insults to its nasal and respiratory system. At the veterinary hospital where I work, bulldogs are even used to study the phenomenon of sleep apnea. The difficulty they have breathing while asleep is so pronounced that most of them die prematurely from heart failure due to chronic oxygen deprivation.[44] These malformations are mainly due to a congenital defect known as chondrodystrophy, a developmental anomaly in the formation of bones that produces gross distortions, particularly in the craniofacial and appendicular skeleton. It is also present, though at different levels of expression, in most other brachycephalic breeds, such as pugs, Boston terriers, boxers, and Pekinese and in those with abnormally stunted limbs including the dachshund and basset hound.[45] In humans this condition causes a severe disability, and considerable research efforts are devoted to finding a cure for it. Yet these animals are being deliberately bred to preserve and even accentuate the same disabling characteristics. If bulldogs were the products of genetic engineering by agripharmaceutical corporations, there would be protest demonstrations throughout the Western world, and rightly so. But because they have been generated by anthropomorphic selection, their handicaps are not only overlooked but even, in some quarters, applauded.

Of course, not all of what we humans do to exaggerate or enhance the anthropomorphic appearance of pet animals is necessarily harmful, at least from the animal's perspective. It is unlikely, for example, that dogs suffer to any appreciable extent from being dressed up like dolls or from being used by their owners as fashion accessories. One could certainly argue that these animals are diminished symbolically by such uses, in much the same way that human dwarves and midgets are degraded by their use in comic theater. But it is very doubtful that the animals are aware of the symbolism or that they care. Altering an animal's physical appearance raises more serious ethical questions, however, when it involves deliberate mutilation. Docking the tails of pets, or surgically removing their claws, could certainly be interpreted as an anthropomorphic intervention. Humans do not possess tails or claws, and it appears that some of us expect our pets to match our own self-image by doing without these natural animal appendages.

Along with anatomy and physical appearance, anthropomorphic selection has also distorted the behavior of pets. Again, some of this is relatively harmless. The proverbial loyalty and fidelity of dogs to their masters and mistresses is almost certainly a product of anthropomorphic selection, as is Sweetpea's uncanny ability to apprehend her owner's unconscious signals. A recent study in Hungary compared the problem-solving abilities of dogs and hand-reared wolves and found that when faced with an insoluble problem such as getting food out of a sealed container, wolves worked persistently at the task and ignored their human handlers. Dogs, on the contrary, struggled briefly with the problem and then looked at their handlers "for assistance"—exactly the same kind of behavior we would expect from a person, especially a young person, in similar straits. The authors interpreted this difference not as a sign of the dog's superior intelligence but rather as a product of evolutionary selection for cooperative, humanlike behavior in the dog.[46] In human social communication, of course, looking is also a sign of liking.[47]

Unfortunately, because these anthropomorphic traits are often accompanied by abnormally accentuated dependency in dogs, they sometimes result in a crippling pathology. Probably the second most common category of problems seen by animal behavior specialists, or so-called pet psychologists, these days is separation anxiety: dogs who panic whenever they are left alone. These animals shred furniture and carpets, rip holes in doors (often injuring themselves in the process), and defecate and urinate all over the house or apartment, so great is their distress at separation.[48] By selecting for animals with exaggerated anthropomorphic (or paedomorphic) appeal, it is probable that we have inadvertently created lines of overdependent dogs who fall apart emotionally when their attachments are threatened. Sadly, the common response to this problem is either to contain it by incarcerating these animals in cages while their owners are out of the house or to subdue it through the use of psychoactive drugs.[49]

The performance of nonanthropomorphic behavior by pets is also a frequent excuse to get rid of them. Whenever there is a mismatch or incompatibility between an animal's behavior and its owner's anthropomorphic expectations, the animal risks either being punished and abused for its perceived "misbehavior" or being disposed of.[50] According to current estimates, approximately 4 million dogs (roughly 7 percent of the total population) are abandoned or relinquished annually to animal shelters in the United States, of which roughly 2.4 million (4.2 percent) are killed.[51] We know from a recent epidemiological survey that so-called behavior problems are the leading cause of canine-human divorce and the second most common reason for disowning a cat.[52] This is precisely what we would expect if anthropomorphism is the primary force cementing these relationships. It could be argued, of course, that as with other selection pressures, there will always be some individuals in the population who are less well adapted to the available niche than others and that a 4.2 percent annual mortality rate is relatively modest compared with what exists in most wild animal populations. Unfortunately, while dissatisfied pet owners and animal shelters may be removing some less well adapted individuals at one end of the life cycle, little is being done at the other end to ensure that pets are bred for compatible aspects of temperament and behavior. Somewhat ironically, in their laudable efforts to reduce a perceived "oversupply" of pets, humane societies and animal protection groups throughout the world have successfully advocated wholesale sterilization of companion animals, thereby eliminating most of the best behaved animals from the breeding population. This has allowed fashion and aesthetics to determine which animals are bred, based on arbitrary standards of physical conformation that have almost nothing to do with adaptive behavior or morphology.

CONCLUSION

The anthropomorphic tendency to attribute human feelings and motivations to nonhuman animals has given rise to a unique set of interspecies relationships that have no precedent elsewhere in the animal kingdom. These human-pet relationships are unique because they are based primarily on the transfer or exchange of social rather than economic or utilitarian provisions between people and animals. For the humans involved in these relationships, anthropomorphism has provided the opportunity to use animals as alternative sources of social support and the means to benefit emotionally and physically from this. For the animals, it has created a novel ecological niche, a set of unusual evolutionary selection pressures, and a variety of corresponding adaptations, some of which are detrimental to the animals' welfare. In this respect, it must be said, pet keeping is no different, and probably no worse, than other ways of using animals for human ends, including farming and biomedical research. Every novel adaptation to a new environment, whether natural or manmade, carries with it certain costs, and it would be unrealistic to imagine that things could be otherwise. It is not unrealistic, however, to question the level of cost that animals should have to incur to participate in such relationships. Regardless of how we use animals, there are ethical limits beyond which we should not go, and those limits should surely disallow us from deliberately breeding animals that suffer from severely painful, distressing, or disabling handicaps, or from surgically mutilating them in the interests of fashion or convenience.

No doubt, in some circumstances, anthropomorphism and pet keeping are powerful antidotes to what Searles once called the "existential loneliness" of the human condition.[53] By enabling us to participate in nonhuman lives not just as observers but as active social partners, anthropomorphism provides us with a unique opportunity to bridge the conceptual and moral gulf that separates humans from other animals. Indeed, it is questionable whether the animal protection and conservation movements would even exist if not for the bond of sympathy engendered for nonhuman animals by anthropomorphic thinking. Sadly, however, instead of accepting and appreciating companion animals for what they are, we seem more inclined to abduct them across the animal-human divide, render them in our own "image," and transform them in the process into a motley collection of deformed or mutilated cultural artifacts.[54] Ironically, the healthy sense of connection with other animal existences that we ought to derive from these relationships is thereby endangered. Instead of enjoying the company of animals for its own sake, we may ultimately find ourselves sharing our lives with an assortment of hybrid monsters: no longer animals so much as strange little people in disguise.

NOTES

1. D. K. Candland, *Feral Children and Clever Animals: Reflections on Human Nature* (Oxford: Oxford University Press, 1993), 111–33.

2. J. A. Serpell, *In the Company of Animals* (Cambridge: Cambridge University Press, 1996), 14.

3. Numerous wholesale and retail Web sites now exist that specialize in fashion wear for pets, for example, http://www.doggonefashions.com.

4. E. Louie, "An Indoor Pet Playground, with Everything but Squirrels to Chase," *New York Times*, 16 November 2000.

5. Figure derived from the Veterinary Hospital of the University of Pennsylvania, April 2001.

6. American Animal Hospital Association, *National Pet Owner Survey* (Denver, Colo.: AAHA, 1996).

7. D. McFarland, ed., *The Oxford Companion to Animal Behaviour* (Oxford: Oxford University Press, 1981), 16–17; R. Lockwood, "Anthropomorphism Is Not a Four-Letter Word," *Advances in Animal Welfare Science, 1985/86* (Washington, D.C.: Humane Society of the United States, 1985), 185–99; J. S. Kennedy, *The New Anthropomorphism* (Cambridge: Cambridge University Press, 1992); R. W. Mitchell, N. Thompson, L. Miles, eds., *Anthropomorphism, Anecdotes, and Animals: The Emperor's New Clothes?* (Albany, N.Y.: SUNY Press, 1997).

8. N. Humphrey, *Consciousness Regained* (Oxford: Oxford University Press, 1983), 6.

9. S. Mithen, *The Prehistory of the Mind: A Search for the Origins of Art, Religion, and Science* (London: Thames and Hudson, 1996), 165–67.

10. Mithen, *Prehistory of the Mind*, 224–26.

11. In a recent article, Hirata et al. describe a case of a wild female chimpanzee apparently capturing and keeping a western tree hyrax as a pet. Such observations clearly pose a fascinating challenge to Mithen's claim that such behavior is distinctively human. See S. Hirata, G. Yamakoshi, S. Fujita, G. Ohashi, and T. Matsuzawa, "Capturing and Toying with Hyraxes (*Dendrohyrax dorsalis*) by Wild Chimpanzees (*Pan troglodytes*) at Bossou, Guinea," *American Journal of Primatology* 53 (2001): 93–97.

12. J. Archer, "Why Do People Love Their Pets," *Evolution and Human Behavior* 18 (2001): 237–59.

13. W. D. Hamilton, "The Genetical Evolution of Social Behavior," *Journal of Theoretical Biology* 7 (1964): 1–32.

14. R. L. Trivers, "The Evolution of Reciprocal Altruism," *Quarterly Review of Biology* 46 (1971): 35–57.

15. J. J. Sacks, L. Sinclair, J. Gilchrist, G. C. Golab. and R. Lockwood, "Breeds of Dogs Involved in Fatal Human Attacks in the United States Between 1979 and 1998," *Journal of the American Veterinary Medical Association* 217 (2000): 836–40.

16. S. James, "Nestle–Ralston Purina Deal Sign of Growing Population," http://www.petsforum.com/petnews/0181c.htm; accessed 27 April 2000.

17. K. Lorenz, "Die angeborenen Formen möglicher Erfahrung," *Zeitschrift für Tierpsychologie* 5 (1943): 235–409; S. J. Gould, "Mickey Mouse Meets Konrad Lorenz," *Natural History* 88 (1979), 30–36; Archer, "Why Do People Love Their Pets?" 237; S. Budiansky, *The Truth About Dogs: An Inquiry Into the Ancestry, Social Conventions, Mental Habits, and Moral Fiber of Canis familiaris* (New York: Viking, 2000).

18. Serpell, *In the Company of Animals*, 73–86.

19. Serpell, *In the Company of Animals*, 23–42.

20. T. F. Garrity and L. Stallones, "Effects of Pet Contact on Human Well-Being: Review of Recent Research," in *Companion Animals in Human Health*, ed. C. C. Wilson and D.C. Turner (Thousand Oaks, Calif.: Sage, 1998), 3–22; E. Friedmann, S. A. Thomas, and T. J. Eddy, "Companion Animals and Human Health: Physical and Cardiovascular Influences," in *Companion Animals and Us*, ed. A. L. Podberscek, E. Paul, and J. A. Serpell (Cambridge: Cambridge University Press, 2000), 125–42.

21. J. M. Siegel, "Stressful Life Events and Use of Physician Services Among the Elderly: The Moderating Role of Pet Ownership," *Journal of Personality and Social Psychology* 58 (1990): 1081–86.

22. J. A. Serpell, "Beneficial Effects of Pet Ownership on Some Aspects of Human Health and Behaviour," *Journal of the Royal Society of Medicine* 84 (1991): 717–20; K. M. Allen, J. Blascovich, J. Tomaka, and R. M. Kelsey, "Presence of Human Friends and Pet Dogs as Moderators of Autonomic Responses to Stress in Women," *Journal of Personality and Social Psychology* 61 (1991): 582–89.

23. M. G. Ory and E. L. Goldberg, "Pet Possession and Life Satisfaction in Elderly Women," in *New Perspectives on Our Lives with Companion Animals*, ed. A. H. Katcher and A. M. Beck (Philadelphia: University of Pennsylvania Press, 1983), 303–17; E. Freidmann and S. A. Thomas, "Pet Ownership, Social Support, and One-Year Survival After Acute Myocardial Infarction in the Cardiac Arrhythmia Suppression Trial (CAST)," *American Journal of Cardiology* 76 (1995): 1213–17.

24. Serpell, *In the Company of Animals*, 108–24; Garrity and Stallones, "Effects of Pet Contact on Human Well-Being," 6–11; G. M. Collis and J. McNicholas, "A Theoretical Basis for Health Benefits of Pet Ownership," *Companion Animals in Human Health*, ed. C. C. Wilson and D. C. Turner (Thousand Oaks, Calif.: Sage, 1998), 105–22; Freidmann and Thomas, "Pet Ownership, Social Support, and One-Year Survival," 1213–17.

25. S. Cobb, "Social Support as a Moderator of Life Stress," *Psychosomatic Medicine* 38 (1976): 300–314.

26. W. Eriksen, "The Role of Social Support in the Pathogenesis of Coronary Heart Disease: A Literature Review," *Family Practice* 11 (1994): 201–9.

27. Collis and McNicholas, "A Theoretical Basis for Health Benefits of Pet Ownership," 114–16.

28. Eriksen, "The Role of Social Support in the Pathogenesis of Coronary Heart Disease," 201–9; B. A. Esterling, J. Kiecolt-Glaser, J. C. Bodnar, and R. Glaser, "Chronic Stress, Social Support, and Persistent Alterations in the Natural Killer Cell Response to Cytokines in Older Adults," *Health Psychology* 13 (1994): 291–328; J. S. House, K. R. Landis, and D. Umberson, "Social Relationships and Health," *Science* 241 (1988): 540–45; C. D. Sherbourne, L. S. Meredith, W. Rogers, and J. E. Ware, "Social Support and Stressful Life Events: Age Differences in Their Effects on Health-Related Quality of Life Among the Chronically Ill," *Quality of Life Research* 1 (1992): 235–46; R. Vilhjalmson, "Life Stress, Social Support, and Clinical Depression: A Reanalysis of the Literature," *Social Science Medicine* 37 (1993): 331–42.

29. R. L. Ader, N. Cohen, and D. Felten, "Psychoneuroimmunology: Interactions Between the Nervous System and the Immune System," *The Lancet* 345 (1995): 99–103.

30. J. A. Serpell, "Humans, Animals, and the Limits of Friendship," in *The Dialectics of Friendship*, ed. R. Porter and S. Tomaselli (London: Routledge, 1989), 111–29.

31. J. A. Serpell, "Evidence for an Association Between Pet Behavior and Owner Attachment Levels," *Applied Animal Behavior Science* 47 (1996): 49–60.

32. R. C. Budge, J. Spicer, B. Jones, and R. St. George, "Health Correlates of Compatibility and Attachment in Human–Companion Animal Relationships," *Society and Animals* 6 (1998): 219–34.

33. S. Bonas, J. McNicholas, and G. M. Collis, "Pets in the Network of Family Relationships: An Empirical Study," in *Companion Animals and Us*, ed. A. L. Podberscek, E. Paul, and J. A. Serpell (Cambridge: Cambridge University Press, 2000), 209–36.

34. "Reliable alliance" refers to a person's belief that the relationship will last; "nurturance" refers to taking care of or protecting others from harm; and "companionship" is defined as spending time with others and doing enjoyable things together.

35. "Instrumental aid" refers to others providing practical help, and "intimacy" concerns confiding in others or sharing private thoughts with them.

36. Serpell, *In the Company of Animals*, 141–43.

37. D. L. Mech, *The Wolf: The Ecology and Behavior of an Endangered Species* (Garden City, N.Y.: The Natural History Press, 1970); L. Boitani, F. Francisci, P. Ciucci, and G. Andreoli, "Population Biology and Ecology of Feral Dogs in Italy," in *The Domestic Dog: Its Evolution, Behaviour, and Interactions with People*, ed. J. A. Serpell (Cambridge: Cambridge University Press, 1995), 218–44; J. A. Serpell, "Domestication and History of the Cat," in *The Domestic Cat: The Biology of Its Behaviour*, ed. D. C. Turner and P. P. G. Bateson (Cambridge: Cambridge University Press, 2000), 180–92.

38. Pet Food Institute, "Pet Incidence Trend Report," http://www.petfoodinstitute.org/pet-data.cfm; accessed 14 February 2000.

39. M. R. Slater, *Community Approaches to Feral Cats: Problems, Alternatives, and Recommendations* (Washington, D.C.: Humane Society Press, 2002), 3–5.

40. It is arguable whether this phenomenon should be labeled "anthropomorphic" or "*paedomorphic*" selection, since much of what is selected for in companion animals is characteristic of juvenile or infantile appearance and behavior. "Anthropomorphic selection" may be the preferable term because the putative goal of selection is to produce an animal that is more humanlike, even if its humanlike features are also childlike or infantile.

41. T. Halliday, "Sexual Selection and Mate Choice," in *Behavioural Ecology: An Evolutionary Approach*, ed. J.R. Krebs and N.B. Davies (Oxford: Blackwell, 1978), 180–213.

42. A. Zahavi, "Mate Selection—a Selection for a Handicap," *Journal of Theoretical Biology* 53 (1975): 205–14.

43. K. S. Thomson, "The Fall and Rise of the English Bulldog," *American Scientist* (May–June 1996): 220–23.

44. K. A. Panckeri, H. M. Schotland, A. I. Pack, and J. C. Hendricks, "Modafinil Decreases Hypersomnolence in the English Bulldog, a Natural Animal Model of Sleep-Disordered Breathing," *Sleep* 19 (1996): 626–31.

45. Thomson, "The Fall and Rise of the English Bulldog," 222–23.

46. A. Miklosi, E. Kubinyi, J. Topal, M. Gacsi, Z. Viranyi, and V. Csanyi, "A Simple Reason for a Big Difference: Wolves Do Not Look Back at Humans, but Dogs Do," *Current Biology* 13 (2003): 763–66.

47. A. Kendon, "Some Functions of Gaze Direction in Social Interaction," *Acta Psychologica* 26 (1967): 22–63.

48. E. A. McCrave, "Diagnostic Criteria for Separation Anxiety in the Dog," *Veterinary Clinics of North America: Small Animal Practice* 21 (1991): 247–55.

49. A. L. Podberscek, Y. Hsu, and J. A. Serpell, "Evaluation of Clomipramine as an Adjunct to Behavioural Therapy in the Treatment of Separation-Related Problems in Dogs," *The Veterinary Record* 145 (1999): 365–69.

50. Serpell, "Evidence for an Association Between Pet Behavior and Owner Attachment Levels," 49–60.

51. G. J. Patronek and A. N. Rowan, "Determining Dog and Cat Numbers and Population Dynamics," *Anthrozoös* 7 (1995): 199–205.

52. L. Spencer, "Behavioral Services in a Practice Lead to Quality Relationships," *Journal of the American Veterinary Medical Association* 203 (1993): 940–41; M. D. Salman, J. G. New, J. M. Scarlett, and P. H. Kass, "Human and Animal Factors Related to the Relinquishment of Dogs and Cats in Twelve Selected Animal Shelters in the United States," *Journal of Applied Animal Welfare Science* 1 (1998): 207–26.

53. H. H. Searles, *The Nonhuman Environment* (New York: International Universities Press, 1960), 122.

54. J. A. Serpell, "Companion Animals as Mediators," in *Companion Animals and Us*, ed. A. L. Podberscek, E. Paul, and J. A. Serpell (Cambridge: Cambridge University Press, 2000), 108–21.

· · · · · · ·

CHAPTER 7

Digital Beasts as Visual Esperanto

Getty Images and the Colonization of Sight

· · · · · · · ·

Cheryce Kramer

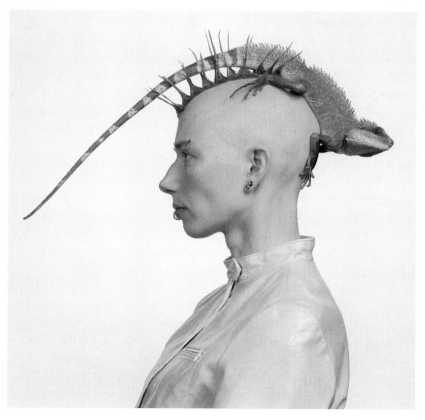

7.1   PUNK. CREDIT: TIM FLACH, GETTY IMAGES.

What do we have here? A stuffed-iguana hat? An attention-seeking punk? Our attention is drawn into the image in search of an answer. The eye travels up the profile, around the reptilian tail, along the arched back, past limpid feet, to the scaly head, and down the neck. Each element contributes a fragment of information from which meaning can be configured.

The photographer contends that we are to read this pose as "a statement of arch-individuality." The message, at a level of affirmative identification, is roughly: I'm a nonconformist free spirit, I wear whatever I like and I pull it off with pizzazz! At another level, however, a metalevel that situates the image within the language game of its creation and exposure, it might equally be interpreted as an oblique commentary on the punk movement—political dissent dead-ended in fetishistic consumption. Walter Benjamin's condemnation of photography as the cardinal fashion victim comes to mind: "The creative source of photography is its preemptory dependence on fashion. 'The world is beautiful'—that is its slogan . . . even in its most dream-bound subject matter anticipating resale value rather than insight."[1]

The iguana-woman image, cast almost entirely in shades of bright and pastel green, is a prime example of photography's "preemptory dependence" on the postures and attitudes of high fashion. Yet the image also seems strangely unmotivated in that there is no discernable profit motive. What are we being sold? Nothing, it would appear. No brand, no product, not even a lifestyle—just punk and beast fused in the formal dynamics of composition, an aesthetic apotheosis arguably achieving what Kant might have termed "purposiveness without purpose." This ostensible indifference is, however, misleading. To take in this image is to engage, as the following elaboration will show, in a commercial transaction of sorts: public demand triggers its supply, and supply reinforces demand. Incrementally, image by image, visual expectations shift, as does the nexus of unspoken shared assumptions within which visually mediated symbolic relations operate.

The photograph arguably furthers a creeping process of enculturation within a milieu of systemically aligned commercial interests. Although this image is off the charts for most applied advertising purposes—"nice eye candy," as they like to say in the visual content industry, but "useless in a business sense," as one picture editor opined—it stands a good chance of being featured in a glossy magazine as a stand-alone, no caption or marketing angle needed. The purpose of circulating such an image is not to move specific products but rather to commodify a frame of mind, to sell a way of seeing the world, to forge an aesthetic consensus in the target audience. In the above quoted "Short History of Photography," Benjamin proposes a mode of resisting the rampant commercialism of the medium of photography: because "the true face of this photographic creativity is the advertisement or the association," he says, "the appropriate reaction to it is its unmasking or fabrication,"[2] a rigorously critical stance every bit as pertinent today as when he was writing in 1931. But how to achieve this mandatory "unmasking" or "fabrication"?

A counterintuitive form of resistance advocated by Béla Balázs in the 1920s urged unconditional surrender to the seduction of images as a precondition for breaking their spell: "Spectators who have never felt their living reality freeze in a moment of eternity and crystallize around an image have never really experienced an image."[3] Where experience "rules," the matter is not to be resolve theoretically. So let us surrender. Connecting the spaces between the lines, new shapes emerge and cycle through countless permutations, a kaleidoscopic gaze in flux. Eventually, a static mental picture takes hold and superimposes itself on the scene: a composite eye has emerged from the mesh of color and form—the lizard forms its eyelid, the spikes its eyelashes, and the woman's head the iris of this strange eye-in-the-sky of interpretive possibilities. Once witnessed, the new image becomes ineradicable. It cannot be unseen. Though auto-generated, it can recalibrate the spectator's sensory purchase of the photograph: what is more, this elusive new eye is as imponderable and pervasive as the politics of sight in the age of the digital distribution of images.

This essay pertains to recent developments in the global trade of commercial images and related changes in the emotional configuration of contemporary subjectivity. In particular, it focuses on a commercial image purveyor, Getty Images, and a new visual brand the company is disseminating. The animal photography of Tim Flach serves as a case study for exemplifying this brand's aesthetic character and exploring its subliminal suggestiveness.[4] The paper argues that when we "think" with Flach's animals, we are rehearsing a decidedly postregional gaze. Methodologically, the paper relates current trends in the regime of sight to predictions made in the last century by early media theorists, especially Adorno, Benjamin, Balázs, and Kracauer. Given the nascent media with which these thinkers were concerned—photography and film—their *visionary observations* were often enough also *observations on vision*, and that is the topic of this essay.

THE CENTRALIZED DIGITAL IMAGE BANK

Tim Flach is not a household name, but his photography circulates through the average household as if he were. His images have a global exposure, reaching picture editors, creative directors, and design groups in all countries through the distributive rationale of a photographic agency. Currently, one of his images is sold somewhere in the world approximately every thirty minutes, a frequency that is steadily increasing. His photography appears on billboards and food packages, in magazines and newspapers, on calendars, postcards, or stamps. When he travels, he invariably sees tokens of his work integrated in local advertising campaigns and associated with a vast range of product lines. Yet the prominence of his work goes mostly unnoticed because he is not credited by name. Even the name of his main distributor, Getty Images, is listed in such small print as to be easily overlooked.

Flach is one of the most highly valued photographers under license with the commercial-image giant Getty Images—a centralized-distribution agency supplying visual content for every kind of illustrated surface. His animal images are part of a media revolution that is currently transforming the licensing and distribution of visual material. This revolution has received little scholarly attention thus far, but its effects are palpable on all sides; a new mechanism of visual content delivery is redecorating the public arenas. To understand this mechanism and its ramifications for the image habitat of the consuming public it is important to understand the nature of stock images. In contrast to commissioned commercial images that are ordered by a customer for a specific purpose, stock consists of a preexisting collection of photographs from which a suitable image is first chosen and then adapted to its print milieu. The difference between them is like the difference between tailor-made clothes and prêt-à-porter. Magazine articles rely primarily on stock imagery to brighten up their copy; big-name companies will commission bespoke visuals for major advertising campaigns but often resort to stock photographs for lower-profile marketing needs.

Historically, stock libraries were small businesses holding limited collections of photographs, often on a restricted range of subjects. Originally these collections were rights-managed, which meant every image was leased with exclusionary clauses restricting access of competitors to one and the same image. Most of the agencies were founded after World War II. But in the early 1990s a royalty-free system emerged based on selling images in bulk with unlimited and unrestricted rights of usage. The divide between rights-managed and royalty-free agencies split the industry into two camps. Over the last decade, however, these two models have been consolidated to form a cohesive new system of distribution. Globalization of the world market and the advent of Internet commerce have enabled the rise of a new kind of photo agency: the centralized digital-image data bank. These are large conglomerates of former stock libraries that license and distribute the images in their collection for worldwide usage. Getty Images (founded in 1995) and Corbis (founded in 1989) are the leading behemoths, peddling everything from historical photographs to contemporary fashion images, lifestyle to wildlife, politics to sports. Between them they are said to supply 70 percent of the images we see, and this figure is set to increase.[5] Their collections comprise more than rights-managed and royalty-free collections; they have also started to develop a line of commissioned photography.

Although Getty Images initially saw itself as an aesthetic innovator in the sphere of stock photography and Corbis strove to position itself as the world's premier virtual museum by acquiring digital rights to grandmasters of every ilk and distinction, the companies have grown to resemble each other in the heat of contest. Their editorial policies are said to be, as are the recipes of Coke and Pepsi, closely guarded trade secrets.[6] Employees are instructed not to comment on the respective house styles. Whereas commercial image distributors used to be known as "photo libraries" or "photo archives," Getty Images and Corbis are often called "image banks." "Image Bank," originally the name of a specific agency founded in 1974, has since come to designate a distinctive new phenomenon in the provision of visual content.

The linguistic shift from "photo library" or "picture archive" to "image bank" is apt, given the cultural authority of financial institutions today as compared with that of archives and libraries.[7] Mark Getty, the founder of Getty Images, was a banker before entering the image business and appears to have imported into the picture-licensing trade many of the models and techniques employed in the financial sector. Just as banks make their profits from interest earned on money in the accounts of clients, so too many of the photographs in the Getty collection are produced by photographers at their own cost; the picture budget is financed from outside the company coffers. The higher risk to the photographers working on a freelance basis is outweighed by the provision of higher royalty fees. By contrast, images specifically and uniquely commissioned by Getty carry smaller royalties (note: stock commissioning should not be confused with commissioning at the top end of the advertising market). The tiered and complicated royalty arrangements of the image banks can be viewed as carefully calculated instruments of risk management in an arena of financial investment.

A recent book with the telling title *Bildwirtschaft*, literally "picture economy," likens the circulation of stock images in society to currency flows in the global economy.

> In being a finite, consumable entity, images are also a kind of currency. They reduce singular events to commensurable dimensions, that is to say, they turn the photo of a person, place, or event into a norm that calls forth its own reactions and fashions, and this, in turn, has a reciprocal influence on the production of images.[8]

If pictures are a form of currency, it is hardly surprising that their circulation should be governed by institutions akin to banks. Indeed, Mitchell quotes French philosopher Jean Baudrillard as arguing that the fine-art museum serves as the gold standard of the fine-art market.[9] But the gold standard is no longer a regulatory factor in world markets either for banking or in the currency of images. High finance is governed by floating exchange rates, and images are valued according to expected visibility: the value of an image today is a function of its "eyeball count," a term used in Internet commerce to describe the number of hits to a Web site.

Commonly likened to "wallpaper" or "canned food," stock was regarded as a trade in stereotypes where the *standard deviation* carried a premium and the unremarkable outperformed the iconic. Paul Frosch, a media theorist specializing in image banks, has pointed out that forgettable images hold a clear business advantage in that they can be recycled, resulting in higher licensing fees for the agency.[10] A stock photograph's "planned obsolescence," to echo Vance Packard, is its capacity to self-eradicate—spectators must forget or, better yet, never even register the presence of an image on their mental radar screens. Marketing experts maintain that this very innocuousness gives stock its subliminal and directive force; its efficacy as an advertising instrument depends on going unnoticed. Unconscious seeing, so the theory goes, renders spectators more susceptible to putative values, promises, and insinuations and bypasses the cognitive censorship that would accompany more attentive modes of visual comprehension.

But these assumptions are undergoing rapid revision. The near-monopoly hold that Getty Images and Corbis have been able to obtain over the image market is having a profound impact, both quantitative and qualitative, on visual landscapes in the information age. While the onus is still on the spectators *not seeing* and *not noticing* certain aspects of their ambient image environment, the cultivation of public inattention is no longer being achieved by deploying innocuous graphic material, at least not exclusively. Rather, a complex and highly self-referential picture language is being developed that draws the spectator's attention to itself and, hence, away from any biases adhering to the image. This qualitative shift will be the focus of the rest of this essay. First, however, it is important to establish the magnitude of quantitative changes under way.

The word in Getty circles is that image consumption has increased tenfold over the last ten years. Howsoever that figure may have been compiled and whatever it may mean, it confirms Benjamin's prediction that "reproducible artwork is, increasingly, the reproduction of works of art geared toward reproducibility."[11] Stock photography is the reductio ad absurdum of reproducing artistic commodities for the sake of reproduction. A further indication that image consumption has multiplied exponentially in recent years is the growing agitation, in the popular press and scholarly circles, regarding the so-called iconic turn. Technically, this term describes the influence of visual forms of communication on consciousness. In its vernacular usage, however, it has come to describe the swamping of the market—and our minds—with unsolicited graphic material.

Given the proliferation of digital cameras and home imaging techniques, it would seem that the sheer diversity of image material would multiply alongside the increase in volume. Instead, variety appears to be dwindling.[12] This development is consistent with Adorno's critique of the ratings-driven culture industry whose narrowing influence he saw exemplified and prefigured in television programming.[13] A recent *Spiegel* magazine article on image banks reports: "In the meantime, even die-hard Getty supporters see that a piece of cultural heritage is in danger. After all, photos are more than archived pixels. 'Most young photo editors are only able to push an order button at the supermarket Getty and Corbis. They aren't aware of agencies like Magnum or Focus anymore,' said Michele Vitucci, previous managing director, Europe, for Getty. 'The language of images is becoming 'ever more uniform.' "[14] It is worth noting that Vitucci has had a long-standing professional association with the Tony Stone collection, Getty's premier image brand—the brand that carries Flach's animals.

Visual content, previously supplied from myriad sources and expressing a multiplicity of perspectives, increasingly reflects the output of two large commercial institutions. Our ambient graphics have the aesthetic coherence of a film dispersed throughout our material environment and arrested in freeze-frame animation. These days, image material as varied as that found in newspapers, commercials, and textbooks ultimately has a common source and progeny. Recycled images in multiple contexts produce patterns of repetition and passive recognition. Image retrieval depends on search engines that rely on the keywords that structure the collection as whole; this is nothing new. But the market domination that centralized image banks have been able to obtain is a novel phenomenon. As images journey into the vast holdings of these companies and back into the public domain, referential regularities arise that obey a fractal algebra of cultural production; these, in turn, establish correlations between images and concepts.[15] "The keywords used to retrieve images become part of the definition of the image and its meaning," says Stephen Mayes, former group creative director at Getty Images.[16]

Even though Getty Images supports an in-house think tank whose members are engaged in trying to predict visual trends and open new image markets, the company can steer and intervene in the larger phenomenon it is servicing only to a limited degree. Using its own financial performance, sales ledgers, and customer feedback as a barometer of the overall market situation, Getty's creative strategy rests on economic pragmatism. As Siegfried Kracauer points out with respect to the film industry, "manufacturers labor to expand their business. That they also produce values does not occur for the sake of the values."[17] Even though the aesthetic and ideological coherence associated with today's visual content industry is comparable to a film, this coherence is an epiphenomenon of the conditions of distribution—no central intelligence can mastermind the process of image alignment.

Coincident with the centralized digital image bank's coming to dominate global delivery of photographic services is a thoroughgoing revision of the character of stock imagery. In 2000, Getty Images introduced a new editorial policy for selecting photographs for inclusion in its commercial archive. Approximately every three to six months, Louis Blackwell, the creative director of Getty Images, issued a brief enjoining photographers to produce visuals that conjure up specified moods, feelings, and aspirations. These one- to two-page briefs were written in a curious, New Age language and deemed confidential, so it is possible only to paraphrase here: feel the rain on your skin; you leave work and run with the release that comes from shouting by a passing train; you have no fear of expressing yourself because you are in touch with an inexhaustible source of creative energy. Each brief was thematically unified around a specific rubric, such as "body," "spirit," "family," or "energy"; the evocatively written texts link spheres of affective resonance with current buzzwords of social and political import. The tone of these briefs has now shifted to a documentary-style, news-bulletin report on current social and demographic trends; the central creative steering office, working in concert with an in-house think tank, draws its inferences on future visual consumption from extensive statistical analyses of the Getty sales records.

For three months Getty photographers devote themselves and their resources to rendering these briefs in visual form. Investment dollars soar in preparation of sets, model hires, and shoot schedules lasting up to several days. At the end of the quarter, submissions are made to Getty and a selection committee chooses entries for inclusion in the online collection, each brief having given rise to thousands of graphic submissions. The proverbial picture worth a thousand words is inverted by a few words spawning thousands of pictures.

The corporate strategy resting upon Blackwell's spiritual meditations is to increase sales by building a new brand of images whose key characteristic is photography that "moves," "touches," or "reaches" the consumer. Old stock is being phased out and replaced by new, conceptually enhanced stock. Since Getty management considers Flach's animal images to be directly "on-brand," his work, to some extent, exemplifies the aesthetic character of this brand.

FLACH'S EMOTICONS ✓

A Flach image is comparable to an *emoticon*—a cryptogram of keyboard characters used to embellish an e-mail message with the emotional grammar of the author's intended tone.[18] Flach utilizes a sophisticated array of techniques both to produce and enhance his images and to signal that a given image has a specific emotional charge. It is possible to detect three main classes of visual cues in his work: *sensory* cues, *gestural* cues, and *treatment* cues—and often several are in play at once.

The most striking and obvious way in which Flach achieves *sensory* identification is by highlighting the eyes. A flash of light invariably accentuates the eye of his animal model, a hint of consciousness, a dart of brightness that he likes to refer to as a "ping." Its prominence in his photographs should not be misconstrued as an "authentic" expression of the animal's untamed spirit. The ping is a detail exceedingly difficult to orchestrate and produce; consequently, the eyes of most animals in wildlife photography look flat, dumb, or muted. Flach applies meticulous care to the problem of illuminating the eyes. The procedure involves an intricate light installation uniquely assembled and consisting of honeycombs, ring flashes, screens, and flags. Before shooting can commence, Flach spends hours "bending the light" so that the eyes of the animal model are illuminated with requisite precision (a procedure which usually tires the subject long before shooting has even begun).

7.2   MONKEY EYES. CREDIT: TIM FLACH, GETTY IMAGES.

Seeing is not the only sensory reality to be visually captioned, however. *Touch* finds suggestive notation too. Take, for example, Flach's photograph of a lurcher shot from below through a glass floor (figure 7.3). The dog's body is suspended in space like an abstracted piece of calligraphy, species attributes attenuated in the neutered creature. Although appearing to be suspended in air, the animal is standing on a transparent surface. Shot from below, its paws are exaggerated in size and darkened in their immediate contact with the glass. This angle places pictorial emphasis on the sense of touch and, hence, on a point of affinity between the dog and the spectators—tactile sensibility.

Flach's photographs also engage sound and hearing. Peering out from its leaf, the red-eyed tree frog looks set to emit a croak. Not a froglike croak, mind you, but a one-liner croak, the opening gambit of a conversation,

7.3   LURCHER. CREDIT: TIM FLACH, PAVEMENT.

something to the effect of: "Hey, babe!" The composition of the photograph revolves around the animal's mouth placed front and center. The framing leaf amplifies its mouth—and the implied croak—through color, shape, and composition.

At the same time, the tree frog's flirtatious alertness engages the spectator in reciprocity. The image communicates by means of a second class of visual references, namely *gestural* cues, a code of communication conveyed through posture, body language, and implied movement. One of the most striking uses of gestural cues in Flach's work is his series on the Australian fruit bat. At the 2001 awards ceremony of London's Association of Photography, the creative press described these bat portraits as the most "human" photographs of the year. Ironically, most of the competing entries showed human beings; Flach's did not.

7.4   RED-EYED TREE FROG. CREDIT: TIM FLACH, GETTY IMAGES.

7.5   Opera bat. Credit: Tim Flach, Getty Images.

7.6   Egyptian bats. Credit: Tim Flach.

The human resemblance of these bats is elusive. It does not attach to any particular features—not the hairy faces, wizened bodies or skinny legs. Rather, their putative humanity is ubiquitous, a function of the distribution of the animal's parts in forming a recognizable whole. These bat poses are organized around a clear center of gravity; like us, they have a vertical stance. Moreover, the photographs have been turned upside down. This inversion of perspective enables the spectator to identify with the animal's comportment in terms of human poses. Every contour is suggestive of the human frame, the innumerable postures it adopts and the infinity of emotional states spectators see coded in those postures.

7.7   COMPASSION BAT. CREDIT: TIM FLACH.

The bats are more striking than human models would be in the same poses. Imagine a man and woman emulating these animals; they would not move the viewer in the same way. Abstracting human forms into bat poses concentrates the mind on the essence of gesture. What remains is the choreography of social relations, a general body language dissociated from the physical vocabulary of a given individual. Whether the viewer is drawn to or repelled by the bats, or both, the animals are neither good looking nor bad looking—just bat looking in a human way.

As Balázs points out, the same holds for all animals on film:

How interesting the physiognomies and facial gestures of animals! And how mysterious that we should be able to understand them! Needless to say, this is based on an analogy. But perhaps this is justified. . . . All animals are actually caricatures of certain human types. . . . [They] carry the physiognomies of humans and, at the same time, keep their own lovable and honest animal faces.[19]

Here Balázs appears to have fallen prey to the anthropomorphism he is at pains to identify. As Flach's bats reveal, both parts of Balázs's so-called analogy are in fact human constructs; we never "understand" the animals.

7.8   MANDRILL. CREDIT: TIM FLACH.

Turn the photographs around and the eloquent bearing of these bats becomes a submission to gravity unintelligible in human terms.

A third method by which Flach encodes his animal emoticons is *treatment*. Rather than relying on the heavy-handed symbolism of props—such as chimpanzees wearing a suit and tie—Flach transposes a visual system of references from the treatment of human subjects to the treatment of animal subjects. The animals function as symbolic placeholders; viewers identify not with the animals themselves but with their placement in a familiar symbolic context. The pictorial language of fashion is thematized in the contrasting blue, red, and yellow coloring of the mandrill against an orange background. In the original color photograph, the animal's natural pigmentation is shown off as an elaborate cosmetic statement; eye shadow, lipstick and platinum-blond hair are alluded to in the garish colors of its nose and beard; its coiffure is styled to meet the exacting standards of a top-end beauty parlor. Other examples of treatment cues include the beguiling finery of a parrot arrested in deep blue and the abstracted geometry of a pigeon in black and white. Here colors, shapes and patterns turn animal forms into emblems of beauty and glamour. The parrot triptych alludes to the sweeping swirling shapes of the catwalk, the bird's feathers form a lavish cloak elegantly draped around its frame.

Another *treatment* cue employed by Flach is the family album, with its characteristic snap-shot rendering of awkward and goofy moments often set in the home or a place of leisure. Flach employs his arsenal of sophisticated, photographic techniques to re-create this semblance of spontaneity. In his photograph, a dog and man kissing resemble a settled, middle-aged couple. They radiate earthy affection, a relationship based on physical immediacy where emotional bonds are upheld by touching, sniffing, and licking. The dog seems human and the human doglike. Treatment cues simultaneously

7.9   PARROTS. CREDIT: TIM FLACH.

7.10 PIGEON. CREDIT: TIM FLACH, GETTY IMAGES.

7.11   MAN AND DOG KISSING. CREDIT: TIM FLACH, GETTY IMAGES.

defamiliarize our readings of the *animals* as well as the *human* frames of
reference: makeup and fashion come to resemble animal plumage, the kiss
an animal's kinship ritual.

FABRICATING SENTIMENT

Flach's work is the product of an image-making collective. From the quarterly call for photographs, to the debriefings with art editors at Getty, to
consultations with animal handlers, fellow photographers, and assistants,
to his high-end commissions in the advertising world, Flach is immersed

in an industry of professionals specialized in tracking, anticipating, and delivering visual content for a consuming public.

His images are not the result of lucky shots, jungle-paparazzi style.[20] Nor does he simply bring a good eye to wildlife situations, documenting with conscientious care an animal's behavior in its natural habitat.[21] He resists the conceit of photography as a neutral, objective recording of observable facts. Constructing the situation, manipulating the image, composing the visual trigger mechanism for producing a predictable emotional response—in short, crafting marketable emoticons—these are the qualities for which he prizes the medium of photography.

Flach's images are produced under conditions of tight quality control. His streamlining of the process is evidenced in his approach to the frame that surrounds the image. Whereas many photographers choose the frames after they have finished shooting their film by cropping the negative, Flach only rarely resorts to later adjustments. He disapproves of separating the shooting from the framing of an image because the frame is integral to the subject matter and determines the distribution of light. In order to accentuate recognition cues by means of highlights, Flach must know exactly how the image is going to be placed on the negative. Ideally, there is no wasted space or rendering of useless information. He focuses the camera on the visual dynamics of the scene on set, especially any anthropomorphic opportunities it may afford.

Over the years, Flach has generated an environment conducive to his peculiar methodology. His studio is a cross between a surgical ward, a Buddhist temple, and a circus tent. Evident in every corner are years of experience with recalcitrant animal models on set. Having obtained possession of an empty warehouse in Shoreditch, London, two hundred square meters of open-plan space divided over two floors with four-meter ceilings, he supervised the renovation of the space. Besides accommodating animals of most any size, the space's glass floor allows pictures to be shot from underneath, enormous light fixtures can be cranked out of the ceiling, and adjustable temperature gauges ensure that the room's temperature is finely variable. Flach has found that temperature, more than any other single factor, allows him to influence the behavior of his animal models. In his studio, animals are confined to a more predictable set of behavioral variables. This control allows him to zero in on the anthropomorphic opportunities on set.

Although Flach has sole possession of the camera, his creative direction is strongly influenced by an image-making collective. For instance, preferences expressed by Getty's picture editors regarding the staging and production of a shoot will take precedence over Flach's own aesthetic judgment. Equally, the expertise possessed by animal handlers regarding the behavior and responses of their charges frequently serves as the stimulus for a shoot's following one path rather than another. In addition there are makeup artists, stage designers, costume makers, set builders, and their various assistants to take into account. The team assembled on the day of the shoot prefigures, in miniature, the market place; like a group dynamic medium (or focus group), its responses help to funnel operative symbols from consumer culture into the image under construction.

The studio itself is also a key player in Flach's image-making collective. It establishes a creative margin of opportunity and puts technology in the service of chance. The camera and the eye are not only distinct modalities of seeing; they operate in different ontological realms, as Benjamin observes: "It is a different nature speaking to the camera than the eye. The difference consists especially therein that a space permeated by consciousness is replaced by one unconsciously permeated."[22] The studio space is "unconsciously permeated" in the sense that it conditions the photographic output generated on its premises and arranges nature in conformity to the dictates of Flach's camera. Temperature, lighting design, and his highly routinized handling of the photographic equipment turn the space into a *dompteur* of sorts, manipulating the animals' behavior for the camera. At the same time, the notion of an "unconsciously permeated" space also applies to the creative situation inside the studio where team dynamics unconsciously intervene in the fabrication of an image able to capture the public imaginary.

At every stage of Flach's image-production process, the emotiveness of the photograph is incrementally enhanced. Although the adjustments made along the way can be infinitely subtle, spectators asked to choose will instinctually agree on the version they prefer. The process is akin to tightening a screw; with every turn the emotional message is more solidly in place. At no stage in this process is Flach alone—he is continually guided, prodded, and encouraged by a team of technical collaborators.

CONCEPT MAPS

Getty photographers think of themselves as "image makers," not photographers. Their creative energy goes into formulating graphics with multivalent commercial applications. Recently, Getty insiders have introduced the notion of a "concept map," or "thought map," to distinguish the new line in sentiment-enriched imagery from old-fashioned stock photography. Getty markets itself as a purveyor of "conceptual images" at the same time that it promotes itself as a supplier of photographs "with a clear emotional message."

This deliberate and systematic collapsing of "concept" and "emotion" throughout the Getty enterprise should give pause to readers and spectators alike. Kracauer has identified the conflating of "concept" and "emotion" as the hallmark of propaganda material. He also notes, however, that the conflation can only be effective if "true emphasis is on visual communication." The more elusive the message of a film, he says, the more directly it imprints itself on "the unconscious drives and bodily reactions" of spectators. By contrast, he argues, a message that appears merely to be illustrated will neither "confound the senses" nor "render the spectator receptive to the ideas being propagated."[23] Kracauer's observations about film apply equally to the global picturescape of stock photography. The iguana woman image, for instance, is elusively vivid yet alludes to nothing in particular.

Getty's creative director Louis Blackwell recently went on record proclaiming Flach's animals to be the sentimental culmination of an artistic journey begun by the French documentary photographer Cartier-Bresson. Blackwell makes this connection despite Cartier-Bresson's vehement repudiation of sentiment in photography: "The only joy in photography is geometry. All the rest is sentiment." In response, Blackwell mounts a spirited "defense of sentiment": "What an outrageous remark! How can the 'only joy' be geometry, and that be somehow elevated to a plane that is so far superior to 'sentiment'? The fact is that it is sentiment that gives photography much of its power."[24] The reasons Blackwell adduces in favor of sentiment are telling in that they equate the value of a photograph with the bottom-line of profit maximization: "Sentiment is the reason that photography works so effectively in the commercial world—whether as a newspaper front or back page image, or as a fashion shoot, or as a billboard ad or as a feature portrait."[25]

Flach's photographs instantiate the Stone Getty project. The company regularly uses his images for purposes of self-promotion. His animal portraits promote a weltanschauung (the literal translation being "a way of looking at the world") that is conducive to Getty's corporate agenda. Not only do these satisfy the distributor's vested interest in promoting visuals that have a long shelf life, the impeccable execution of Flach's work conveys a professionalism, precision, and deliverability consonant with the company's aims. Most important, these images reify the workings of power, in that they depict unruly animals tamed by the disciplining routines of a photographic studio. Flach's aesthetics of power and control facilitate Getty's exercise thereof.

Nobel Prize–winning author Elias Canetti penned an aphorism that could easily be applied to Flach—a person who "thinks in animals as others think in concepts."[26] But what does it mean to "think in animals"? Flach would say he is "formulating a visual language structure that has emotional resonance." What he means is that his photographs are not only emotive but also didactic; they "formulate a visual language structure" in that they both depict animal forms and express a theory of pictures. Supposing, therefore, as Mitchell contends, that every ideology is an iconology and vice versa, it behooves the spectator to ask what ideology is being promoted by the theory of pictures that Flach's animals self-consciously promote.[27]

Flach himself maintains that his animals are "a mirror of the human condition in its rawest form." He thinks of his work as a conduit to emotional truths because it taps into the core of his spectators' affective responses. Not striving to capture the animals in their natural state, however this may be defined, he is concerned with the exploration of human nature, no doubt an equally problematic category. Looking at animals through Flach's eyes is similar to experiencing animals in a petting zoo, in that spectators do not encounter a representation of the natural world but the staging of an ideology.[28] Yet unlike the aesthetics of display practiced in contemporary zoos, where moated exhibits have replaced iron-bar cages, the stylization and distortion techniques utilized by Flach positively broadcast that he has no pretensions at conventional animal naturalism.

Nevertheless, Flach is advocating a naturalism of sorts, namely that of the *emotional connection*. The problem with his take on naturalism is that, like any naturalizing rhetoric, it posits as fixed and universal categories of understanding that are, in fact, culturally determined. An emotional response, according to Flach, is proof positive that a given image expresses eternal values, the strength of response being directly proportional to the truth content of the image. Although the response no doubt reveals that a chord has been struck in a given spectator on a given occasion, there is nothing fixed or eternal about the conditions under which this affective event takes place. Human nature is highly variable and inconstant. Individuals change over the course of their lifetimes, and so do societies. The most constant feature of our emotional experience may be our belief in its constancy. Emotional responses present themselves as so utterly autonomous in experience that it is virtually impossible to comprehend them as being highly mediated and conditioned by external factors. Yet the orchestrated transience of our attractions—the ever-changing fashions in clothes, lifestyles, and causes to which we feel drawn—belie the private character of this emotional experience.

The question of "what images are," Mitchell writes, must be considered in light of the question of "what human nature is or might become." The act of seeing an image, animal or not, is inseparable from the act of projecting meaning onto the same, and the configuration of that meaning is a function of the existing symbolic order at a given historical moment. "Images," according to Mitchell, "are not just a particular kind of sign, but something like an actor on the historical stage, a presence or character endowed with legendary status."[29] We, as spectators, turn them into such: first, we endow them with meaning based on our own conditioned responses, and then, we misread these same meanings as eternal verities. In this regard, Mitchell concurs with Balázs, who, writing seventy years earlier, likened our proclivity to invest images with personal significance to applied physiognomy, that is, the art of deciphering a person's character from the lines in his or her face. Balázs, echoing Kant, insists that a phenomenal reflexivity akin to physiognomical perception animates each and every sensory event: "Just as time and space are fundamental categories of perception that cannot be eliminated from our world of experience, so the physiognomical attaches itself to every phenomenon. It is a necessary condition of our perception."[30]

Both Mitchell's "heroic images" and Balázs's "physiognomical sight" admonish spectators to bear in mind that all meaning is projected meaning, even if it seems *natural* to the spectator, an *instrinsic* feature of the image itself. It is, therefore, necessary to distinguish between two distinct modalities of physiognomical projection, the *topical* and the *medial*. Connecting with Flach's animal portraits in human terms, that is, at the emotikon level discussed earlier, animals as anthropomorphic vehicles of emotion, involves *topical* projection in that it pertains to the subject matter depicted and concerns our relationship with other species. Believing these same photographs to mirror the human condition involves *medial* projection in that it pertains to our assessment of the medium itself and posits photography as a vehicle capable of storing such profound, almost religious content. By focusing the spectator's attention so narrowly on the process of anthropomorphic identification, Flach's animals end up blunting awareness of the secondary leap of faith implicit in experiencing the medium of photography as a conduit to the eternally human.

An alternative reading of the notion of a *concept map*, then, is that any given image can be understood as a map through a terrain of topical-medial meanings working in concert. Flach's elaboration of visual techniques for *thinking with animals* distracts the viewer from the fact that they are also inevitably *thinking with media*. Reflexive energy is channeled into the animal's uncanny humanity but not into the symbolic function of the picture. These pictures are able to steer the spectator's attention away from any corollary suggestiveness adhering to the image. Employing Flach's animals literally as concept maps, that is, maps through a terrain of implied concepts, it becomes possible to explore the constellation of symbolic meanings immanent in the medium he has developed. These meanings are a product of the manner in which his body of work circulates in a global system of image distribution.

WHAT HUMAN CONDITION?

Flach's positioning as a creative professional defies traditional distinctions between high and low culture; he is anonymously associated with a vast range of products and services and, at the same time, featured in museums like the National Portrait Gallery in London, at the other. Some of the same images for hire from Getty Images sell on the fine-art market in signed, limited editions. Adorno would abhor such two-timing as the triumph of "pseudo-culture."[31] Snobbery aside, this collapsing of cultural distinctions has far-reaching implications for the revelatory potential of Flach's animals and for why a close reading of them can enhance our understanding of current cultural trends. The anthropomorphic quality of his images suggests that their appeal trades on human self-understanding; the international scope of his popularity betokens a global phenomenon. So what does the mirror reflect? What specific *thinking with animals* is occasioned by his images? Or in other words, what concept of humanity is enshrined by his images?

Kangaroos, red-eyed tree frogs, ants, and lizards all form parts of Flach's bestiary corpus. The images he enters into the Getty Images collection generate a particularly high ratio of profits per image and maintain their

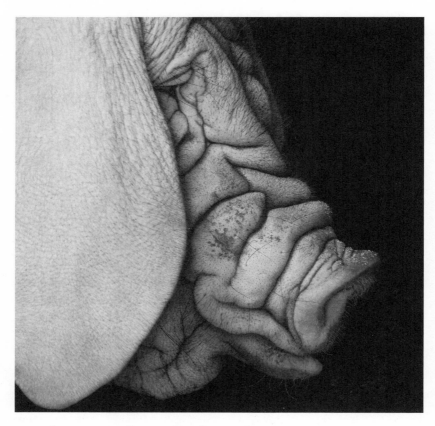

7.12   CHINESE PIG. CREDIT: TIM FLACH, GETTY IMAGES.

popularity over exceptionally long periods. Unlike photographs of human beings, whose referential scope tends to be constrained by the markers of class, gender, race, age, and nationality, photographs of animals rehearse a realm of interpretive conventions that can bypass human stereotypes.

Of course, animal imagery is laden with its own layers of cultural meaning rooted in religion, heritage, and politics (the sinfulness of the snake and the eeriness of the bat in the western tradition; the coding of animals as "domestic," "agricultural," or "wild"; the conservationist efforts to elevate certain species in the public imaginary, such as the "gentle" elephant and the "noble" primate). But Flach's stylized portraits strive to extract the animals from their existing frames of reference, thereby divesting them of their conventional symbolism. Metamorphosed into surrogate humans, they express a state of putative emotional "innocence": the wrinkled pig, an evocation of age without biography or history; the monkey licking its thumb (see figure 7.13), a tribute to well-being without

7.13   MONKEY LICKING. CREDIT: TIM FLACH, GETTY IMAGES.

7.14 MONKEY LAUGHTER. CREDIT: TIM FLACH, GETTY IMAGES.

sacrifice or compromise; the screaming monkey (see figure 7.14), a meditation on vulnerability without exposure or risk.

These images of apes are compelling. And so is the implied possibility of a visual Esperanto in whose universalizable embrace all humans being can be accommodated. At the same time, it is remarkable that this vision should so captivate the public imagination. In *The Interpretation of Cultures*, Clifford Geertz argues that the notion of a human being without culture is a contradiction in terms. His developmental argument is that because the human brain and human culture were coeval evolutionary adaptations, a "cultureless human being would probably turn out to be not an intrinsically talented though unfulfilled ape, but a wholly mindless and consequently unworkable monstrosity."[32] Yet Flach, working in concert with Getty Images, seems to be promoting just that—a vision of experience sterilized of "contaminating" cultural influences.

Needless to say, this supracultural stance is itself a cultural act. Culture is not restricted to specific rites or ways of doing things; rather, it encompasses the formative activities of humans, whatever these may be. If humans, or the institutions they develop, efface the specificities of local-historical customs, taste, and so on, then the instruments and acts of erasure are themselves cultural products and acts. Which forms of cultural practice may be preferable, or more conducive to human happiness, is a question whose treatment exceeds the scope of this article. That the Fordist and Taylorist innovations in twentieth century industrial production tapped human labor in ways that would agitate against personal and cultural individuation is widely acknowledged. That the media would be integral to upholding and furthering this trend by shaping public opinion has long been apparent to critically minded media theorists.

The effectiveness and popularity of Flach's animal images across all sectors of society and in different national contexts and their simultaneous foregrounding in the self-promotion of Getty Images reveal a profound alignment between corporate interests and private values. Nevertheless, diversity still abounds. As market analyses across all sectors of consumption show, Flach's animals do not reflect an extant social situation; cultural specificity is still a relevant factor in consumer behavior. This diversity is, however, under threat. A growing body of literature and evidence attests that cultural variety and local traditions are being transmuted, and eroded, in the corporate race for global market share. Flach's animals are not only further evidence of this trend, they are an integral part of the mechanism propelling this alignment.

The global consumer culture that Flach's animals embody and promote has its own characteristic values. These are particularly apparent with respect to sexual conduct and scientific developments. Two examples will suffice to illustrate how these values play out with respect to Flach's animals. Again, it is worth noting that the deflective tactic of topical-medial ambiguity obtains. While spectators marvel at Flach's extraordinary imagery, the mediation of an associated set of messages can easily go unheeded. By flirting with the transgression of a taboo—specifically bestiality—viewers are caught off-guard, their senses confounded along the propagandistic lines described by Kracauer.

Flach's licking horse lips are a lusty and playful revisiting of the canonical licking lips imagery that has accompanied our advertising culture since the original Rolling Stones album to which it obliquely refers. The image could figure in the promotion of a brand of gourmet ice creams or as an illustration for a magazine article on tongue piercing. Behind its multiple possible applications resonates a codified allusion to the human kiss as the

7.15 HORSE TONGUE. CREDIT: TIM FLACH, GETTY IMAGES.

foreplay to sexual intercourse, an activity ultimately ensuring the perpetu-
ation of the species. But looking this gift horse in the mouth, the spectator
finds a suggestion more indecent and transgressive than many a centerfold
spread in the glossies. There is a chain of events hinted at here which, taken
to its final conclusion, issues forth in a horse and human embrace reminiscent of Catherine the Great. Yet the picture's intrinsic humor blunts any
edge of affront. The sexuality implicit in this scene is purely recreational;
crossing a species boundary, it can serve no procreative ends. This image
exists within and itself perpetuates a nexus of social arrangements, rep-
resentational conventions, and ideological constellations in which procreative sexuality has become an exceptional type of encounter and scoring
orgasms the pastime of choice.

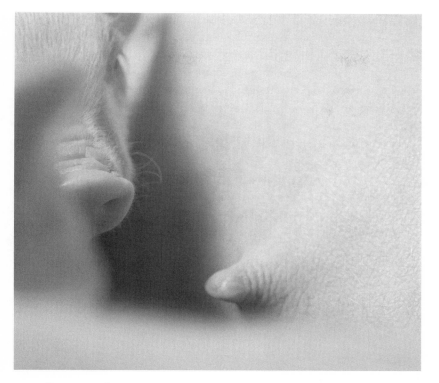

7.16 PIG TEAT. CREDIT: TIM FLACH, GETTY IMAGES.

The blurring of erotic boundaries performed in the next concept map goes so far as to warrant a designated term, "pornomorphism." The same audience that finds pleasure in the picture of pork teats at an aesthetic level might well reject, or at least pause to consider in more critical terms, the picture's suggestive content. The nipple looks startlingly similar to that of a human breast. The color tones, hairlessness, and hygienic care evidenced in this scene place the spectator firmly in the arena of human skin rather than pig hide. Close examination of the mammary, itself involving sexually charged mental deliberations, reveals this teat to be attached to the udder of a pig. Despite the piglet in near proximity, the visual ambiguity remains. This is not an optical *illusion* in gestalt-psychological terms, where the teat is either rabbit or duck but never both at the same time. Rather, this is an optical *allusion* to a world in which species boundaries have been reduced to changes along a sequence of genetic code. The nipple is *both* that of a human and that of a pig, two species fused in a single breast. Skin grafts, often involving a pig's skin, and organ transplants between animal species come to mind as well as genetic engineering with its myriad reproductive

technologies. Innovations in the medical and biological technologies together with the vast social upheavals they entail are here cast in the natural-
ized visual vocabulary of a barnyard *Madonna con bambino*.

The point is not that this photograph, like a Trojan horse, slips the
viewer a subversive political message behind an innocent scene of nursing.
Flach's images do not contain messages in the transmission sense of send-
er/receiver. Rather, they are meaningful, and what is more, commercially
successful, insofar as they reflect and reinforce an extant order of symbolic
relations through which the viewers, the image brokers, the technical assistants on the day of the shoot, and the photographer himself all make sense
of the world. Flach's pig nipple compels attention because the jumbling of
categories performed by this photograph is already well underway in the
societies to be serviced by that image. As George Orwell concludes in his
1946 novel *Animal Farm*: "The creatures outside looked from pig to man,
and from man to pig, and from pig to man again; but already it was impossible to say which was which."

"TASTE IS IDEOLOGY"

As pictures about pictures, Flach's animals convey a sentimental education,
a schooling for the emotions. Unlike the fusion achieved in Orwell's vision,
these photographs invite and positively instruct spectators to project levels
of meaning presumably not shared by the animal models themselves. This
discrepancy between the spectator and the animal model re-enshrines that
long-established and much-defended gulf separating the human animal
from all other animals, at least as imagined by the former.[33] These humanlike animals accentuate the uniqueness of being human. In so doing, they
also further a mental isolationism that not only separates the human animal from all other animals but also spectators from one another.

Flach's animals separate us from other species even as they urge emotional identification. In the process, empathy, the binding and unifying force
par excellence, is converted into its opposite, a distancing mechanism that
instrumentalizes the animal form for the sake of momentary emotional
gratification. The viewer is moved to project sentimental significance onto a
scene that simultaneously undermines the validity of the sentiment in question. Flach's animal images invite a wholly one-sided emotional event to take
place. The affective experience they afford is unashamedly spectator-cen-
tered. His photographs are the cardinal expression of a new set of emotional
responses that have arisen in the dialectical interaction between a consump-
tion-powered media machine and the target audience whose desires it both

reflects and structures. In Balázs's words: "Aesthetic taste is a self-defense mechanism of the spiritual organism. Even the tastes of a class are an expression of the struggle for that class's survival. Taste is ideology."[34]

To adapt Benjamin's famous phrase, Flach's animals represent sentiment in the age of its digital proliferation. Changes in the technological conditions of producing and disseminating images have entailed changes in the collective configuration of visual perception. Flach's photography, in its factorization through the distributive arms of Getty Images, can be understood as a carefully crafted prosthetic replacement for meaningful emotional exchange. To the extent that spectators look at Flach's pictures and suspend disbelief, they enter into a technologically assisted process of narcissistic self-projection. As concept maps, his images can be understood as commodified guides to visual apperception assisting the public imaginary to envisage trends whose consequences, though already felt, are only beginning to be articulated in graphic form.

Flach's anthropomorphic style of photography is in sync with Getty's ambition to serve as a centralized mechanism for boosting consumption through emotional manipulation. In pumping subliminal positivity, like citrus aroma, into the marketplace, Getty Images is fundamentally transforming the diet of images we, the seeing and consuming public, ingest on a daily basis as we walk down the street, do our shopping, surf the Internet, and so on. We neither see the progeny of the images bombarding us nor are we aware that these images may be gradually and imperceptibly recalibrating our emotional literacy. As Benjamin observes, "the masses are a matrix out of which all habitual understandings with respect to works of art are currently emerging newly born. Quantity has switched into quality: the much larger number of participants has resulted in a different kind of participation."[35]

Stephen Mayes likens stock photography to "a cultural stream of consciousness. . . . It is hardly considered and yet it is all around us, a mirror that seems to reflect the world but which actually reflects our ideas of how we would like the world to be."[36] Mayes's aperçu draws attention to the ubiquity of commercial imagery and its cohesive nature. Yet his claim that the mirror "reflects our ideas of how we would *like* to the world to be" is tendentious. To the extent that stock photography can be compared to a mirror at all, it is a mirror that deliberately distorts and selectively filters the information it transmits. In believing that the desires portrayed in stock land are, indeed, our own authentic desires reflected back at us, we are succumbing to the lure of the *topical* over the *medial*.

Flach's animal photography is but one vector of change in the silent transformation of our visually mediated emotional responses. Yet by probing the symbolic content of his images, spectators can learn to recognize how emotional identification with these animals may be rendering them affectively susceptible to values operative in an increasingly global society—values whose implications for the organization of regional public spaces and social institutions they may not want to endorse uncritically.

CONCLUSION

By occasioning a psychological event in the spectator—in this case, seeing human attributes in animal forms—Flach's concept maps enable us to experience ourselves, momentarily, as *perceiving* animals comprehending the environment through strata of emotional projection. The last photograph here summarizes, by way of visual metaphor, the anthropomorphic faculty characterizing the human animal and so assiduously cultivated throughout Flach's portfolio of work. Instead of projecting human qualities onto an animal model, this photograph of a man's neck and shoulders invites spectators to reflect on the phenomenal reality of being human and the human propensity to see, as Balázs would have it, physiognomic monsters where there are only shadows. Ironically, as Flach's animals show, spectators are perhaps equally prone to see only shadows where there may lurk ideological monsters.

The aim of this essay has been to demonstrate that there is something fishy about animals, especially as portrayed by Flach. Thinking with them we invariably seem to allegorize about ourselves. Balázs attributes the singular magic of animals on film to their unselfconscious immediacy:

> The particular thrill of observing animals on film consists in knowing that they are not playing at something but actually living. They know nothing about the apparatus and strut their stuff with naïve earnestness. Even when their performance is drilled, only we know that it is theater. They don't demur and are deadly serious about everything. Every actor's aim is to arouse the illusion that his grimaces are no mere "impersonations" but rather the expression of authentically present feeling. Yet no actor is able to outdo the animals in this respect. The latter know no illusion, only real facts. All artifice is absent; we are eavesdropping on nature.[37]

But again Balázs seems to have succumbed to the subliminal process he seeks to examine. Consistent with his own critical media theory, a more accurate conclusion would have been, "All artifice *seems* absent, we *feel* as

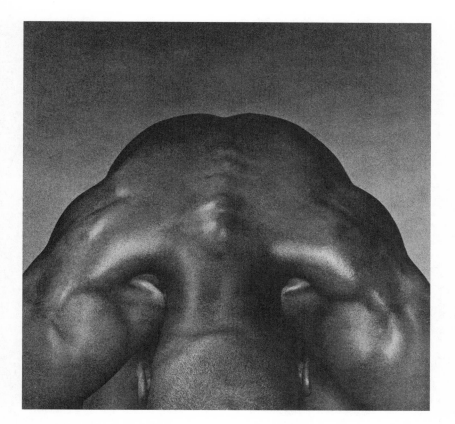

7.17   WALRUS. CREDIT: TIM FLACH, GETTY IMAGES.

if we were eavesdropping on nature." This subtle distinction must be born in mind if we want to enjoy the complex resonance of Flach's digital beasts without falling prey to the powers they unwittingly serve.

NOTES

The author would like to thank Tim Flach and Getty Images for permission to reproduce the photographs used in this article. It has not been possible to print the photographs in their original color version. But for anyone interested in seeing the original images, please visit www.timflach.com. The author would also like to thank the following people for their invaluable help and feedback on early drafts of this paper: Matthias Bruhn, Lorraine Daston, Roberto Farneti, Karen Kramer, Gregg Mitman, Tania Munz, Michele Vitucci, and Heike Weber.

1. Walter Benjamin, *Medienästhetische Schriften* (Frankfurt am Main: Suhrkamp Verlag, 2002), 314. In this paper all translations from German texts have been made by the author.

2. "Fabrication" is a translation of Benjamin's term "*Konstruktion.*"

3. Béla Balázs, *Ein Baedeker der Seele: Und andere Feuilletons aus den Jahren 1920–1926*, ed. Hanno Loewy (Berlin: Das Arsenal, 2002), 28.

4. Much of this paper is drawn from personal observations the author made over a one-year period (2001–2002) while collaborating with Tim Flach on an exhibition project entitled *AcroBats*. The author is indebted to Flach for the numerous insights he shared about his work and the stock industry. In the course of this collaboration, the author also had occasion to observe and interact with other Getty photographers and employees at the Getty headquarters in London. Most recently, the author has benefited from interviews with influential figures in the field of visual-content delivery, especially Louis Blackwell, Stephen Mayes, and Michele Vitucci.

5. Paul Frosch, "Rhetorics of the Overlooked: On the Communicative Modes of Stock Advertising Images," *Journal of Consumer Culture* 2, no. 2 (July 2002): 174.

6. Opinions differ among those working in the industry; while some would argue that the editorial policies are still carefully guarded secrets and claim to know a Getty or a Corbis picture on sight, others maintain that the secret is long out and, indeed, that the visual output of the two companies is indistinguishable.

7. Banks are responsible for managing our most precious assets, not only money, data and images but also vital organic substances, as evidenced by the notions of gene banks, sperm banks, and blood banks. The invocation of a "bank," at least in the western world, implies the existence of a vast system of controls and accountability structures combined with a service model providing ready access to a given commodity or resource.

8. Matthias Bruhn, *Bildwirtschaft: Verwaltung und Verwertung der Sichtbarkeit* (Weimar: Verlag und Datenbank für Geisteswissenschaften, 2003), 18.

9. W. J. T. Mitchell, *Iconology: Image, Text, Ideology* (Chicago: University of Chicago Press, 1986), 203.

10. Frosch, "Rhetorics of the Overlooked," 175.

11. Walter Benjamin, "Das Kunstwerk im Zeitalter seiner technischen Reproduzierbarkeit," in *Illuminationen: Ausgewählte Schriften 1, Suhrkamp Taschenbuch* (1955; reprint, Frankfurt: Suhrkamp Verlag, 1977), 144.

12. Bruhn, *Bildwirtschaft*, 67.

13. Theodor W. Adorno, "Fernsehen Als Ideologie," in his *Kulturkritik und Gesellschaft* (Frankfurt: Suhrkamp Verlag, 1977), 518–32.

14. Nils Klawitter, "Bilder-Stürmer in Not," *Der Spiegel* 26, no. 23 (June 2003): 142.

15. Bruhn, *Bildwirtschaft*, 43, 48.

16. Stephen Mayes, "Masterclass Piece," Lecture delivered at Joop Swart Masterclass 2002, World Press Photo Organisation, Amsterdam, November 2002.

17. Siegfried Kracauer, *Das Ornament der Masse* (Frankfurt: Suhrkamp, 1963), 54.

18. For a listing of recognized emoticons, see http://www.windweaver.com/emoticon.htm.

19. Béla Balázs, *Der Geist des Films* (1930; reprint, Frankfurt: Suhrkamp, 2001), 77.

20. Catherine A. Lutz and Jane L. Collins, *Reading National Geographic* (Chicago: University of Chicago Press, 1993), 64.

21. Gregg Mitman, *Reel Nature: America's Romance with Wildlife on Film* (Boston: Harvard University Press, 1999).

22. Benjamin, "Das Kunstwerk," 162.

23. Siegfried Kracauer, *Theorie des Films: Die Errettung der äußeren Wirklichkeit* (Frankfurt: Suhrkamp, 1964), 219.

24. Louis Blackwell, "In Defence of Sentiment," *Pictured*, no. 1 (2003): 50.

25. Blackwell, "In Defence of Sentiment," 50.

26. Elias Canetti, *Über Tiere* (Munich: Carl Hanser Verlag, 2002).

27. Mitchell, *Iconology*, 164.

28. John Berger, *About Looking* (New York: Pantheon Books, 1980).

29. Mitchell, *Iconology*, 9.

30. Balázs, *Der Geist des Films*, 70.

31. Robert W. Witkin, *Adorno on Popular Culture* (London: Routledge, 2003), 30–31.

32. Clifford Geertz, *The Interpretation of Cultures: Selected Essays* (1973; reprint, London: Fontana Press, 1993), 68.

33. Anna L. Peterson, *Being Human. Ethics, Environment, and Our Place in the World* (Berkeley and Los Angeles: University of California Press, 2001).

34. Balázs, *Der Geist des Films*, 145.

35. Benjamin, "Das Kunstwerk," 165.

36. Stephen Mayes, "i SAY: Through the Looking Glass (Darkly)," *Photo District News NY* 6, no. 6 (December–January 2001): 17.

37. Balázs, *Der Geist des Films*, 76.

PART IV

THINKING WITH ANIMALS
IN FILM

· · · · · · · ·

CHAPTER 8

Pachyderm Personalities

The Media of Science, Politics, and Conservation

· · · · · · · · ·

Gregg Mitman

"I defy any one to look upon elephants without a sense of wonder. Their very enormity, their clumsiness, their giant stature, represent a mass of liberty that sets you dreaming. They're . . . yes, they're the last individuals.

"No, mademoiselle, I don't capture elephants. I content myself with living among them. I like them. I like looking at them, listening to them, watching them on the horizon. To tell you the truth, I'd give anything to become an elephant myself."

—ROMAIN GARY, *The Roots of Heaven*

To become an elephant: a fictional idea when Romain Gary published his internationally best-selling novel in 1958, this became an important scientific question a decade later among a generation of elephant researchers inspired by Gary's novel to pursue their own single-minded cause to save the African elephant. The Los Angeles premiere of the Discovery Channel's forty-minute large-format film, *Africa's Elephant Kingdom*, in May 1998, drew upon thirty years of ethological research to bring viewers an intimate portrait of elephant family life and social relations told through the eyes of Old Bull, a sixty-year-old male elephant in Amboseli National Park who "lived through World War II, the Mau-Mau rebellion and the independence movement in Kenya."[1] Filmmaker Tim Cowling spoke of the challenges of being like a "wide-angle eye inside an elephant."[2] To aid him in thinking, seeing, feeling like an elephant, Cowling had at his disposal the film's scientific consultant, Iain Douglas-Hamilton, who had spent his entire adult life living among the elephants, waging guerilla warfare in their defense, and helping orchestrate a worldwide ban on the elephant-ivory trade. In describing a scene from *Africa's Elephant Kingdom* when a mother makes a futile attempt to lift her dying infant off the ground and is, in an alleged gesture of compassion, touched by an elephant from another family, Douglas-Hamilton remarks: "They can't tell us what was going on in their heads, but to me it looked as if they understood very well what she was feeling. And animals that can do that are really very high on the order of consciousness, animals that have the mind and tools to be able to reconstruct what is going on in the mind of another animal's head."[3]

Douglas-Hamilton was speaking not just of the elephant's abilities to transcend individual experience but of his abilities and those of a handful of researchers—Cynthia Moss, Joyce Poole, Katy Payne—to cross the species divide. In the thirty years since Douglas-Hamilton first began his pioneering study of the Lake Manyara elephants, a detailed, intimate understanding of elephants as individuals has emerged. The introduction of a number of innovative methodological field techniques related to communications technology drew researchers not only into the world of animal communication but into the mass-communications industry. This alliance has forged new networks in the practice and promotion of conservation biology where personalities and emotions, prominent features in the "highly personalized topography" of media culture, have also become distinguishing landmarks in elephant research and conservation.[4]

Unlike other areas of science and public policy, the authority and expertise of scientist-activists like Iain Douglas-Hamilton and Cynthia Moss among politicians and the general public derives not from their detachment but from their long years of intimate associations with elephants in the wild. Just as Hollywood stars encourage a sense of intimacy with their audience, so too do these biologists achieve fame through their ability to bring humans into intimate contact with elephants.[5] It is the very interplay between elephant and human, as biologists take on characteristics of elephants and vice versa, that has been of critical importance in the rise to stardom of both researchers and their extended elephant families. While an appeal to numbers has often shored up the authority and expertise of scientists in the political realm, in the case of elephant conservation, anthropomorphism and emotion, more than numbers, have lent greater credence to science in the public sphere.[6] It is the morphic aspects of anthropomorphism that interest me in this essay, along with the transformative aspects of photography and film in altering the topographic spaces where biological knowledge gets produced and consumed. In their deployment of film and photography as instruments of research and weapons of activism, ethologists and the media networks that sustain their work and image have fashioned themselves and their subjects into popular celebrities, creating new systems of patronage and research that do not fit readily into the standard funding patterns or research practices of twentieth-century life science.

THE FAMILY THAT LIVES WITH ELEPHANTS

DAUGHTER: What does "objective" mean?

FATHER: Well. It means that you look very hard at those things which you choose to look at.

DAUGHTER: That sounds right. But how do the objective people choose which things they will be objective about?

FATHER: Well. They choose those things about which it is easy to be objective.

DAUGHTER: You mean easy for them?

FATHER: Yes.

DAUGHTER: But how do you KNOW that those are the easy things?

FATHER: I suppose they try different things and find out by experience.

DAUGHTER: So, it's a subjective choice?

FATHER: Oh, yes. All experience is subjective.

DAUGHTER: But it's HUMAN and subjective. They decide which bits of animal behavior to be objective about by consulting human subjective experience. Didn't you say that anthropomorphism is a bad thing?

FATHER: Yes—but they do try to be not human.[7]

The above—an excerpt from Gregory Bateson's metalogue to a 1965 international conference on "Approaches to Animal Communication" sponsored by the Wenner-Gren Foundation for Anthropological Research—appeared at a time when the mechanomorphism of classical ethology had begun to show signs of strain. In regarding animals as "limited to existing and reacting" rather than viewing them as "thinking and feeling," ethologists like Konrad Lorenz and Niko Tinbergen had developed an approach to the study of animal behavior that yielded impressive results in understanding the role of communication in the animal world.[8] But, as the Bateson metalogue implies, it did so at a cost, excluding any reference to the individual subjective experience of either the animal or human. Bateson's metalogue calls into question criticisms of anthropomorphism by suggesting that excluding various behaviors from study, what Frans de Waal has labeled anthropodenial, is as much a subjective act as is anthropomorphism. In the daughter-father conversations that followed, the problem of subjectivity—not of the observer but of the individual animal, inaccessible to human experience—became a topic of discussion. It is this focus on individuality in ethological research, which lends itself so readily to "the individualizing production aesthetic of television culture," that is of central importance to the production of celebrity scientists and elephants.[9]

Historians have yet to explore when and why questions of subjective emotional and mental states became once again legitimate, albeit controversial lines of inquiry within ethology and comparative psychology, but one important factor is surely the long-term behavioral field studies that began in the 1960s and relied upon the identification, recognition, and naming of individual animals, most notably the primate studies of Jane Goodall and George Schaller. While Tinbergen followed individuals to understand signals of communication among herring gulls, his interest in the individual was only as a marker of species-specific behavior. In the act of naming, however, Goodall, Schaller, and others offered the possibility of understanding individuals not as simply placeholders of animal behavior but as subjective beings. Schaller himself remarked that only by looking at gorillas as "living, feeling beings" was he "able to enter into the life of the group with comprehension, instead of remaining an ignorant spectator," although he reserved such reflections for his popular 1964 book *The Year of the Gorilla* and not his scientific monograph.[10] When Iain Douglas-Hamilton set out in 1965 to pursue his doctoral research on the behavioral ecology of elephants in Lake Manyara National Park, he was among the first of a generation of ethologists and behavioral ecologists to focus on individual life histories in understanding complex social relationships.

Douglas-Hamilton's initial interest was not individual elephants. Rather, his dissertation research was undertaken on behalf of John Owen, director of Tanzania National Parks, to advise on whether the elephant population in Lake Manyara needed to be culled based upon "knowledge of rates of habitat change and elephant population dynamics."[11] A quick, two-day aerial census of large mammals in Lake Manyara conducted by Murray Watson of the Serengeti Research Project and Myles Turner of Tanzania National Parks in April 1965 had produced estimates of twelve elephants per square mile, the largest density to be found in all of East Africa. Unless the herds of elephant and buffalo were reduced, Watson and Turner believed that the plains game populations of wildebeest and zebra faced imminent extinction.[12]

The recommendations of Watson and Turner for Lake Manyara appeared at a time when a heated controversy over management of elephant populations in East Africa was stirring, which culminated in a bitter public dispute. Tsavo National Park, located 150 kilometers to the northeast of Lake Manyara in Kenya, was the largest national park in East Africa. Established in 1948, Tsavo became a favored spot for elephant poaching, with an estimated 3,000 elephants killed between 1954 and 1957. In 1956, special antipoaching teams organized by David Sheldrick, a former British military office, professional hunter, and warden of the eastern district of Tsavo National Park, significantly curtailed the poaching activities of local Waliangulu and Wakamba tribes. By the early 1960s, an estimated 10,000 elephants inhabited Tsavo as their movements became more restricted by poaching activities and habitat loss outside the park's boundaries and as wells drilled inside the park became attractive watering holes. In 1948, when the park was established, the vegetation of Tsavo was largely woodland, consisting of thick commiphora and acacia trees that made wildlife viewing difficult for tourists. By the early 1960s, however, as a result of a drought and an increasing elephant population, eastern sections of the park looked like a "lunar landscape," as elephants destroyed large numbers of baobab, commiphora, and acacia trees, converting what was once bush country into grassland.[13]

In the early 1960s, the trustees of Kenya National Parks believed the deteriorating landscape in Tsavo East warranted the killing of 2,000 elephants to bring the population in line with the area's carrying capacity. Originally supportive of culling, Sheldrick began to have doubts as the rains returned and the country became a lush, open grassland, attractive to both grazing wildlife populations and tourists. Sheldrick wondered whether woodland represented the natural climax community or whether the region was marked by a repeating vegetation cycle from woodland to open savanna, aided by elephants. If the latter, then a reduction in the elephant population instituted a management scheme that hindered rather than abetted "natural" ecological processes and cycles. His reluctance to support the wholesale slaughter of elephants in Tsavo, known as "cropping" in wildlife-management circles, which he believed would undermine the park's successful antipoaching efforts, prompted the Kenya national government, with the assistance of the Ford Foundation, to fund a research study to investigate the problem.

Richard M. Laws, a Cambridge biologist with an expertise in marine mammal populations in the Antarctic, was selected as director of the Tsavo Research Project in 1966. In 1961, Laws had abandoned the icy waters of the Antarctic for the tropics when he accepted the directorship of Cambridge

University's Nuffield Unit of Tropical Animal Ecology in Uganda. It was in Murchison Falls National Park in Uganda that Laws first perfected his techniques for studying the population ecology, conservation, and management of elephants, methods he transferred to the study of the elephant problem in Tsavo. To arrive at a detailed understanding of elephant population dynamics, including social structure, age structure, growth, population size, and mortality and reproductive rates, Laws conducted aerial census surveys and large-scale sampling that involved killing hundreds of elephants. Laws contracted Ian Parker's firm, Wildlife Services Limited, to crop elephants and assist in performing speedy postmortems. Using semiautomatic rifles, Parker and his team could kill a family of ten or more elephants within thirty seconds. Scientific sampling techniques that gathered data on age, sex, and body size of elephants proved a lucrative business, since Parker's company harvested the ivory, meat, and hides for sale (figure 8.1). In a three-month period in 1965, Parker and Laws fine-tuned their sampling techniques, killing 563 elephants in Murchison Falls National Park. Convinced that the methods Laws and Parker had refined were sufficiently efficient and humane, the National Park trustees granted the Nuffield Unit of Tropical Animal Ecology and Wildlife Services Limited a contract to kill a total of 2,000 elephants over the course of the next two years for cropping purposes and scientific investigation.[14] When Laws took up his new post at Tsavo in 1966, he requested and was granted a permit to kill 300 elephants for experimental, scientific purposes. In July of 1967, when he asked to extend that number to 1,800 elephants for simultaneous cropping and scientific research, Sheldrick and the National Park trustees objected. Laws resigned his position, accusing Sheldrick and others of adopting an attitude that was "irrational and entirely based on emotion." "It is sad to consider that the fate of these impressive populations of elephants and other species depends on emotion and politics," he continued, "rather than study, rationale debate, decision, and action."[15]

In the quantitative methods Laws utilized for obtaining knowledge about elephant population dynamics, individuals did not count. This was, in fact, why Laws could move so easily between marine mammals and elephants; his approach was derived foremost from statistical methods in population ecology, where patterns of numbers, rather than a detailed understanding of individual organisms and their behaviors, mattered most. Laws strongly believed numbers offered an "objective scientific approach" to the problem of elephant management, in contrast to the "wooly thinking" of preservationists like Sheldrick. And although Laws's appeal to politicians and the public was far removed from the intimate knowledge of pachyderm personalities for which ethologists like Iain Douglas-Hamilton

8.1 ELEPHANT CULLS OFFERED A METHODOLOGICAL TOOL FOR
COLLECTING STATISTICAL INFORMATION ON THE ANIMALS' SEX, AGE,
AND BODY SIZE. COURTESY OF IAIN DOUGLAS-HAMILTON, ORIA
DOUGLAS-HAMILTON, AND THEIR CHARITABLE ORGANIZATION, SAVE
THE ELEPHANTS.

would become so well known, his approach, grounded in population statistics, nevertheless relied upon an emotional response in winning support
for his views.[16]

The "calculated aesthetic distance" so central to Laws's scientific study
and management of East African elephants found its artistic expression in
the work of Peter Beard.[17] A Yale graduate, Beard followed in the path of
a previous generation of wealthy sportsmen and went to Africa on safari
in search of manhood. He settled in Kenya in the 1960s next to Karen
Blixen's farm, enchanted by the vanishing life in Blixen's *Out of Africa*.
In 1966, his talents as a big-game hunter earned him a place among the
staff of Wildlife Services Limited to assist in the scientific cropping of
elephants in Murchison Falls National Park. In his 1977 edition of *The
End of the Game*, a historical, photographic record of Africa's vanishing wildlife and people first published in 1963, Beard added a haunting
series of photographs and an epilogue by Richard Laws that seemed to
confirm Laws's conviction that the greatest threat to Africa's elephant
populations was not poaching but the increasing population-growth
rates of elephants coupled with habitat destruction. The drought years of
1969 and 1970 in Tsavo resulted in an estimated 6,000 elephants' dying

of starvation and a desert wasteland. Beard's aerial photographs of this death and destruction in Tsavo, on exhibit at the Manhattan International Center for Photography in 1978, haunted viewers not because of their intimacy but because of their detachment. The sheer number of photographs captured a stark, impersonal side to a disaster that was at once natural and manmade, which Beard and Laws hoped would call politicians and the public to action. Like Laws's population statistics, Beard's photographs played upon an aesthetics of detached objectivity meant to enlist public support (figure 8.2). Only culling, Laws believed, could save the elephants.[18] In 1996, in an exhibition of his work in Paris, Beard extended that recommendation to the human race as well. Asked about Africa's current ecological problems, Beard remarked: "Agents of mortality is what we need now. We should be campaigning for smallpox and cancer."[19] In advancing their cause, neither Laws nor Beard adopted ecological or photographic techniques that focused upon intimate, individual portraits. Beard, a regular in New York City's legendary Studio 54 and friend of celebrities such as Mick Jagger and Jackie Onassis, knew well that the camera's intimacy, which he readily put to work as a famed international fashion photographer, would only hinder public support of the elephant-culling operations he and Laws endorsed.

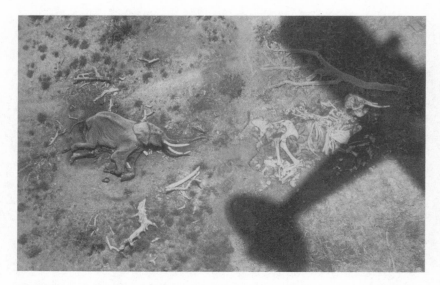

8.2   THE CALCULATED AESTHETIC DISTANCE OF POPULATION ECOLOGY, AIDED BY THE AIRPLANE, FOUND ITS ARTISTIC EXPRESSION IN THE WORK OF PETER BEARD. COURTESY OF PETER BEARD/ART AND COMMERCE ANTHOLOGY.

Douglas-Hamilton pursued his doctoral research amidst this ongoing controversy over the need and merits of scientific culling. The question his work meant to resolve was whether elephants would naturally regulate their population size as they reached the ecosystem's carrying capacity or whether humans would need to intercede. Framed within a debate in population ecology over the significance of density-dependent versus density-independent factors regulating population numbers, and following closely upon the heels of V. C. Wynne-Edwards's book *Animal Dispersion in Relation to Social Behavior*,[20] Douglas-Hamilton's study focused upon elephant social organization in order to determine the influence of social behavior upon population structure and size. Although he used aerial census techniques to arrive at population estimates, Douglas-Hamilton chose as his primary unit of analysis individuals within a population. Only by following individuals and analyzing their behaviors could he arrive at a better understanding of elephant social dynamics. By the time he completed his study in 1972, he could individually recognize and identify 300 elephants in 25 family groups out of an estimated population of 420 elephants in Lake Manyara National Park.

The "calculated aesthetic distance" of Beard's photographs stood in contrast to the intimate elephant portraits Iain Douglas-Hamilton and his wife Oria made as part of a recognition system devised to identify individuals within a family group. Oria, whose cousin Jean de Brunhoff created the children's stories about Babar the elephant, found her skills as a former fashion photographer well-suited to the demands of Iain's field study. Close-up photographs of elephants revealed characteristic features of the ears and tusks that were distinctive enough to serve as reliable markers of individuals (figure 8.3). Although Douglas-Hamilton first resorted to a numbering system, he found that assigning names proved a much more effective mnemonic device for remembering individuals. To my knowledge, his dissertation is the first to be written and published under his adviser Niko Tinbergen that actually referenced animals by personal names instead of numbers.

In naming female elephants—like Boadicea, the queen of the elephant matriarchs in Lake Manyara, named after the fierce ancient British queen who led the Iceni Celts against the conquering Romans in A.D. 61—and in his use of close-up photographs shot with the eye of a former fashion photographer, Douglas-Hamilton foregrounded personality and emotion in his analysis of elephant social life (figure 8.4). Earlier in his life, Niko Tinbergen, Douglas-Hamilton's mentor, had worked arduously to develop an "objectivist study of innate behavior among animals." By the early 1970s, however, Tinbergen suggested that without the "emotional, personal

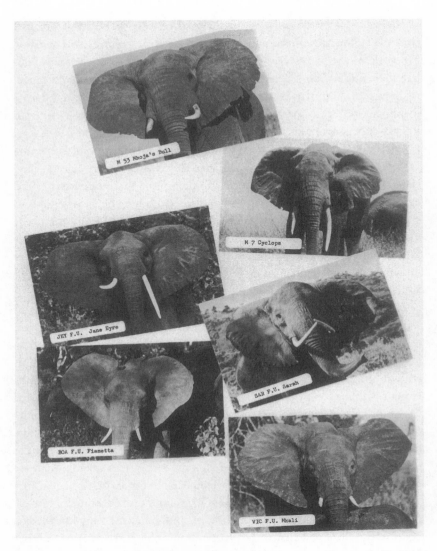

8.3 CLOSE-UP PHOTOGRAPHS OF ELEPHANTS TAKEN BY IAIN AND ORIA DOUGLAS-HAMILTON SERVED AS AN IMPORTANT RECOGNITION SYSTEM FOR BOTH IDENTIFYING INDIVIDUAL ELEPHANTS AND CAPTURING THEIR INDIVIDUALITIES. COURTESY OF IAIN DOUGLAS-HAMILTON, ORIA DOUGLAS-HAMILTON, AND THEIR CHARITABLE ORGANIZATION, SAVE THE ELEPHANTS.

involvement" of Douglas-Hamilton, "no man could have had the perse-verence [sic] to carry out this type of study." Douglas-Hamilton similarly remarked that despite his strict scientific training at Oxford "not to give human interpretations to animal behaviour, it was impossible not to an-thropmorphize." As Tinbergen came to recognize, Douglas-Hamilton's emotional attachment to individual animals was precisely what led him to a detailed understanding of elephant behavior and social life far beyond what any biologist had previously described.[21] His intimate portrait of indi-vidual elephants through both the camera and the pen also made his work appeal more to film and television crews than the work of biologists like Laws, whose quantitative approach to elephant research and conservation did not fit easily into the narrative and visual conventions of the commer-cial media industry.

In his intimate associations with elephants for a period of four and a half years, Douglas-Hamilton found elephant social life to be organized around tightly knit matriarchal family units that had distinct but widely overlap-ping home ranges and would associate in larger kinship groups without any territorial aggression. Note that unlike Richard Laws, the sum total of individuals in Douglas-Hamilton's study resulted in an elephant society, not a population. The prolonged years of dependence, Douglas-Hamilton observed, of calves upon mothers and older siblings led him to believe that elephants displayed a high order of intelligence acquired through learned experience. With one particular female, Virgo, Douglas-Hamilton felt he was on "the brink of an understanding" as she came to greet him with her trunk and a warm gush of air.[22] But crossing the species divide always proved an elusive goal, even as his family lived among the elephants and adopted certain aspects of their way of life. In *The Family that Lives with Elephants*, a half-hour episode of *Suvival* that aired on British television in 1975, for example, Oria Douglas-Hamilton speaks of how "as a mother observing elephants," she became "much more aware of the importance of tactile care, because baby elephants . . . always had a young female who would touch them, put their trunks around them. . . . It was this special tactile care," she observed, "that I was trying to relate to the way I brought up my children because this I thought was important. Just as important as it is for elephants to live close to each other, it was important for us to live close to each other"[23] (see figure 8.5). It is curious, yet perhaps not un-surprising, that an article published in *Psychology Today* in the early 1970s referred to Iain Douglas-Hamilton as an anthropologist. But had elephants become human or had he become elephant? This was always the danger of going native.[24]

8.4   Boadicea, the queen of the elephant matriarchs in Lake
Manyara. Courtesy of Iain Douglas-Hamilton, Oria Douglas-
Hamilton, and their charitable organization, Save the
Elephants.

8.5   CROSSING THE SPECIES DIVIDE. COURTESY OF IAIN DOUGLAS-
HAMILTON, ORIA DOUGLAS-HAMILTON, AND THEIR CHARITABLE
ORGANIZATION, SAVE THE ELEPHANTS.

BATTLE FOR THE ELEPHANTS

*"It seems to me that what you and your husband are doing, count-
ing elephants, is not going to solve the problem. You need proper
people and proper guns."*
    —J. A. MULL, 1981, IN IAIN AND ORIA
    DOUGLAS-HAMILTON, *Battle for the Elephants*

During the 1970s, a second generation of ethologists and behavioral ecologists, who became equally important celebrities in the fight to save the
elephant, furthered the work Iain Douglas-Hamilton had begun. Cynthia
Moss, the guardian of elephant herds in Amboseli National Park, was
first introduced to the study of elephant behavior during eight months
spent with Iain Douglas-Hamilton in the field in 1968. A former theater
reporter for *Newsweek*, she gathered around her a handful of other researchers, including Joyce Poole and Katy Payne, devoted to the study
of elephant social behavior and communication. Through these studies,
which have lent support to the view that elephants are "extremely social, long-lived beings whose intelligence is formed by deep memories

and passions," these researchers have also come to actively defend and promote the moral standing and rights of elephants.[25]

The lives of these researchers have in fact become so enmeshed with those of the elephants that it is sometimes difficult to discern the boundaries between the two. Moss has remarked how "studying elephants is a bit like watching a soap opera," as researchers engage in gossip about their favorite animals. One day the conversation might turn to Lolita's coming into estrus and being chased by "dinky little bulls"; the next day, to Jezebel and who she was seen with. These were not random names but chosen to convey something of individual animal personalities. As for anthropomorphism, Moss and others argue that any such fears are unwarranted. Moss, who adopted Iain Douglas-Hamilton's technique of naming individual female elephants, had little concerns that such names would impose a "person's characteristic on the animal." Instead, Moss remarked that she had the opposite problem. "When I am introduced to a person named Amy or Amelia or Alison, across my mind's eye flashes the head and ears of that elephant." These elephantic associations extended to researchers themselves. M13, a large male bull in Amboseli, for example, became affectionally known as Iain among this tight-knit group of female researchers. Alphanumeric codes, rather than human names, were more commonly used to refer to male elephants, indicating how tangential researchers considered them to be in this matrilineal society.[26]

During the late 1970s and 1980s, Douglas-Hamilton's life did indeed begin to resemble that of the "rogue elephant" Morel, the protagonist in Romain Gary's novel who would do "anything to become an elephant" and launches a crusade in their defense.[27] On the basis of his dissertation research, Douglas-Hamilton concluded that there was no evidence to suggest that elephants would naturally regulate their population size through behavioral mechanisms such as territoriality or aggression as they approached the upper limit of available food supply. The high densities of elephants in Lake Manyara National Park were having a destructive impact on the *Acacia tortilis* woodland, but Douglas-Hamilton strongly opposed the culling measures advocated by Laws because of their impact on the elephants' complex social organization. Instead, he urged the Tanzania National Parks to extend the park's range to the southwest by buying back eighty square kilometers of farmland and establishing access routes to the Marang Forest. When a drought, similar to that which ravaged Tsavo in the early 1970s hit Manyara in 1976, escalating woodland destruction, Douglas-Hamilton reluctantly advised Derek Bryceson, director of Tanzania National Parks, to institute a culling program. He insisted, however, that his study groups in the central and northern regions of the park be left intact. Only elephants in the southern portions of the park, which were recent refugees and thus unknown to Douglas-Hamilton, were to be shot. Although the rains returned the following spring, briefly sparing the Manyara elephants, soaring ivory prices were taking an increased toll on elephant populations across the African continent. Abandoning the cause of the Lake Manyara elephants, Douglas-Hamilton launched a concerted effort on behalf of the entire species.[28]

In moving from the individual to the species, Douglas-Hamilton "regrettably" abandoned his "intimate study of known elephants" and took to the air, compiling the first continental census of African elephants, organized through the International Union for the Conservation of Nature with funds from the New York Zoological Society and the World Wildlife Fund.[29] The distance from his beloved elephants was both literal and figurative. Between 1976 and 1979, using a combination of standardized aerial census techniques and a network of scientific informants, he gathered numbers to arrive at an estimate of 1.3 million elephants remaining in Africa. If the numbers seemed high, Douglas-Hamilton was convinced that they showed an alarming declining trend, precipitated first and foremost in his opinion by poaching and an expanding ivory trade.

His pan-African survey nearly complete, Douglas-Hamilton flew to Washington, D.C., in December 1977 to testify before a congressional committee to debate whether the African elephant should be listed as a threatened or endangered species under the Endangered Species Act, effectively banning U.S. imports of ivory and other elephant products. The committee also faced the question of whether the United States should petition member countries of the Convention on International Trade in Endangered Species of Wild Flora and Fauna to raise the status of the African elephant from appendix II to appendix I, which would severely restrict the worldwide ivory trade. Two years later, he returned, this time to testify on behalf of a bill introduced to Congress to provide for the control of the import and export of elephants and elephant products into and out of the United States.

Minnesota Representative James Oberstar succinctly captured the protocol of science in the legislative arena when he remarked to Douglas-Hamilton: "It must be quite a contrast to sit here in the rather arid committee hearing room discussing the fate of the elephants, among whom you have lived for such a time, and with whom you had such a close relationship being able virtually to talk to them. I cite the contrast between the enormous study you have done and the relationship you had in the world of animals with the way we are trying to protect them in this legislation."[30] Oberstar was referring to the reams of reports grounded in statistics of elephant population sizes, densities, and ivory sales and trade that formed the basis of hearing testimonies, including those of Douglas-Hamilton. But it was not numbers but a concern for individual elephants that motivated the public, who sent 4,000 letters to the committee chairman in support of House Bill 4685. This was the subtext of Oberstar's remark. Oberstar knew and respected Douglas-Hamilton not because of his census but because he was a charismatic ethologist, featured on television, in the pages of *National Geographic*, and in his best-selling book as the man who lived with elephants. Within the committee hearing room, however, the only scientific game in town in the late 1970s was statistics. To resort to anything but a "numbers game," Douglas-Hamilton would have appeared more like a diplomat sent on behalf of the elephants than a credible scientific witness.[31] Only on rare occasions did the testimony appeal to the mental and emotional life of elephants. In 400 pages of congressional hearings, the only explicit reference to elephants as individual beings came from Christine Stevens, founder of the Animal Welfare Institute, who lamented that in the hearings so little was heard about "the elephants themselves." Ten years later, the playing field would look quite different.[32]

Douglas-Hamilton played the numbers game and lost. House Bill 4685 was defeated. More devastating, however, was the lack of support for his million-dollar Elephant Action Plan and the questioning of his census figures at the first full meeting in 1981 of the IUCN's African Elephant Specialist Group, which Douglas-Hamilton cochaired. To Douglas-Hamilton's surprise and dismay, Ian Parker, contracted by the Elephant Specialist Group to provide an economic and statistical analysis of the ivory trade, launched a vociferous attack on the pan-African survey and suggested that the ivory crisis had been completely fabricated by Douglas-Hamilton. According to Parker's calculations, the African elephant faced no threat of extinction and the ivory trade was operating within sustainable limits.[33] As the tide turned in Parker's favor, Douglas-Hamilton lost his chairmanship of the African Elephant Specialist Group. Determined to take "real action," he headed for Uganda to save the remnant elephant population in Murchison Falls National Park from extinction.[34] Armed with G3 and AK-47 automatic rifles rather than numbers, he organized a paramilitary operation to protect the 160 elephants left after the fall of Idi Amin's brutal regime and threatened by the outbreak of violence that ensued.

CONCLUSION

In 1987, at a meeting of the IUCN African Elephant and Rhino Specialist Group in Nyeri, Douglas-Hamilton found scientific opinion turning once again in his favor. Successor to the African Elephant Specialist Group, the

AERSG had commissioned in the mid-1980s, under David Western's chairmanship, a census of forest-elephant populations in the Congo Basin. Accurate estimates of forest-elephant populations had proven difficult, and Western, an ecosystem ecologist and prominent leader in international conservation circles, believed such numbers held the key to knowing whether Douglas-Hamilton's predictions about an impending crisis were warranted. In addition to Douglas-Hamilton, Western also appointed Cynthia Moss to the AERSG. Moss's appointment was significant, since she represented another "champion of elephants as individuals" on the committee, in contrast to members like Western, for whom only numbers provided a "watertight scientific case." When the AERSG met in Nyeri, they were armed with new estimates at the population size of Africa's forest elephants, which put the total African elephant population at around 800,000, well below the maximum sustainable yield of the world ivory trade. A scientific consensus emerged at the AERSG meeting that the rapid decline in the population of the African elephant was due, in large part, to the ivory trade.[35]

Western attributes the scientific consensus among members of the AERSG to the incontrovertible estimates of forest-elephant populations. Douglas-Hamilton, Moss, Poole, and others at the meeting whose scientific studies approached elephants as individuals have a different perspective. Poole's presentation at the AERSG referred little to population dynamics or the ivory trade. Instead it focused on the complex social life and communication found among the elephants of Amboseli National Park and their moral status. After the AERSG meeting, Douglas-Hamilton, Moss, Payne, and Poole banded together to launch a public outreach campaign to generate a groundswell of support to raise the status of the elephant from appendix II to appendix I at the upcoming 1989 Convention on International Trade in Endangered Species meeting in Lausanne, Switzerland.

In viewing elephants as individuals, Douglas-Hamilton, Moss, Payne, and Poole forged a critical alliance with animal rights groups and the media, outside the traditional network of scientists and international environmental organizations. Moss's hugely successful 1988 book *Elephant Memories* did much to promote pachyderm personalities and instill in the public a belief in their moral rights. Moss convinced the African Wildlife Foundation, a small, 24,000-member conservation group, to launch an advertising campaign in the spring of 1988 denouncing the ivory trade and alerting the public to its impact on elephants. One year later, it stepped up its efforts with a full-page ad in the Sunday *New York Times*, which featured Joyce Poole's photograph of a poached elephant with its face hacked off. The Douglas-Hamilton's Boadicea also became a featured celebrity in the ad campaign aimed to dissuade the public from buying ivory. Christine

Stevens, who was at the Washington center of the "Humaniacs," the derogatory label environmental groups like the World Wildlife Fund (WWF) commonly use to refer to animal rights organizations, helped organize the Humane Society, Friends of Animals, and the Animal Welfare Institute in their filing a petition with the Interior Department in the spring of 1989 to have the elephant declared an endangered species.[36] Ten years before, Douglas-Hamilton had grounded his case in statistics and aligned himself with established international environmental organizations like the WWF. But as the Humaniacs were quickly stealing the thunder from these groups over a worldwide ivory ban, Douglas-Hamilton found that his ethological and behavioral studies of individual elephants were far more compelling to powerful lobby groups and media organizations inside and outside of Washington than the methods of population ecologists. When CITES convened at Lausserne, Switzerland, in October of 1989, the moral rights of elephants were explicitly on the agenda for the first time.

Since the 1989 CITES convention, Douglas-Hamilton and Moss have traded upon their personalities and that of their elephants, as well as their photographic techniques, in enlisting the support of PBS, the BBC, the Discovery Channel, and Chivas Regal, to name a few, in funding and promoting their research and conservation efforts. The Discovery Channel's Web site for "Africa's Elephant Kingdom," for example, contains direct links to Iain Douglas-Hamilton's organization, Save the Elephants, where viewers can follow, thanks to the GPS, the movements of particular elephants accompanied by film clips of some featured elephant celebrities, like Esidai, and send in a contribution to help her cause. At Scirocco House, Oria's family estate on the shores of Lake Naivasha, wealthy tourists can dine with these Discovery Channel celebrities, lodge in one of their guest houses, and go on an elephant-watching safari. They can also pay homage to the legendary star Boadicaea, the grand matriarch of Manyara, whose skull sits on the veranda, staring toward Mount Longonot. In the fall of 2001, frequenters of eBay could bid for an exclusive five-day safari with the Douglas-Hamiltons that included a stay at their home and a trip to the Samburu Elephant Camp. Among the other events included in the Chivas 200 charity auction: a seven-day Tanzania safari that included a two-day visit with chimpanzee celebrity Jane Goodall at the celebrated Gombe reserve and a dinner with model and film star Charlize Theron that went for £26,300. A click on *Nature*'s Web site for Cynthia Moss's film *The Elephants of Africa* takes you through a series of hyperlinks into a host of organizations, including the Africa Wildlife Foundation and Moss's activist organization, the African Elephant Conservation Trust, where viewers can subscribe to receive recent news about the Amboseli elephants and contribute to their survival.[37]

Once on the fringes of traditional networks of power within science and conservation, Douglas-Hamilton and Moss have become powerful forces in the world of elephant conservation and research. Their success suggests the manifold ways that media networks have become an instrumental part of doing science. In the case of elephants, the research methods and techniques of ethologists, unlike population ecologists, are calibrated closely with the aesthetics and conventions of fashion photography, television, and film. Trading upon intimacy, individuals, and emotions, scientist-activists like Douglas-Hamilton and Moss have found themselves and the elephants they live with active participants in and beneficiaries of celebrity culture. We should not view this as an isolated incident of the media's powerful foothold in shaping the practice and vision of science. In media-chic fields like primatology, paleontology, and oceanography, the cultures of science and commercial media are rapidly converging. Recently, Discovery Communications, the parent company of the Discovery Channel, the Learning Channel, Animal Planet, and ten other networks provided the funding for Montana State University to launch the first MFA program of its kind in science and natural-history filmmaking. Hoping to recruit prospective filmmakers with degrees in science, the program is designed to train filmmakers "who walk the walk and talk the talk" of science.[38] And media giants like Discovery Communications are as likely to be on the list of contributors as the National Science Foundation in fostering and promoting research in certain fields. The most recent Discovery Channel/BBC epic series, *The Blue Planet*, for example, surpasses the great natural-history museum expeditions of the early twentieth century in publicity, personnel, and patronage. While few scientists have yet to worry about the paparazzi, the star-struck world of television and film are nevertheless transforming research practices and careers, as well as the subjects and sites of scientific research.[39]

NOTES

1. http://elephant.discovery.com/behind/notes.html.

2. http://elephant.discovery.com/behind/behind.html.

3. http://webcast.ucsd.edu:8080/ramgen/UCSD_TV/4618/Guestbook_DouglasHamilt.rm.

4. David L. Andrews and Steven J. Jackson, eds., *Sport Stars: The Cultural Politics of Sporting Celebrity* (London: Routledge, 2001), 3.

5. On the rise of celebrity culture and the importance of film and television technologies, see Jib Fowles, *Star Struck: Celebrity Performers and the American Public* (Washington, D.C.: Smithsonian Institution Press, 1992).

6. On the history of mechanical objectivity, see Lorraine Daston and Peter Galison, "The Image of Objectivity," *Representations* 40 (1992): 81–128; Theodore M. Porter, *Trust in Numbers: The Pursuit of Objectivity in Science and Public Life* (Princeton, N.J.: Princeton University Press, 1995).

7. Gregory Bateson, "Metalogue: What is an Instinct?" in *Approaches to Animal Communication*, ed. Thomas A. Sebeok and Alexandra Ramsay (The Hague: Mouton, 1969), 20.

8. Donald Griffin, *Animal Minds* (Chicago: University of Chicago Press, 1992), 234. On mechanomorphism and classical ethology, see Eileen Crist, *Images of Animals: Anthropomorphism and Animal Mind* (Philadelphia: Temple University Press, 1999).

9. Andews and Jackson, eds., *Sport Stars*, 4.

10. George Schaller, *The Year of the Gorilla* (Chicago: University of Chicago Press, 1964), 176. Sarah Blaffer Hrdy notes that it was through her identification of and with individual female primates that traditional scientific theories about female monogamy were overturned. See, Sarah B. Hrdy, *The Woman That Never Evolved* (Cambridge, Mass.: Harvard University Press, 1981). On the place of individuals in naturalistic field studies and popular natural history, see Gregg Mitman, "Life in the Field: The Sensuous Body as Popular Naturalist's Guide," in *Primate Encounters: Models of Science, Gender, and Society*, ed. Shirley C. Strum and Linda Marie Fedigan (Chicago: University of Chicago Press, 2000), 421–35.

11. Iain Douglas-Hamilton, "On the Ecology and Behavior of the African Elephant," Ph.D. diss., Oxford University, 1972.

12. R. M. Watson and M. I. M. Turner, "A Count of the Large Mammals of the Lake Manyara National Park: Results and Discussion," *East African Wildlife Journal* 3 (1965): 95–98.

13. Daphne Sheldrick, *The Tsavo Story* (London: Collins and Harvill Press, 1973), 113. Also see Daniel B. Botkin, *Discordant Harmonies* (New York: Oxford University Press, 1990), 15–26; Christopher Campbell, "A Place for Elephants: Science, Sentiment, and Local Knowledge," master's thesis, University of Oklahoma, 1999.

14. R. M. Law, I. S. C. Parker, and R. C. B. Johnstone, *Elephants and Their Habitats: The Ecology of Elephants in North Bunyoro, Uganda* (Oxford: Clarendon Press, 1975); S. K. Eltringham, "The Work of the Nuffield Unit of Tropical Animal Ecology in the Uganda National Parks," *J. Reproduction and Fertility, Supplemental* 6 (1969): 483–86.

15. R. M. Laws, "Elephants and Men in East Africa" (lecture, University of Saskatchewan, 23 October 1969), 5–6. Also see R. M. Laws, "The Tsavo Research Project," *J. Reprod. Fert. Suppl.* 6 (1969): 495–531.

16. Laws, "Elephants and Men in East Africa," 18.

17. Congress, House Subcommittee on Fisheries and Wildlife Conservation and the Environment and the Committee on Merchant Marine and Fisheries, *African Elephants—December 13, 1977: Hearings Before the Subcommittee on Fisheries and Wildlife Conservation and the Environment and the Committee on Merchant Marine and Fisheries*, 95 Cong., 1977, serial no. 95–50, 159.

18. Peter H. Beard, *The End of the Game* (New York: Doubleday, 1977).

19. http://www.cnn.com/WORLD/9611/09/african.photog.

20. V. C. Wynne-Edwards, *Animal Dispersion in Relation to Social Behavior* (Edinburgh; Oliver and Boyd, 1962).

21. Douglas-Hamilton, *Among the Elephants*, 15, 44.

22. Iain Douglas-Hamilton and Oria Douglas-Hamilton, *Battle for the Elephants* (New York: Viking, 1992), 27.

23. "The Family That Lives with Elephants," *Survival*, Anglia/Survival, 1975.

24. Jack C. Horn, "Unforgettable Elephants," *Psychology Today* (April 1977): 88.

25. Katy Payne, "Caring Beasts . . . ," *Washington Post*, 8 April 2000. See, for example, Cynthia Moss, *Elephant Memories: Thirteen Years in the Life of an Elephant Family* (New York: William Morrow, 1988); Cynthia Moss, *Echo of the Elephants: The Story of an Elephant Family* (New York: William Morrow, 1992); Katy Payne, *Silent Thunder: In the Presence of Elephants* (New York: Simon & Schuster, 1998); Joyce Poole, *Coming of Age with Elephants* (New York: Hyperion, 1996).

26. Moss, *Elephant Memories*, 139, 37.

27. Romain Gary, *The Roots of Heaven* (New York: Simon and Schuster, 1958), 6, 37.

28. Even in his doctoral thesis, published in 1972, Douglas-Hamilton recommended that if in the future a culling program was established in Lake Manyara National Park, the northern and central clans should be left untouched. Douglas-Hamilton, "On the Ecology and Behavior of the African Elephant," 215–16.

29. Congress, House Subcommittee on Fisheries and Wildlife Conservation and the Environment and the Committee on Merchant Marine and Fisheries, *African Elephants—December 13, 1977*, 38.

30. Congress, House Committee on Merchant Marine and Fisheries, *Elephants: Hearings*, 96 Cong., serial no. 96–13, 76.

31. Douglas-Hamilton and Douglas-Hamilton, *Battle for the Elephants*, 251.

32. Congress, House Committee on Merchant Marine and Fisheries, *Elephants: Hearings*, 96 Cong., 234.

33. Ian Parker and Mohamed Amin, *Ivory Crisis* (London: The Hogarth Press, 1983).

34. Douglas-Hamilton and Douglas-Hamilton, *Battle for the Elephants*, 187.

35. Douglas-Hamilton and Douglas-Hamilton, *Battle for the Elephants*, 250. David Western, *In the Dust of Kilimanjaro* (Washington, D.C.: Island Press, 1997), 197.

36. On the ad campaign, see Raymond Bonner, *At the Hand of Man: Peril and Hope for Africa's Wildlife* (New York: Alfred A. Knopf, 1993), 117–21; Douglas-Hamilton and Douglas-Hamilton, *Battle for the Elephants*, 329–30.

37. http://elephant.discovery.com; http://www.pbs.org/wnet/nature/elephants/index.html; http://www.elephanttrust.org/; http://www.pbs.org/wnet/nature/echo/index.html.

38. http://naturefilm.montana.edu/pifaq.htm.

39. Other fields that I think would be fruitful to explore include paleontology, primatology, and oceanography, each of which has close links to commercial media in both the funding and promotion of research.

· · · · · · · · ·

CHAPTER 9

Reflections on Anthropomorphism in
The Disenchanted Forest

· · · · · · · · ·

Sarita Siegel

The Disenchanted Forest is a documentary film that I made in 2002, broadcast to over 250 countries worldwide on standard and satellite television via National Geographic International and National Geographic US. The film takes viewers on a journey chronicling the rehabilitation of formerly captive orangutans in Indonesian Borneo. The film explores the drama, knowledge, and wonderment embodied in interactions between human and nonhuman species. Audiences are transported deep into the Bornean rainforest where Dr. Anne Russon has studied orangutan intelligence and psychology for fourteen years. Dr. Russon understands intimately how infant orangutans suffer at the hands of the illegal pet trade. Taken from the forest, these orphaned orangutans are forced into a human world during crucial developmental years, far removed from the physical and social environment of their kin. Anne Russon's research provides vital information for Dr. Willie Smits, director of The Wanariset Orangutan Reintroduction Project, an organization committed to preserving orangutan habitat and helping orphaned orangutans relearn the skills they need to survive in the protected forests of Borneo. *The Disenchanted Forest* brings viewers inside the world of formerly captive orangutans and the complex problems they face in regaining forest lives after living in human captivity.

Film is a medium of the arts and humanities, yet it also exists to communicate information to audiences across broad cultural, social, and age groups. Knowing I intended to place my documentary on the international satellite and cable broadcast market, I had to "hook" audiences by appealing to universal human experiences. Carefully crafted scenes that combine

9.1   ANNE RUSSON AND SITI. PHOTO BY SARITA SIEGEL.

video images and interviews in meaningful ways bring audiences into the world of orangutans and imbue the film with subjectivity, emotionality, and wonderment. Strong human and animal characters establish an emotional identification with the audience. Anthropomorphic metaphors, anecdotes, and analogies are extremely useful when combining image and narration as a means of portraying complex orangutan "personalities," who might otherwise be seen as unremarkable when viewed by an audience untrained in observing such complex creatures. In this way, the unique cross-species interface in orangutan research and rehabilitation unfolds as an accessible story in a global television marketplace.

During the filming and production of *The Disenchanted Forest*, I found it impossible as a filmmaker not to be anthropomorphic in how I perceived the orangutans and how I depicted them in my film. Aware that it would be ridiculous to impress the conscious "personality" of humankind upon a community of orangutans, I carefully used anthropomorphism in my documentary as a tool of communication and comparison rather than making explicit claims or dangerous and incorrect implications that the orangutan subjects are "just like us." In this way, beneath the surface of the story, the orangutan characters can be appreciated as universal figures in a parable that reveals a disquieting message of a survival and struggle within an altered and degrading world. The following essay offers the reader a close-up, personal look into the worlds of orangutans and natural-history filmmaking, exploring the role anthropomorphism plays in the filmmaker's craft.

The making of a film has three main stages. The first stage is preproduction, when the idea is developed and shoots are scheduled and prepared for. The production period follows, when shoots are undertaken. Postproduction is the final stage, when footage is edited, color corrected, and sound work is undertaken in readiness for delivery to a broadcaster or distributor.

Through all of these phases the film is in a state of becoming, and many factors can influence the final product. The story and the themes in *The Disenchanted Forest* grew in complexity with every stage of the process. My initial intention was to make a film about the threats to orangutans and their habitat. When I first conceived of this project, I was heavily influenced by the dangers that threaten orangutan survival. I was inspired to make the film by viewing news footage of singed orangutans huddled together in charred landscapes as Borneo's 1997 forest fires raged out of control. Because these images of orangutans suffering like human refugees affected me so deeply, I imagined that anthropomorphic association would be a useful dramatic tool in conveying their story to a wider audience.

In the initial stage of writing proposals for funding and eliciting interest from television broadcasters, anthropomorphic language was of immense value. Film proposals must be written with colorful and enhanced language that evokes the potential of a film before it has been shot. Many months of research and writing are put into authoring a proposal that will allow funding bodies and broadcast committees to visualize the film and be moved emotionally. Filmmakers must build a sense of drama in proposals to inspire confidence that the film they intend to make is something audiences will want to see. I naively assumed that a seemingly innate human fascination with great apes would mean that orangutan rehabilitation would be a popular subject for audiences. I was surprised to learn otherwise. One broadcast corporation informed me that great apes were a "hard sell" to television audiences. Undeterred, I moved ahead with the first interviews and production shoots without any broadcast commitment. Throughout the subsequent months, I traveled into the world of orangutans in Borneo, during which, my simple concept of a film on orangutan conservation developed into something much more layered, complex, and urgent.

PRODUCTION OF THE DOCUMENTARY

The proliferation of nature films on cable television and the lack of control that scientists have in the final products has frightened some primatologists away from interfacing with the media. Natural-history films are sometimes criticized as simplistic evangelical endeavors that focus on favored animals to prove that these animals have feelings and purpose. Distortions of science do indeed occur when interviews and footage of primates are filtered through broadcast committees who transform documentary films to suit their own corporate political and social agendas.

Aware of the fact that Anne Russon might be hesitant to involve herself in a documentary production, I contacted her and arranged our first meeting. In my first interview with Russon, I was surprised to hear her speech was peppered with anthropomorphic language. It was clear that orangutans' similarity to humans needed to be acknowledged and used as a comparative tool rather than treated as something to sneer at or disregard. Russon finds it natural and effective to discuss orangutans using anthropomorphic semantics. Anne refers to the juveniles as the "little guys." A large male brachiating through the trees is likened to "a slow motion ballet" and orangutans are "incredible chefs" when describing their dexterity in food processing. In a candid interview, Anne describes herself noting "that an orangutan is happy, or depressed, that an orangutan made a joke, or is not motivated today" (Russon 1998).

As a general rule in her teaching life, Russon projects human attributes onto the orangutans for descriptive purposes that recognize the recent evolutionary roots of primate and human behavior. H. Lyn Miles articulates the position that anthropomorphism and anecdotes told by researchers can "illuminate the science rather than fabricate it" (Miles 1997). As a filmmaker seeking to make a film that would resonate with human audiences, I saw no reason not to follow her example and use anthropomorphic and anecdotal comparisons as a communication tool.

I was pleased to discover that anthropomorphic associations and metaphors were increasingly acceptable in primatology. I was particularly amused when Anne enhanced her stories about the orangutans and their activities by using allusions to human fables or popular literature. One of her favorite references was to William Golding's book *Lord of the Flies* when speaking of the strange rehabilitant orangutan communities that have developed in the forest, as the juvenile and adolescent orphans struggled to learn to sustain themselves independently of human aid. Once I had spent a little time in the rainforest at the rehabilitation site, I decided this comparison was remarkably apt. The group of orphans had very little forest knowledge and did things that orangutans who grew up in the rainforest never would. Former captives are often seen walking on the ground upright, falling out of trees, and walking past foods that they should know are edible. Bento is the "child king" of that community—at the tender age of ten, the oldest and most knowledgeable of the rehabilitated orangutans.

I did not want the interpretation of this allusion to *Lord of the Flies* to be too literal or detailed, fearing that it would limit the audiences' perception of the orangutan community. During the script-writing phase, my editor at *National Geographic* was excited by the allusions to the book. However, she also questioned my use of "child king," knowing that Jack, the red headed "chieftain" in Golding's novel, had become a savage despot. We were careful not to imply that Bento might become deluded. Such a literal projection would have overshadowed the unique attributes and struggles of individual orangutans that I had come to know. I was not prepared to make specific connections between human nature in the absence of order and authority and that of a community of juvenile orangutans, although I probably could have. Most primates live in highly structured societies, and the loss or absence of group members with powerful social positions can open the door to similar aberrations. The comparison remained in the script, but it was used only vaguely.

Prior to beginning this film, I thought human and great ape differences might be highlighted in order to achieve objectivity in scientific discourse. However, in the post-Darwinian era primatology has transformed its focus, practice, and basic premise. With the acceptance of our close relation to great apes, primate studies are now closely tied to the promise of furthering our understanding of human evolution. The contemplation of an animal mind is now widely discussed in animal-behavior research. Inquiries often focus on the specific definition of the thought processes that animals use to handle information and how these might be compared to human thought (Byrne 2000, 300). In the search for research paradigms to compare and articulate great ape cognition and behavior, there is increasing selective use of human psychological models. In particular, the Piagetian framework, which outlines a progressive series of steps of mental development that are interlinked and cumulative, is now used in the analysis of observational data that primatologists collect in their fieldwork. (Byrne 2000)

Anne Russon explains how anthropomorphic comparisons function to articulate her analysis of orangutan thought processes:

> We cannot assume that how we think is necessarily how orangutans think, because they live in a world that is very different to our own. But, if you work on the premise that to predict how species will behave, the smart thing to do is to assume that it will behave like other species that it most resembles. Based on how closely the non-human great apes are related to other living species genealogically, in terms of how recently they shared a common ancestor with other species, they are more closely related to humans than they are to any non-human

species. On that basis, for the great apes, the proper assumption is anthropomorphism. Part of the reason I like to do it [anthropomorphize] is that it suggests you might look a little differently at them. Rather than saying it's just an animal out there, if you instead make the comment that Bento is having a nice time looking at the sunset, that credits him with more consciousness than saying he was just sitting there waving his legs around. (Russon 1999a)

Anthropomorphic interpretation and individual incidents are colorful and effective ways of describing her orangutan subjects' behavior. In the field of primate cognition and psychology, they become particularly useful devices when scientists speak about their work to a broad public audience.

I was particularly influenced by the identification of the mental similarities between humans and great apes and used this concept to expand and strengthen my film's narrative. Historically, humans have been fascinated with great apes as "higher" thinkers. Orangutans are among the most intelligent primates and are often described as mechanical geniuses and the most cerebral of all the great apes (Russon 2000a). Eager to weave themes of intelligence and psychology into the documentary, I pursued Dr. Anne Russon, Dr. Carey Yeager, and Dr. Carel van Schaik to fully understand the implications of captivity and rehabilitation on orangutan mental development.

"Culture" emerged from these discussions on cognition and mental development with my scientific consultants as a dominant theme. Culture has been perceived as a uniquely human capacity that allows us to accumulate knowledge and share it socially (Russon 1999a). It is becoming increasingly accepted that humans share "culture" with all of the great apes and, indeed, with many nonhuman species. Orangutans learn the skills for surviving in their habitat from elders and peers. Information is passed communicatively from one individual to another, with fairly complex relationships and cognitive or intellectual abilities behind that communication (Russon 1999a). The themes of culture, cognition, and psychological development were interwoven during the film's editing to illustrate the complexity of the challenges faced during the process of rehabilitating formerly captive orangutans.

As culture, cognition, and individual psychology are so closely related to the human experience, anthropomorphic associations are naturally embedded in the film's narrative to communicate the magnitude and complexity of orangutan thought processes. Wherever possible in the script and interviews, I used anecdotes and comparisons that connected with the human experiences of loss of culture. Audiences see a lonely orangutan infant in diapers on a medical table, clenching its fist in a state of stress and possible despair. This image is made more effective by Anne Russon's voice-over description of the captive process. She compares the destruction of the fragile cultural systems that the infants rely upon in the forest to the shattering of Humpty Dumpty (Russon 2000b). The script of *The Disenchanted Forest* developed some parallels with human stories of displaced peoples and cultural loss.

In the cultural vacuum that is created for orangutan orphans removed from their forest lives, it is not surprising to see them engage in the human cultural world that is available to them in captivity. I observed numerous infant and juvenile orangutans in the throes of transforming into "little people" as they spent their formative years imitating humans. Carel van Schaik describes their state of mind as "psychologically feeling like they are humans" (Van Schaik 2000). On occasion, captive orangutans confiscated by the Ministry of Forestry of Indonesia have been removed from the breasts of women who were nursing them as their own. These orangutan infants are surrogate babies for women who cannot have children. These captives are acculturated to a human world rather than an orangutan world. Russon tells a story of one orangutan, after being returned to the forest, who was visited every birthday by his human "mother" and presented with a birthday cake. Judi, an adolescent female who had been reared by a military man, was another orangutan who existed in the borderland between human and primate. Judi smoked cigarettes and for years after she had been released into the forest would pilfer cigarettes off forestry staff. Another orangutan female had been brought up in a convent and had an ascetic demeanor. She had learned to pray and regularly avoided men. The use of orangutans as infantile actors for selfishly devised roles in human families brings intelligent but compliant young animals into an alien human world. This process is degrading and can ultimately be dangerous, when once harmless infants inevitably develop into full-grown cheek-pad males.

It was clear to me that I would have to make some difficult choices in the depiction of orangutans who were living heavily anthropomorphized lives. It is hugely appealing for audiences to see humanlike behavior, antics, and attributes. However, I made a principled choice to accompany scenes of overtly anthropomorphized orangutans with bits of narration and interviews explaining the dangers of indulging in this form of oversimplified entertainment. My most memorable example of standing on such a principle was in the portrayal of Camp Leakey's inhabitants.

In 1998 I traveled to the traditional research and rehabilitation site at Camp Leakey with a cameraperson to film reintroduced orangutans. We traveled into Tanjung Puting National Park by boat up the Sekonyer River, which swirled with muddy toxic effluvia that flowed downstream from an

9.2   CAMP LEAKEY. PHOTO BY SARITA SIEGEL.

illegal gold mine. After turning up a clear, tea-colored tributary, we arrived at Camp Leakey's dock. All Camp Leakey's orangutan residents have
names, reputations, and thoroughly documented lives. As we disembarked
at the dock we were met by Princess, the most famous of Camp Leakey's
overtly anthropomorphized orangutans. Princess, the red queen in this
wonderland of wiry-coated former captives, escorted us up the ironwood
causeway to the cluster of rickety cabins that is the camp.

Anne describes being at Camp Leakey as "like being in the bar scene in
Star Wars" (Russon 1999a). This colorful, twentieth-century, western analogy
perfectly describes a place "where humans and exiled forest creatures live together in a sketchy 'no-mans' land, somewhere between human and natural
worlds" (Haraway 1989,132). Princess passed her days interacting with ecotourists in Ameslan (American sign language), washing pots and pans, or she
might be found at the dock helping wash laundry or taking a ride in a camp
canoe. Kusasi, a huge, cheek-padded male, sulked like a child in his hideout
under the camp canteen. We filmed a young female, Melli, lathering up and
washing her hair. In the final edit, a female orangutan smiles a wide foamy
grin while she vigorously brushes her teeth. This was a truly startling introduction to a species that sits with ease at the edge of being almost human.

In the days we spent filming at traditional rehabilitation sites like Camp Leakey, it was immediately clear that allowing former captives to continue living acculturated human lives did not provide a useful remedy for orangutans whose lives had been severely disabled by captivity. Traditional rehabilitation wrongly assumes that former captives will automatically return to forest lives of their own volition. Meanwhile, daily picnics are held at the edge of the mysterious forest. Attended by forest rangers and camera-toting ecotourists, Camp Leakey's orangutans converge in a clearing to eat rice and bananas. These orangutans easily choose human culture instead of a return to forest lives. "Human handouts are far easier to obtain than learning to balance on a branch in the canopy to extract pulp out of a particularly difficult fruit. It is not surprising that ex-captives became hangers on, moochers and thieves, who continue to live in purgatory between human and natural worlds" (Russon 1999a). One orangutan that we filmed at Tanjung Harapan stepped so far into the human world that it cost him his life. Gistok was so used to human company and food provisioning that he was killed while breaking into the kitchen of a logging camp in search of a favorite food. The frightened loggers apparently hacked him to death.

Stations such as Camp Leakey now languish as vestiges of the old way of rehabilitation. Many of Camp Leakey's former captives were never restored to free forest lives. Rehabilitant females are unable to pass on forest skills to their offspring, creating what amounts to a welfare state for orangutans, with second-generation, third-generation, and potentially fourth-generation rehabilitants (Yeager 1999). The rehabilitants at Camp Leakey have been sacrificed as "ambassadors" for the remaining populations of wild-born orangutans. Their value as ambassadors lies in raising awareness about conservation issues. Unknowingly, they perform "ambassadorial duties" when they engage in amusing and endearing anthropomorphic activities that entertain ecotourists. These images appear regularly in the media to convince general audiences of high-level orangutan intelligence. Complex, humanlike intelligence elicits empathy in audiences, who are then more likely to be interested in and educated about the threats to the species. Thus, time and money spent on rehabilitation and the conservation of the species is largely justified in the public domain.

However, one cannot help but wonder how much Camp Leakey's overtly anthropomorphized orangutans really contribute to meaningful communication between the species. Orangutans transformed into little "people" offer few insights into the orangutan worldview. To understand orangutan cognition and behavior and come closer to "thinking with orangutans" or viewing the world from the other's point of view, we would do better to study orangutans who are at ease with a human presence but have regained their own forest culture. For this reason, in *The Disenchanted Forest* I portrayed the overt anthropomorphism of traditional rehabilitation as a demeaning and debilitating spectacle, where orangutans strut and fret like human actors on the doorstep of their natural forest world.

On returning to Borneo the following year, I went directly to Wanariset Orangutan Reintroduction Project. With the voracious pet trade in Indonesia, it is becoming increasingly dangerous and difficult to rescue orphaned orangutans. Teams of forestry police confiscate infant orangutans from desperate conditions in animal markets or find them packed into overcrowded airline crates for transport to foreign countries. The "lucky" ones live pampered lives as surrogate children in wealthy private homes.

In recent years rehabilitation programs have gone through a period of remodeling, fueled by the knowledge that orangutans fare better when efforts are made to encourage them back into their own cultural world. Willie Smit's Wanariset Project was returning unprecedented numbers of orphans to free forest lives. To date, more than 800 captive orangutans have been accepted at Wanariset, where they undergo a lengthy process of reenculturation back into an orangutan way of life.

On our first day at Wanariset we filmed the arrival of six newly confiscated orangutans. Frightened and exhausted, they huddled together in the shadows of the transport crates after the long journey from the distant town of Palangkaraya. Coaxed into the arms of Wanariset's technicians, the orphans were swiftly put through the necessary medical checks, finishing with a compulsory stint in quarantine. The technicians' encouraging voices accompanied by gentle touching and holding made the medical checks more bearable for the tired and traumatized orangutans.

Orangutans suffer many of the same problems as humans when they are socially or psychologically abused. The effect of being torn from the body of the mother orangutan when she is shot from the trees can be a debilitating long-term emotional scar. It is very difficult for rehabilitation to mimic the natural situation where orangutan infants instinctively cling to their mother in the early years of life. However, at Wanariset human surrogate mothers carry traumatized infants for weeks to try to recreate the mother-infant bond that was lost when they were taken from the forest. The young women portrayed in the film have remarkably patient and empathic natures and are forging remarkable bonds in the fluid borderland between human and animal. Although this relationship is anthropomorphized, I decided to portray it positively in the film because it does not generate misunderstanding and the relationship enhances the infants' development. The audience's own sense of nurturing is brought out by watching young women caring for orangutan infants as they might care for their own children. It is also

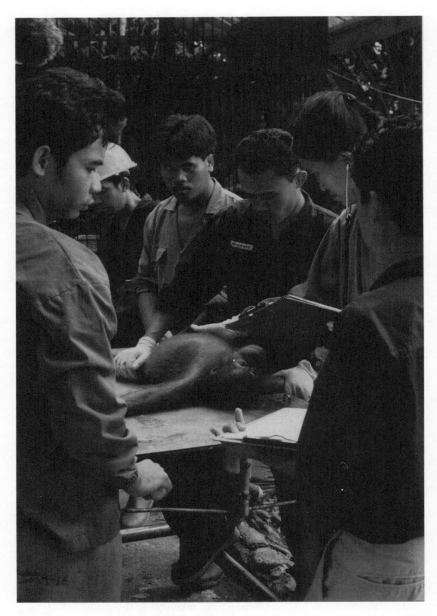

9.3   WANARISET MEDICAL CHECKS. PHOTO BY SARITA SIEGEL.

an appealing portrayal of an irresistible cross-species relationship between the orangutan babies and their female human caretakers. For the infants, these weeks of care and comfort are the last opportunity to take part in a human social world. Independence is encouraged with the more confident infants, and they are soon put into socialization cages with their peers. The large cages at Wanariset were overflowing with orphans, and all of them were greedy for attention and activity.

The human-orangutan relationship continues in a positive way at Wanariset. Although handling and human interaction become less available, humans continue to be effective teachers for the orphans. Being a cultural species, captive orangutans readily imitate human teachers or models. In one scene, Willie Smit demonstrates to young orangutans how to eat a leaf. Lined up along a log, they watch Smits closely and immediately imitate him. In this way they are regaining lost knowledge of the forest; however, audiences cannot help but draw comparisons with their own experiences of seeing children learning at school.

Documentary filmmakers rely on screenings with test audiences to discover what is working and what is not in terms of storyline, character selection, and editing and stylistic choices. Scenes of playful infants tumbling over small trees, pumping water, hanging from rotating merry-go-rounds, and swinging along ropes were the most effective in terms of engaging a test audience. Diaper-wearing infants, a necessity with recurrent parasitic infection, also appeal to viewers, as if we are watching our own human babies. Anthropomorphic images entertain and engage the audiences, who can then more easily appreciate and understand the obstacles the infants must overcome as they are encouraged back into an orangutan social world. The identification with human babies is unavoidable when we see an infant screaming across a field toward the clinic at the Nyaru Menteng Orangutan Reintroduction Project. Having lost contact with its favorite surrogate mother, this infant has a desperate mission, much as a human child would if it had lost its mother. Audiences are drawn to the baby's helplessness and relate to its predicament. Russon compares an orphan struggling to play while clinging to a comfort rag with Linus and his security blanket. This allusion to *Peanuts* was widely appealing to test audiences in America. A high point in the edited film is when rehabilitator Lone Droscher Nielson tickles the orangutan Noor, eliciting breathy giggles and a broad grin. If audiences identify with the infants' humanlike desperation and neediness, they respond equally well to displays of joyful play.

Although we allowed the audience to draw their own conclusions from the images we presented, in the narration of these scenes I was careful not to impose overt claims of human capacities on these infants. For example,

9.4 INFANTS AT PLAY. PHOTO BY SARITA SIEGEL.

in one interview, with guidance from Anne Russon, we opted to edit out the claim that the infants "have nightmares" and instead noted that they "wake up screaming sometimes." The screaming implies that they have nightmares, but because we are unable to prove why orangutan orphans scream, we chose not to make an overtly anthropomorphic claim. Anne guided me in my use of appropriate language for descriptive purposes: comparison and metaphorical language was acceptable, but making an unverifiable claim that an orangutan possessed a subconscious mind was pushing the limits of scientific acceptability.

We were granted access to the remote world of orangutans released from captivity through Russon and the forest technicians from Wanariset. With a small crew and a PD150 digital camera, we "hitched a ride" with Russon as she set off on the long journey into a remote forest camp in the Sungai Wain and the Meratus Forest in northeast Borneo, where the formerly captive orangutans Siti, Bento, Gomez, Maya, and Mono were busy reestablishing forest lives. When the orphans are old enough and skilled enough in forest survival, they are released into protected rainforests to resume independent forest lives.

While my small crew consciously avoided disrupting the small orangutan community, it was immediately clear that the orangutans were as interested in us as we were in them. Clearly there was going to be some degree of interaction, although it was our responsibility to keep the disturbance to a minimum. There is a moment in the film when a young

9.5 ANNE RUSSON AND SARITA SIEGEL. PHOTO BY TAGGART SIEGEL.

female, Siti, reaches out to touch the microphone and pushes it into the camera's frame. In that poignant moment, she shows us up as voyeurs and participates in the filming with an uncanny sense of humor and interest. In the same way, Russon's observational fieldwork requires acceptance by the small, widely dispersed group of orangutans deep in the rainforest. Anne speaks candidly about her interaction with her subjects. "Great apes, orangutans and humans all rely very heavily on interpersonal relationships. If I didn't have a relationship with the orangutans, I couldn't follow them because they wouldn't let me. They wouldn't let me come close to see what they do" (Russon 2000b). Without the orangutans' accepting humans into their world, there would be no possibility of Anne achieving the degree of understanding she has of their minds and their unique behavior.

Through her years of observation, Russon has become an authority on each "personality" and individual history. She knew Bento in his early days as a lazy "shmuck" who later became a knowledgeable "child king" in the strange *Lord of the Flies* community. Maya, Seni, and Mono were all playful sources of humor; Luther was shy and evasive; and Gomez was a vulnerable forest novice. Russon becomes animated when talking of the special bond she formed with Siti, whose sharp wits and trickster character endeared her to everyone. After conducting detailed interviews with Russon, I was able to build a profile of each orangutan's physical, emotional, and mental state. These characters came to populate the documentary's narrative.

Once I arrived in the forest, I began observing these personalities myself. Much as we may meet a person whose reputation precedes them, I responded to the forest orangutans with Russon's descriptions in mind. Without fail, each individual in the rehabilitation forest displayed traits that supported Russon's typecasting. Gomez stole toothpaste from the trash and sat beyond our reach sucking the contents. As we arrived, Bento observed us from a prime position on a tree overlooking the cable car. Siti displayed remarkable tenacity by eating varied and difficult foods, and Luther evaded us at every opportunity.

EDITING AND POSTPRODUCTION PHASE

After having collected more than seventy hours of interviews and footage, I set about editing the raw material into a coherent story. Before beginning with an editor, I had to make vital decisions about premise, structure, themes, style, and content. I wanted the basic premise of *The Disenchanted Forest* to reflect the two-way traffic across the divides of human and animal, culture and nature, domestic and wild. During filming in captivity and rehabilitation situations, I saw many instances of the human-nonhuman divide being fluid and indistinct. I did not want to portray a compartmentalized world where humankind resides in a civilized cultural world and animals are relegated to bestial realms. Russon comments that because orangutans are so like us they blur the boundary between what is human and what is animal (Russon 2000b). I decided that the premise of the film would be that humans are animals and that animals can be humanlike.

In light of the impending extinction crisis that faces the remaining orangutan populations, it was imperative that themes of orangutan psychology, culture, and rehabilitation in *The Disenchanted Forest* be explored within a wider framework of species and habitat conservation. Orangutan studies are now conducted with an appreciation of the diminishing rainforest habitat and the collapse of wild populations into fragmented communities. Carel van Schaik articulates primatologists' fears for the future: "This really is the worst decade in the orangutans' history. Aggressive habitat destruction, in addition to poaching of infants, has meant that in the last seven years we have seen a 46 percent decline of orangutans. If that is extrapolated, orangutans are likely to be gone within about a decade" (Van Schaik 2000).

My editor and I were halfway through the edit when National Geographic International became involved in this project. Because the film was a long way toward completion, their editorial control was not nearly as far-reaching as it would have been had I sold the idea to them before I began preproduction. Nevertheless, once independent filmmakers sign a contract that agrees to the political, technical, and bureaucratic constraints set out by the broadcaster, our work is inevitably altered in ways that suit the sociopolitical agenda of a large, multinational corporate entity.

Negotiations ensued whereby my "cut" was altered to fit National Geographic's standards. It was pointed out in initial conversations that National Geographic prides itself on creating immediate and intimate experiences of the world for worldwide audiences. Because *The Disenchanted Forest* would be viewed on cable television in more than 250 countries, National Geographic wanted to transform hard science into something general audiences could identify with and enthuse about. In short, National Geographic wanted heroes, visionaries, and an angle of "hope" in this film. I must admit that at first this seemed ridiculous, having just returned from Borneo where the last remaining stands of ramin hardwood were being logged illegally from national parks.

After submitting my cut for review, e-mail revision notes appeared on my laptop in various tones of encouragement and disapproval. Eventually, the beginning and the end of the film received the most revision. I was asked to create an opening that would "hook" the audience in the first few minutes of the film. Notably, throughout the film anthropomorphic images became more evident. It seemed that wherever there were cute anthropomorphic orangutan infants or allusions to western myth and fable, such as *Lord of the Flies*, "Humpty Dumpty," and *Peanuts*, I would receive praise from the committee. At the same time, I was politely asked to trim "didactic" talking-head theoretical or scientific interviews. As I had initially been attracted to making this film by the very discussion of culture, intelligence, and cognition, I resisted the broadcaster's demands to simplify the complex issues of culture and cognition in orangutans. I argued with my National Geographic "point person" over devoting adequate screen time to the fascinating world of scientific observation and analysis. The ensuing negotiations via phone conversations and edit notes ultimately transformed the structure and content to assimilate more entertaining footage of anthropomorphic infants in rehabilitation centers, though the final film still retained more complex ideas about orangutan culture and cognition.

During the editing process, "voice over" narration was recorded and interviews and footage were combined and manipulated to develop human and orangutan characters and weave their stories together to create the film's narrative. To illustrate by example how anthropomorphism functions as a communication tool in this process, I will introduce several orangutan characters that predominate in *The Disenchanted Forest* story.

By projecting anthropomorphic associations onto these characters, viewers are linked emotionally to the orangutan subjects, thus engaging them in an amusing and educational way.

When National Geographic requested a hero character for the film to pivot around, at first they suggested an orangutan. I had not intended to use this angle during the shoot but impulsively suggested trying to build a story around Siti. My editor and I spent some trying weeks halfheartedly attempting to construct this device, knowing that we neither had the footage to support this nor the desire to make Siti a great ape "celebrity." Upon submission of the next rough cut, National Geographic acknowledged that it was a bad idea and allowed me to resume my original structure. Nevertheless, Siti remains a major character in the film. I believe it is partly her humanlike qualities that made her so appealing to the National Geographic committee and allowed the film to engage audiences. Close-up shots of her almond eyes promise potential cross-species communication as Russon encounters her in the forest. Her dark, enigmatic stare prompts Anne's comment, "to go out into the forest and see an adult female orangutan, standing up in front of you, almost with her hands on her hips, looking you right in the eye. You know there is a powerful mind out there in front of you. And you can't feel superior anymore. It's a very humbling experience to do that. One of my favorite experiences in the world is to go and be with another species as an equal or maybe even a lesser being" (Russon 2000b).

9.6   SITI. PHOTO BY SARITA SIEGEL.

Siti became the success story, an orphan who came into Wanariset knowing nothing. "She must have been taken captive when she was under a year old because she came to Wanariset when she was still a tiny little baby. So she had virtually no living memory of ever having lived in the forest and she had to start from scratch" (Russon 1999a). Russon describes, in anthropomorphic terms, how "Siti had a temperament or a 'personality' that gave her a big boost in terms of her chance of getting somewhere, because she really wanted to learn things. Siti would be down there beating it out with the boys when all the other little females were hiding away. She'd be right in there because she wanted to see how things were done." With human-oriented narration over footage such as Siti elbowing her way through a group of youngsters to get to a bucket of milk, audiences witness her journey through rehabilitation and are proud of her determination to relearn forest skills.

In the film we develop Siti's vulnerability when she was released into the forest. At first she was timid and unconfident and remained close to the security of the human technicians. At night she slept on the release cage, wrapped up with Ida, another juvenile. However, within the first year Siti began to behave more confidently in the forest. She began to explore various ways of obtaining food. Russon observed her developing survival techniques. "She watched and scrounged palm foods off a little friend. Within two weeks she had mastered extracting pulp from tough palm stalks. Siti made use of older, more knowledgeable orangutans to provide her with new avenues of learning" (Russon 1999a). Audiences have an empathetic response to her character traits, particularly when they accept the human-like intentionality of her actions. Russon speaks of Siti's "dedication" to working on her forest skills, as if she had a goal in mind. Through Russon's intimate descriptions we are told the story of a tenacious, determined character who invested effort in learning, practicing, and problem solving in order to set herself up to survive successfully as a forest-dwelling adult.

Audiences are brought intimately into Siti's world when they hear descriptions of her actions and struggles in language that does not strip her of her sentient capacity. When Siti needed emotional comfort, she spent time grooming with Judy, an older female (Russon 2000b). Because she resembles us in her response to her difficult circumstances, we invest in her emotionally. Siti becomes our protagonist in the drama of orangutan forest adaptation. We can understand her loneliness and fear and are proud that she heroically rises to the challenge of adapting to forest life.

If Gomez were a mythic character in a romantic epic, he would play the part of the underdog. Like a newly released criminal, he faced free life in the forest with fear and uncertainty. The first morning we encountered

9.7   FORLORN GOMEZ. PHOTO BY SARITA SIEGEL.

Gomez—hanging on the rail of the verandah at base camp—he struck me as a vulnerable novice in the forest. Scarred welts across his back spoke of an abused life in captivity. Lacking orangutan friends and teachers within his peer group, he hung around the human technicians, resisting the moment he would have to survive alone. Gomez often hovered around the base camp hut, waiting opportunistically for discarded comestibles. One morning, as we were all diverted momentarily, Gomez slid toward the rubbish tin and grabbed a crumpled tube of toothpaste. Chased by technicians, he fled to the top of a tree and sat sucking on his winnings. With toothpaste drizzling down his chin, Gomez will always remain in my mind's eye as the product of man's selfish urge to incarcerate and torment another free creature.

We were treated to many colorful anthropomorphic stories from Russon about Bento. Sadly, many of them did not make it to the final cut. One in particular that I could not retain in the film was the story of Bento's return to the forest after recuperating from an injury at Wanariset's clinic:

> I went when they took Bento back into the forest to see how he would do. After about three or four days I think he decided he didn't like it there, because he started walking out of the forest. He actually got all the way down to the post that we stay in, which is on the way out. We managed to get him back to where he should have been once, then

9.8 BENTO. PHOTO BY SARITA SIEGEL.

half way back a second time, but the third time he wouldn't follow us at all. The next day he was out of the forest trying to climb into a car. Now it's invention to say what that was about, but I figured he wanted to go back to Wanariset. He thought it was Club Med in there, he didn't have to build a nest, it was nice and warm, no rain on him, people brought him food everyday. He was always a lazy food thief.

(Russon 2000b)

Anne imposes human intentionality upon Bento; the story leads us to think that maybe he was capable of hitching a ride or driving himself back to Wanariset. Anne acknowledges her grossly oversimplified tale of Bento's intended escape and her invention of Bento's anthropomorphic attributes. It is a humorous and communicative story, and furthermore it is true. The manner in which Anne tells the story credits Bento with more consciousness than he otherwise might have been given. It also conveys the degree of change he experienced as he developed from a lazy neophyte to the oldest, most knowledgeable orangutan in the release community.

Anne describes how Bento grew from being lazy and ignorant to the "child king" of the strange community of formerly captive orangutan juveniles. Bento transmits survival knowledge to naive orangutans who gradually reestablish a vital cultural system deep in the forest. Bento is the boy who "made good" when the odds were stacked against him. By linking Bento's development to a mythic "child king," we tie into allegorical symbolism. Perhaps initially, Bento's magnetism lies in his blossoming power in the forest community. However, it is his mythic aspect, the nature of his struggle and the ways he reacts to his predicament by turning it into ultimate success, which provides the dramatic elements of the hero's journey that we invest in as an audience. I hesitate to claim that Bento encourages us to learn about ourselves, but I think on some level we indeed tap into his story and connect somewhere beyond our physical differences to a core similarity.

Finally, I would like to comment briefly upon two orangutans in the forest community, Romanis and Buddha. Their story illustrated that emotionality and friendship are essential components of the survival of the former captives.

Romanis and Buddha were very close friends as infants at Wanariset. When they were released into the forest they always made nests together and slept together. One day, the forest technicians noticed Buddha was absent and it was eventually discovered that a pig had killed him. His body lay close to the tree where Romanis sat crying.

For a month afterwards Romanis would just sit and would barely move or eat as he missed his friend extremely.   (Smits 1999).

We identify with Romanis's grief and are perhaps relieved to know that our great ape cousins also carry the burden of awareness and deep emotion.

This was also evident in the remarkable story told by Willie Smits about encountering Uce, the first orangutan rehabilitant he released, some years later in the forest. Uce came to Willie Smits and offered her baby to him and then, remarkably, led him to a licuala palm and offered him a leaf. Willie interpreted this as an intentional message to him that she had not forgotten him because he had done the very same thing for her when he released her into the forest years before. Her memory and emotional attachment to Willie provide audiences with a powerful story, which allows them to momentarily traverse species boundaries.

The Disenchanted Forest accompanies Lone Droscher-Nielsen and Odom from Ngaru Menteng Reintroduction Clinic when they escort a young female orangutan, Inung, into a protected forest "halfway house." In this authentic forest "play school," orphans develop their forest knowledge and establish social relationships. Inung's journey back into true forest habitat is symbolic of the vast psychological leap she must navigate in a transition from a human world back into an orangutan social world.

The choice of shots help to portray Inung's abandoning of the human world, where we feel close to her, to a more remote view where we have to let her return to her own orangutan forest world. Close-up shots are heavy with Inung's wonder and trepidation as she is driven into the forest and carried along the wooden pathways into the release site. The audience is drawn intimately into Inung's journey by depicting the scene largely from her point of view. Rather than portraying a truly animal point of view, we opted to depict one that humans would identify with. If I had provided a specifically orangutan point of view, it might have consisted of languid, long shots from high in the trees accompanied by a soundtrack of crunching leaves. Instead Inung's point of view as she clings to Odom's neck, staring up at the unfamiliar environment, is more reminiscent of a child clinging to a parent on the first day of school. Through association with their own human experiences, audiences identify with Inung's journey into what is to her an unfamiliar realm.

Once Inung is released, wide shots supplant more intimate close-ups of Inung's journey as Odom releases her gently onto the trunk of a tree. The camera's view takes a more distant recording of the event as Inung is swept up by a group of eager orangutan playmates. They pursue her up the tree until it collapses under their weight and orangutans rain down onto

9.9   INUNG. PHOTO BY SOPHIE MOUNIER.

the forest floor. The shift from intimate close-up shots and Inung's point-of-view shots to more distant wide shots of many orangutans illustrates Inung's transition from the human world back into the forest world.

Rehabilitation experts and animal behaviorists in the past have mistakenly assessed the ease with which orangutans can adapt to human or orangutan cultural worlds at will.

> One of the big problems that everybody has run across with all of the great apes, orangutans included, is that they are species that don't fit our normal break down of the world into humans and animals. For a long time it has been recognized that they bridge the boundary, and I think we still face that problem when we deal with them. On the one hand, we recognize that they take on humanlike characteristics very easily, so we see them as very human. On the other hand, when the ex-captives are sent back to the wild, I think sometimes the idea is that they should suddenly become animal, and that is a distinctly different category than human. It is very easy to fall into the notion that animals have instincts and animals just do their thing, so if we put them in the forest then they will be orangutans again. However, if a lot of their abilities come from learning, and if a lot of their abilities are learned from the world that they live in, then just putting them back in the forest is not going to immediately turn them back into wild orangutans. Their abilities are ones they acquired in the context of the human world and the individuals that they look to as their models or teachers are humans, not other orangutans.
>
> (Russon 1999a).

This quotation encapsulates the practical complexity of returning captive orangutans to free forest lives.

The portrayal of this traffic across the boundaries of human and animal manifests as anthropomorphism in *The Disenchanted Forest*. This documentary depicts the life stories of individuals whose characters and temperaments are articulated in human-derived semantics. Heroic, noble Bento contrasts with naive underdog Gomez. Tenacious Siti succeeds in striking out alone where younger Noor struggles to sever herself from her dependency upon human caretakers. Love-struck Uce communicates her fond memories of Willie Smits by offering a leaf gift. Anthropomorphic associations in this documentary underscore our relatedness and similarity and perpetuate the sense of connection between humans and great apes.

The fact that humans impose symbolic associations upon the great apes is a boon as far as making the story work in film. But I also felt that to a

9.10 Gomez walking away. Photo by Sarita Siegel.

large extent it might be justified. The more time I spent with orangutans, the more firmly I was convinced that great apes possess intentionality, self-awareness, complex modes of communication, a theory of mind, a sense of humor, and a need for emotional support, as well as many other human-like traits. For these reasons I felt anthropomorphic analogy and anecdotes were relevant and helpful in understanding the minds and behavior of the orangutans in *The Disenchanted Forest*. I hope that by illuminating orang-utan mental processes to audiences in this documentary, we may continue to dream of cross-species communication or thinking with "the other."

In the "packaging" of nature and conservation for broadcast to a world-wide audience, documentary filmmakers play a role in the "production of meaning" for great apes. As we move into a global era dominated by a Western perspective, the representation of great apes in documentaries and media is going to be viewed by global audiences and absorbed into popular culture for better or for worse. For this reason, I advocate continuing a close association of science and documentary filmmaking. Documentaries are the conduit through which scientists and pragmatists like Anne Russon and Willie Smits, who know the complexities of issues like orangutan culture and conserva-tion, have an opportunity to impart that story to a global community.

As science becomes increasingly accepting of filmmakers' needs to communicate with broad audiences via vivid and accessible language that contains metaphors and analogies, which are or may be anthropomorphic, we should see increased cooperation between science and media in aid of conservation efforts. With increasing interconnection of these areas of ex-pertise, we can contribute to the common goal of bringing audiences inti-mately into the world of orangutans in the hopes that it may be useful in the care and conservation of this magnificent species in the remnants of rainforest that endure in Borneo and Sumatra.

REFERENCES

Byrne, Richard. 2000. "Changing Views on Imitation in Primates. In *Primate Encounters: Models of Science, Gender, and Society*, ed. Shirley Strum and Linda M. Fedigan, 269–309. Chcicago: University of Chicago Press.

Disenchanted Forest, The. Prod. and dir. Sarita Siegel. 53 min. Bullfrog Films and Cube International. 2002.

Galdikas-Brindamour, B. 1975. "Orangutans, Indonesia's 'People of the forest.'" *National Geographic* 148:444–73.

Groves, C. P. 1989. *A Theory of Human and Primate Evolution*. Oxford: Oxford University Press.

Haraway, Donna. 1989. *Primate Visions*. New York: Routledge, Chapman & Hall..

Kennedy, J. S. 1992. *The New Anthropomorphism*. Cambridge: Cambridge University Press.

Miles, H. Lyn. 1997. "Anthropomorphism, Apes, and Language." In *Anthropomorphism, Anecdotes, and Animals*, ed. Robert W. Mitchell, Nicholas S. Thompson, and H. Lyn Miles, 383–404. Albany: State University of New York Press.

Mitman, G., 2000. "Section 5: E-mail Exachanges." In *Primate Encounters: Models of Science, Gender, and Society*, ed. Shirley C. Strums: *Models of Science, Gender, and Society*, ed. Shirley Strum and Linda M. Fedigan. Chcicago: University of Chicago Press.

——. 1999. *Reel Nature: America's Romance with Wildlife on Film*. Cambridge, Mass.: Harvard University Press.

Pilbeam, D. 1996. "Genetic and Morphological Records of the Hominoidea and Hominid Origins: A Synthesis." *Molecular Phylogenetics and Evolution* 5, no. 1:155–68.

Rijksen, H. D., and E. Meijaard. 1999. *Our Vanishing Relative: The Status of Wild Orangutans at the Close of the Twentieth Century*. Dordrecht, The Netherlands: Kluwer.

Russon, Anne. 1998. Interview with author. Toronto. Digital video recording.

——. 1999a. Interview with author. Wanariset. Digital video recording.

——. 1999b. *Orangutans, Wizards of the Rainforest* (Toronto: Key Porter Books, 1999).

——. 2000a. "Comparative Developmental Perspectives on Culture: The Great Apes." In *Between Biology and Culture: Perspectives on Ontogenetic Development*, ed. Heidi Keller, Ype H. Poortinga, and Axel Schoelmerich, 30–56. Cambridge: Cambridge University Press.

——. 2000b. Interview with author. Suniga Wain Forest, Borneo. Digital video recording.

Smits, Willie. 1999. Interview with author. Wanariset. Digital video recording.

Van Schaik, Carel. 2000. Interview with author. San Francisco. Digital video recording.

Yeager, Carey. 1999. Interview with author. Sekonyer River research camp. Digital video recording.